EVERYONE'S
SEEN MY TITS

EVERYONE'S SEEN MY TITS

Stories and Reflections
from an Unlikely Feminist

KEELEY HAZELL

GRAND
CENTRAL

New York Boston

For my mother. You're a legend. I hope you know that.

———————

Copyright © 2025 by Keeley Hazell

Jacket design and illustration by Caitlin Sacks. Jacket copyright © 2025 by Hachette Book Group, Inc.

Hachette Book Group supports the right to free expression and the value of copyright. The purpose of copyright is to encourage writers and artists to produce the creative works that enrich our culture.

The scanning, uploading, and distribution of this book without permission is a theft of the author's intellectual property. If you would like permission to use material from the book (other than for review purposes), please contact permissions@hbgusa.com. Thank you for your support of the author's rights.

Grand Central Publishing
Hachette Book Group
1290 Avenue of the Americas, New York, NY 10104
grandcentralpublishing.com
@grandcentralpub

First Edition: August 2025

Grand Central Publishing is a division of Hachette Book Group, Inc. The Grand Central Publishing name and logo is a registered trademark of Hachette Book Group, Inc.

The publisher is not responsible for websites (or their content) that are not owned by the publisher.

Grand Central Publishing books may be purchased in bulk for business, educational, or promotional use. For information, please contact your local bookseller or the Hachette Book Group Special Markets Department at special.markets@hbgusa.com.

Print book interior design by Amy Quinn

Library of Congress Cataloging-in-Publication Data

Names: Hazell, Keeley author
Title: Everyone's seen my tits : stories and reflections from an unlikely feminist / Keeley Hazell.
Description: First edition. | New York : GCP, 2025.
Identifiers: LCCN 2025009453 | ISBN 9781538742686 hardcover | ISBN 9781538742709 ebook
Subjects: LCSH: Hazell, Keeley | Television actors and actresses—Great Britain—Biography | Motion picture actors and actresses—Great Britain—Biography | Models (Persons)—Great Britain—Biography | Feminists—Great Britain—Biography | LCGFT: Autobiographies | Essays
Classification: LCC PN1992.4.H39 A3 2025 | DDC 791.4302/8092 [B]—dc23/eng/20250603
LC record available at https://lccn.loc.gov/2025009453

ISBNs: 9781538742686 (hardcover), 9781538742709 (ebook)

Printed in the United States of America

LSC-C

Printing 1, 2025

Contents

Part Three

Woman

Tits Up

It's funny where your tits can get you. Well, maybe "funny" isn't the optimal word to be used here, but in my case, it was funny in a sort of "absurd funny" kind of way that the soft, protruding tissue on my chest ultimately led me here to the Soho Hotel in Central London. Without my breasts, who knows where I would have ended up? I didn't grow up going to five-star hotels, I can tell you that. I might have grown up in London, but my London and *this* London are very different. This world was foreign. It was posh. It screamed money. Where I grew up—southeast of the river—people locked their car doors when they stopped at a red light to ensure they weren't stolen. I was lucky if my mum brought us a KFC family bucket for dinner. My people had meal tickets, not reservations. We didn't do sit-down dinners—it was chicken shops, kebabs, and crime. People sold drugs, got into fights, drank themselves silly, and went to jail. There wasn't much else to do.

But then, because of my tits, everything changed overnight. I went from living on a council estate to owning a luxurious apartment overlooking the Thames. I had a moderate amount of fame and more MySpace friend requests than I could accept. According to *FHM* magazine, I was the second-sexiest woman in the world and the ninth-most-eligible bachelorette. Hot, successful, and famous men wanted to date me. And I wished, *ohhhhhh how I wished*, that I had been running wild and collecting funny stories to share with my friends. You know, the kind of stories that leave people in stitches when you tell them that some guy you met on a train insisted on kissing you with an ice cube in his mouth or the boy you fancied from that movie you loved when you were younger only has sex from behind while listening to a book on tape. These funny stories *could have been mine*, but instead, I was celibate. Over a year without so much as a kiss. The idea of sex had traumatized me so deeply that even the thought of going on a date and kissing someone new had me breaking out in hives and ready to run into a convent. And I was only twenty-one. *Twenty-one!* I was supposed to be living my best life, or as I like to say, my "breast" life. I was inside this fancy-arse hotel, and yet I was depressed. And just when I thought it couldn't get any worse, Anna walked in to depress me even further.

Anna was in her midthirties (or maybe forties; who knows, I was never that good at guessing someone's age). She oozed sophistication and looked every inch the journalist and writer who wrote pieces of merit for the highbrow British newspaper she worked for. I imagined her writing witty, intellectual articles on current affairs. And how pissed off she must have been that her editor had sent her to interview me.

Me: a Page 3 and glamour model.

For those unfamiliar, Page 3 was a feature in *The Sun*, a Rupert Murdoch–owned tabloid, showcasing topless female models on its third page from 1970 to 2015. Controversial yet iconic, it launched many models, some as young as sixteen, into the public eye—often making them household names.

Glamour modeling includes Page 3 but also refers to modeling in publications like *FHM*, *Maxim*, or what many called the "lads' mags." While these magazines didn't always feature topless photos, they still emphasized a model's attractiveness over elements like fashion or branding.

So there I was: a topless titty model. And wait for it…I'd just released my first single, "Voyeur," and a raunchy music video to go along with it.

It makes me cringe greatly to write those words. I must confess, I have the musical talent of a slug and the singing voice of a drowning rabbit, and as for my dancing, well, I've often been asked by panicked friends if I'm okay. But I was severely desperate.

Soooooo desperate. Let me tell you how desperate I was: I'd been known to say that there was no way on earth you would catch me dead releasing a single. I knew my limitations, I knew how much shit I would get, and I swore there was no way I'd humiliate myself like that. But then my ex did something that made every bit of that embarrassment pale in comparison. What he did wasn't just humiliating—it was devastating. It was the reason I was popping an antidepressant every morning, seeing a therapist once a week, a hypnotherapist twice a week, and paying a life coach/healer/unlicensed counselor called Pat seventy-five pounds a fortnight to cure me by making me cups of English

Breakfast tea. I was doing all of this because my ex broke into my home with a knife, and then he sold a video of the two of us having sex to a national newspaper. He violated me in a way that was unforgivable, and I couldn't stop it. The video spread online like a highly contagious disease. The pain and public humiliation were insurmountable. The world assumed I wanted it. *The world thought I'd released it.* In their eyes I was topless in the newspaper, showing my tits off to everyone, so of course I was the kind of girl who'd release a sex tape because, duh, I was obviously a fame-hungry attention-seeking whore who must've been trying to be the next Pamela Anderson, or Paris Hilton, or—my favorite accusation—Kim Kardashian, which is wild because my tape came out *before* Kim's, so unless I was a time traveler, that one's impossible. But there you have it—apparently, I was trying to be Kim months before anyone knew who she was.

When the video came out, I felt like I had no control, no way to fight back. So I did what desperate people do—I grasped at anything to bury it, to divert attention. That's how I found myself singing titillating lyrics into a microphone before having my voice completely autotuned; then I danced around in my underwear in a music video—that I personally paid for—because that's what desperate, traumatized people do.

Of course, it was an awful, exploitative idea that my manager had convinced me was genius. "Releasing a music video will replace the *other* video online, and the people who know will forget and the people who don't know, won't," he said, and I stupidly went along with it because, at the time, I was too busy crying to come up with ideas that didn't involve me crying. Now that I had released my terrible new single and music video, I had to promote it. *That's* why I was in the Soho Hotel meeting Anna. I was here to talk about my new career as a singer—how exciting for both of us.

The interview started off worse than I imagined. I stood up from my seat, and I was preparing my hand to greet her when she aggressively threw her black handbag down in the middle of the square wooden table. Her brown eyes looked me up and down. It was an assessment I didn't particularly like, though one I was used to. It felt part and parcel of being female: the scanning, the once-over, the picking apart everything about me before deciding whether she liked me.

(And I got the vibe that she didn't, so that made two of us.)

After noticing her disdain for my existence, I decided to be friendly—kill with kindness and all. "I like your Prada handbag," I said cheerfully. "My friend just purchased the same one."

She immediately shut me down, replying in her posh, money-eyed British accent—the kind of accent that only comes with rich parents and access to a private education: "She couldn't have because it's *old*."

I was about to say, well, I think hers might have come from a market stall in Thailand, but I didn't get to say this because she didn't give me a chance. Instead, she pulled out her notepad and pen, followed by a little black voice recorder, and jumped right in with her questions. Thankfully many didn't make the final cut.

"Do you think rape is associated with Page 3?"

I didn't know if Anna was serious, so I stared at her for a second, trying to get some form of indication from her oval, stoic face. When I realized she possessed no capacity for joking, I said, "Excuse me?"

She spelled it out for me like I was in preschool, "DO...
YOU...THINK...MEN...RAPE...WOMEN...
BECAUSE...OF...PAGE 3?"

I looked at her in disbelief. The condescension was bad enough,
but did she just seriously ask me if I thought the job I had as
a Page 3 model contributed in some way to rape? I didn't even
know how to begin answering the question. Was that a thing
people actually thought?!? Was I being accused of playing a part
in one of the most awful things a man can do to a woman? Did
my job in any way contribute to...*rape??*

"No," I said bashfully and looked down at the green skirt I
was wearing; it was a sickening thought and a question laced
with accusations that left me uneasy. I had never encountered
the belief that there was a link between the mass circulation of
images of women appearing semi-naked on Page 3 and sexual
violence (I later learned that there is no evidence to support this
theory), and having not been exposed, I hadn't been able to for-
mulate any thoughts or opinions on the matter. I'd barely had an
education; before I left school at sixteen, I'd spent so little time
on campus that court proceedings had been taken against my
mother to send her to jail. Lucky for her, I turned sixteen before
her court date and was legally allowed to leave school. Otherwise, it could have been bye-bye, Amber Jane. (That's my mother's name, by the way.) But, anyway, I don't want to do my school
a disservice; they did teach us about women's rights; the lesson
went something like "Women couldn't vote, and now they can.
Hurray for women." At least it was more detailed than our one
and only female sex education class, where they taught us how to
put a condom on a banana and then sent us on our way. While I

knew what rape was, I'd never questioned *why* men raped or had a detailed conversation about the psychology behind it. I'd never questioned why there were photos of topless women in a national newspaper. They were just there. Photos of tits in the newspaper had been around since I was born, just like cars and electricity.

My parents' education wasn't any better. While they both had access to schools, the education they received was below basic. My dad had never been taught how to read and write, and the only thing my mother learned in her adolescence was how to down a pint. It wasn't exactly like I'd been nurtured in an environment that cultivated these conversations and ideas.

Page 3.

Rape.

What the...?!

I sat there completely sideswiped, and Anna pressed on with her questions.

"Do you think men see you as an object?"

I swallowed hard, then muttered weakly, "I don't think men see me as an object." She looked at me, sneered, and then rolled her eyes. *This* is why my mother hates posh people, I thought. *This* is why. "They always think they're better than the likes of us—the working-class people," she'd told me as a child. "They look down on us. We're the scum of the earth to them."

I felt very uneasy, so I fixed my eyes on Anna's bag and waited for the next question. I kept staring at the Prada triangle until the letters became blurry. Then, finally, the question of all questions came. A question I will never forget.

"Are you a feminist?" she said, leaning back in her chair and crossing her arms. I repeated the question in my head before darting my eyes around the room and squirming in my chair, unsure how to answer. Was I a feminist? How did I know if I was a feminist? And more important, what the heck was a feminist? Oh crap, what was a feminist?? I had to know what it meant! Hadn't I heard that word somewhere before??? Was it a French word?!? It had to relate to my line of work somehow, but how? *Come on*, I thought, *you* have *to know what this word means.*

Truth be told, I had no clue. Growing up poor, you're too busy worrying about putting food on the table and keeping a roof over your head, you don't have much time to think about anything else. Survival comes first, always. Sure, you see the inequality—it's impossible to miss. But the words to explain it? They're not in your vocabulary. Life as a boy was different from life as a girl. We all knew that. Us girls would talk about how unfair it was, how men seemed to have it easier. But where I came from, no one sat around on a Friday night, drinking cheap cider and tossing around words like "feminist."

Working-class women just weren't doing that.

Anna waited for an answer, but one wasn't coming. We sat there in silence as I racked my brain, trying to understand what "feminist" meant. She kept looking at me in anticipation, and I kept stumbling, trying to bide my time. I knew I had one of two options: I was either a feminist or I wasn't. But if I said I WAS a feminist, and it meant something offensive like "racist," then that was bad, really, really bad. Then, out of nowhere, a miracle happened, and it came to me...A light bulb went off in my head: Feminist means "nudist." It means someone who likes taking their clothes off in public places. I knew I'd get it!!

"I'm not a feminist," I replied proudly, "but I can see why

people would think I am one." Anna raised her left eyebrow in a way that suggested she was impressed, or at least that's how I interpreted it. I sat there chuffed. In my mind, she was trying to ask me if I was a nudist because of my job, which made sense, but she was obviously trying to trick me by using this big, fancy French word.

Anna leaned forward slightly and uncrossed her arms. "Why would people think you're a feminist?" she asked with such intent that I began to question if I had, in fact, gotten the meaning of the word right, but at this point, I couldn't ask her. It was clear that she already thought I was a moron—I couldn't serve myself up on a plate for her amusement. And if the last time I'd asked someone what a word meant was anything to go by (I was eighteen, and it was narcotics), I had been scolded with so much ridicule that I'd rather pretend to know what the word meant than go through that again. Sometimes it's just easier to pretend you know what a word means or that you've seen the movie, you know.

"Because...because, I guess, hmm, well, I think...that maybe my line of work just gives off the impression that I'm a feminist."

She picked up her pen and started scribbling in her notepad. I watched the pen touch the paper, and I tried to see what she was writing. I couldn't make out a single word but feared it might be: *Keeley is completely thick and doesn't have a clue what she is talking about, which is why she is a glamour model. The stereotype of the bimbo topless model is confirmed. We can all go home.* This fear only made me more determined to nail the rest of the interview to prove myself. I had never been asked questions like this before, and I wanted to be able to answer them in an eloquent, intellectual,

Jane Austen novel–like fashion. I was ready—up for the challenge. I psyched myself up and waited for the next question.

"Do you ever wonder what men are thinking when they look at your pictures?" Anna asked with the intonation of a police officer, and I crumbled. My brain was suddenly filled with flashbacks of "tribute" videos I'd seen of men touching themselves while looking at topless photos of me before ejaculating all over my tits. I wanted to put my fingers in my ears and scream. My body felt hot, and I lost all confidence in my ability to form sentences and had to stop myself from replying, *That my hair looks nice?*

After a few more questions—all centered around whether or not I thought my music video was soft porn—the interview concluded, and Anna and her old-but-real Prada bag departed the Soho Hotel. I sat there feeling mentally raped and furious. I watched her back as she receded around the corner and listened to the tapping of her shoes as they faintly disappeared into the distance.

I went and got the tube and returned home to my lonely, sterile apartment in Canary Wharf, a part of London to be visited if you worked in banking but, under no circumstances, lived in. I sat on my sofa and typed "feminist" into the search engine on my laptop. I crossed my fingers and prayed it meant the French word for nudist. *Please mean nudist; please mean nudist.* The search engine loaded, and when the response came up, "A person who supports feminism," I wasn't immediately disheartened because I thought, *Huh, well, it could be a person that supports people being naked?* So I searched the word "feminism" and discovered the real meaning. I stared at the screen, rolled off my sofa onto my salt-and-pepper rug, and let out a cry. Wow, I was an idiot. I felt so stupid.

"A person who supports equal pay between men and women" was the definition on the website I was looking at; on others, it was described as the advocacy of women's rights on the basis of the equality of the sexes. HOW it had nothing to do with nudity was beyond me. WHY there was even a term needed to describe a person who believed in equal pay between men and women who were both doing the same job was so baffling to me, and at the same time, it wasn't. I was born with a vagina and knew what that experience was like even if I didn't yet have the vocabulary to articulate it.

Anxiously, I started rubbing the scar on my nose with my index finger. I pushed my finger deep into the scar groove and then along my nose, feeling where I had broken it. I rubbed my finger along my scar until it started to make me feel sick to my stomach, and then I decided to take a trip to the library to look for feminist literature, so I'd never be caught off guard again.

The selection of books was small. There was only one shelf with maybe ten or twenty books on the subject. Most of them had titles I couldn't understand, like *The Feminine Mystique*. I mistook it as "The Feminine Mystic" and flicked through, thinking that maybe I would find a detailed description of my horoscope inside. I picked up a book on objectification and put it under my arm, and I grabbed two other books, thinking I would start there. I presented my library card and checked them out.

Then, that evening, I sat on my sofa with the books, a dictionary, a notebook, a pen, and a pencil. I turned pages and read randomly. I looked up words I didn't know the meaning of and tried to understand them—words that made me wonder if English was actually my second language.

I grappled with the concept of objectification. The idea that some men could view women purely as objects, without considering anything else about them—their personality, intelligence, individuality, or God forbid, the fact that they have their own thoughts and feelings. *Yep, I can relate to that*, I thought, before suddenly remembering the short movie idea I'd come up with when I was trying to think of ways to bury the sex tape; I'd play a girl who was completely naked in a bedroom, crying my eyes out and slitting her wrists with a knife, screaming, "*IS THIS WHAT YOU WANT!*" Admittedly, *it was a little dark*, but I wanted to convey that I was more than just a body to be admired and looked at. Something I hadn't achieved in my music video as I danced around in my underwear and sang, "*I don't care, you can stare.*"

Over the next few months I kept reading, and I started to see the threads that tied my experiences to something larger—to structures and systems and culturally ingrained ways of thinking. I started to understand the apparent differences between men and women and how they were treated and viewed when it came to sex and sexuality. And honestly, my mind was blown and my eyes opened. Suddenly, feminism explained everything I had felt my whole life and had been unable to express. When I learned the meaning of the word "patriarchy," I threw my hands up into the air. *Now I get it!!!* It was like I'd just found Christ. Except—and this is one big exception—when people find Christ, they often feel a profound sense of peace, forgiveness, and renewal. There's typically a deep emotional relief, and I can't say I felt the same way when I found feminism. My findings left me frustrated and angry.

Feeling like being a woman was just one big trap. Like a too-good-to-be-true competition where you won an all-exclusive holiday to Mallorca, but the hotel's next available date was thirty years later.

I kept replaying the interview with Anna in my head, over and over, stuck in an endless loop of rumination. Each time I'd answer her questions differently. Sometimes I would yell or scream. Oftentimes I'd calmly explain things I'd learned since then. On rare occasions, I'd imagine us having long conversations over a glass of wine about living under the patriarchy or how working-class women experience gender oppression differently from middle and upper-class women. Mostly, though, I would find myself defending my job and my decisions. I'd mentally map out how capitalism, class, beauty standards, and patriarchy all shaped my career choice. I'd tell her that my profession had far more to do with financial necessity than with any lofty ideals—that this was a class issue, and how dare middle-class women who have more resources and opportunities shame women who don't.

But no matter how many ways I justified myself or broke down society to understand it, I kept coming back to that one loaded question: "Are you a feminist?" and I didn't know how to answer. Yes, I believed in equality and equal pay between men and women, but did I align with the woman who claimed to speak on behalf of "all women" but somehow excluded me from that group because they blamed girls who posed nude for rape culture? Or who blamed women who seemingly played into these oppressive systems for the lack of progression of the movement? Not particularly.

Sometimes we don't have conclusive answers because we're still figuring it out. And at twenty-one I was still figuring a lot of things out. Heck, I was still waiting for my frontal lobe to finish developing. But if there was one thing learning about feminism gave me, it was the permission to ask myself questions—about who I was and what I wanted. Not long after this fatal interview, I quit topless modeling and moved halfway across the world. For the first time, I took control of my life and did something out of desire, not necessity. But even then it came with complications because the world is what the world is. And as infuriating as that can be, you still must learn to live in it.

Part One

Child

Daddy's Disappointment

"Now, listen, do you hear me? You're wearing a new top. And if you get this down ya—that's it. Your dummy is going out that window," Dad says, stressed. He sits behind the steering wheel. My mother sits in the passenger seat. These are the positions they always assume when Dad is in the car. Dad says women are terrible drivers and shouldn't be allowed on the road. I'm strapped in a car seat behind him with a dummy in my mouth. A dummy is what us Brits call a pacifier. My older sister, Deborah, is sitting on a booster seat next to me. We're by our block of flats. We've just come from somewhere and we're about to go somewhere else— I don't know where. I don't remember getting into the car or where we just came from. All I know is we've made a quick pit stop to eat because we haven't, and that involves chocolate. I have the memory of an elephant when it comes to chocolate, so this moment sticks with me.

My mother unwraps a Kit Kat bar, pulling the wrapper off and removing the silver foil. Dad keeps going, "I'm not playing

around. I don't want to see any of this over you." Dad's obsessed
with us looking presentable.

I nod, understanding the concept but kinda not. I'm two, I've
only just learned how to pee on a potty, and I'm not sure I've even
figured that out properly. Besides, I'm not really listening because
there's a chocolate bar in front of me, and I'm completely dazzled
by it. I came out of the womb obsessed with chocolate. Chocolate
is my everything. I love it so much; it's the greatest thing on the
planet. I'm so obsessed with it that when I turn ten, I follow my
mother around the kitchen, repeating, "Can I have some chocolate cake now? Can I have some chocolate cake now?" like a heroin addict trying to get a hit. I repeat it so many times that, in an
attempt to shut me up, she grabs my face and squirts washing-up
liquid in my mouth. I can taste bubbles for days, but my love of
chocolate never fades. I'm willing to risk anything for chocolate. I
spit my dummy out of my mouth as I reach both hands forward.

"Careful," Mother says, handing the Kit Kat bar to me.

I grip it tightly and carefully put it in my mouth, biting the
top. The taste of the chocolate swirls around my mouth. It's heav-
enly. It's blowing my mind. I'm careful as I take another bite,
making sure not to get it on me. I take another bite and then
another until suddenly Deborah, eating her chocolate bar next
to me, says, "Keeley got it on her top!" I'm shocked and betrayed
that she's ratted me out. I'm only just learning that she's such a
grass.

My father cocks his head around quickly to look at my top. His
voice is loud and sharper than before. "What did I tell you?" he
says. For a short and pretty-looking man, Dad can make the hairs
on your arms stand up. He has a presence that, if he channeled

it differently, could make him a world leader or, at least, an army general.

I try to look at my top, but I see nothing. I look at my hands—covered in chocolate. I don't know how, but it's there.

"I told you not to get that on ya!" he spits in my direction. He's in a rage. I sit there, frozen, not knowing what to do. "Where's your dummy?" he asks, losing his shit. I don't speak, so he turns around, lifting himself up out of his seat. His thick hand reaches into my car seat, grabs my dummy, then turns back around and starts unwinding the car window. His arm goes around and around the black handle as the glass inches down, disappearing out of sight and letting a breeze enter the vehicle, I feel it move through my hair. I can't see his face, only the back of his head through the headrest. He's losing it at Mother, or maybe it's at me. "I bloody knew she couldn't be trusted! I told you we shouldn't have given it to her!" He catapults my dummy out of the car window as hard as he can, and I watch it land on the thick green grass where I play with the other kids who live in our block of council flats. I stare at it longingly. I'm confused. I didn't mean to get the chocolate over me. I tried my best and failed. And now I've lost my dummy. My lips quiver, and I start crying.

My mother bends down to get something off the floor as Dad rolls the window back up. "Well, great, now I'm the one who's gonna have to listen to her whining while you're at work," Mother says. She produces a wet wipe and turns around to face me. "Give me that," she says in a low tone before taking the remains of the chocolate bar off me and cleaning my hands. I'm so upset. "Keeley, come on." She sighs heavily and blinks, shaking her head from side to side like she's defeated.

"You should have been careful," Deborah says, finishing her chocolate bar. Watching her eat hers makes me wail harder.

"Stop your crying now!" Dad yells as he turns the key in the ignition.

I'm so scared, so scared by him that I halt my tears as the engine roars to life. I learn then to muffle them in front of him. Mother puts the chocolate bar and the wet wipe together and looks at them, frazzled, unsure where to dispose of them.

"That's the last time she's having a dummy. Don't you be giving her another one," Dad warns, and Mother grunts like a child who's been told off. "If I see you giving her a dummy, *that's it.*"

I know what "that's it" means even then; it means if my mother doesn't do what he says, she'll be punished for it. I know the drill. My father's word is final, and we must obey, or we will be punished. My mother sits there completely silent, her eyes lowered, her shoulders collapsing into her chest, curling around so that her back is rounded out. I want to be close to her, to grab on to her and never let go.

Deborah goes to speak. "I didn't..." is all that comes out of her mouth before Mother turns around and politely "Shhhhhs" her, saying, "Not now." She knows what will happen if we annoy Dad further, and she's trying to calm him. We all have to be quiet to steady him. It's a routine I know well.

Deborah doesn't listen and instead takes her shot. "I didn't get any on me." She beams proudly.

"That's great—now, will you give it a rest," Mother says softly. Any happiness in the car has been sucked out and replaced with a somber terror.

Dad is still reeling from my mistake. "I can't believe she got chocolate on that new top," he says. I look out the window at my dummy.

I love chocolate, but that's my dummy! I sleep with that thing. It is the only thing that I want right now. The only thing that will comfort me. That's the last time I see it. My mother will never give it to me again.

Daddy Issues

I hate my father. I really do, and if he were your father, you might hate him, too. I wrote this poem when I was twelve. I think the more nuanced and accurate description of our relationship would be, "I love my father. I hate my father. I love my father. I hate my father." But, as you can see, this version doesn't rhyme, so I settled on the first because if you're going to hate on a parent you might as well be creative about it.

My dad, Roy, embodies a peculiar mix of being both simple and complex. He's charming and funny, but also aloof and uninterested. He has little to no understanding of my interests, yet he never forgets birthdays or Christmases. If I got stuck in Wales and needed a ride home, he's the person I'd call. If I need to move, my car breaks down, or I need a punching bag hung from the ceiling, Dad's the man I can rely on. Great with a screwdriver but not so great with words.

When I was a kid, whenever I asked him a question, he would reply, "Who's asking? The police?" When I asked him where he was going, he would respond, "To see a man about a dog." He's a very private man. You can't get much out of him. He's reserved to a fault—the poster boy for the British stiff upper lip. Still, to this day, I've never seen him cry, not even when the girl he left us for died of cancer at twenty-eight. I didn't see so much as a tear. And I looked. *Trust me*, I looked.

Dad was born in South East London, back when it was home to some of the most notorious gangsters. When the Kray twins were glorified, and acts of violence meant you could rise to power. In a throwback to another era of masculinity, one where "toxic masculinity" was simply known as "being a man." Vulnerability was weakness. The only acceptable emotion was anger.

No one was scarier to me than my dad. I was terrified of him. He had a temper, a short fuse. He would be calm and quiet watching TV, and before you even saw a flicker of emotion, his anger would explode, and bang, he'd whack you. And I'd shit myself with fear. It would happen so quickly that you were unnerved merely because you didn't see it coming, like an actor jumping out at you in a haunted house. I also never knew what he would be angry about. I could get into serious trouble in school, and he wouldn't give a shit, he'd laugh about it, but I could make too much noise when I was eating and that would be it. Being around him was like walking through a field of land mines, not knowing if or when one was going to go off.

Dad grew up in a working-class family—one of five. They all lived under one roof with my grandmother's parents and her siblings packed into bedrooms like sardines. His father died when he was a teenager. And his older sister drank herself to death. He's dyslexic—which, if inherited, is likely where I get it from—but he didn't know until much later. He couldn't read or write until his late teens. Education wasn't seen as important. I'm not entirely sure his parents went to school. And why would they? Why'd you need to get an education when all you're going to get is a job at a factory?

It was a different way of life; getting caned or beaten was the norm. It is this form of punishment that he passed down to us—though his cane was a wooden meter stick and a gigantic wooden spoon. Deborah and I would get whacked by either one of them. Or sometimes we'd get a shoe thrown at us. (This was my family's version of dodgeball.) If none of those were on hand, you'd get it with the metal part of the vacuum cleaner or a whipping with the belt. We'd get smacked and kicked, all the usual forms of corporal punishment.

On one occasion, Deborah flicked a hair tie in Dad's face. He was livid. Deborah knew she was in trouble, so she ran and locked herself in the toilet. Dad kicked the door down in a fit of rage, and then he beat the shit out of her with a metal clothing horse. That one hurt; even I felt it as I sat in the kitchen as silent as a mouse, praying I didn't get it.

One thing that I couldn't stand was that there was no rhyme or reason as to why you would get a beating. It wasn't strictly discipline; it was predicated on Dad's moods, which were more unpredictable than the British weather. And yet, despite growing up in the same household with the same father, Deborah, who is two and a half years older than me, loved Daddy dearly. I could never understand it. To her, Dad was God; he could do no wrong.

She was Daddy's little girl, the type who would buy him "the best Dad in the world" cards for Father's Day and tell him how great he was. She wanted to be around him at all times, and I, who thought he was a mean prick, wanted to be as far away from him as possible. I was so terrified when I was little, that I would glue myself to my mother's side like a stick insect in the hopes he wouldn't come near me. When Mother had to go to work in the evenings and leave me in the care of Dad, I would hold on to her legs and beg her, "Please don't leave me with him! Please take me with you!" Dad's response to this was either to find it funny and tease me or, when he had enough, he'd shout, "Stop your whining and let go of your mother's legs or else!"

As I got older, I learned that showing my fear or vulnerability to my dad was like willingly giving all of my weapons to the enemy. So I started masking it. "It doesn't hurt," I'd say as my father whacked me with the meter stick, or, "Oh, did you actually hit me? I don't feel anything." I kept up the act for as long as I could. Forget tennis lessons or horse riding; I was mastering the art of defiance. I became so determined to be the sort of person to remain undefeated even if I was beaten to my final breath. Sometimes I'd succeed; other times Dad would just continue to whack me until I'd plead mercy.

I always hated myself so much for surrendering. After he'd forced me to apologize, I'd retreat to my room, open my wardrobe to find an old landline phone, stick it in the wall, and call Childline. I knew the number by heart. I'd called them so many times. I was determined to hold my father accountable and to stand up for myself, but whenever someone spoke, I would slam the phone down and unplug it. I wanted so bad to escape but the thought of being taken away and ending up in foster care and getting placed in a home with some weirdo or creep or—God forbid—a vegetarian, I just couldn't risk it. Plus, I was loyal like a dog. I believed you stood by your family no matter what. Even if they murder someone, you stand by their side. Blood is thicker than water.

My mother had it worse than us girls; our beatings could be chalked up to "how it was back then," and I guess, in some regard, so could Mum's, since throughout history domestic violence was often seen as a husband's right. I might have been born in 1986, when UK laws were changing to address domestic violence, but in South East London, we had never heard of these new laws, and it might as well have been happening on another planet for all the good it did for us.

Men from my parents' generation grew up passing down advice to one another: "If your wife gives you any trouble, you just knock her about a bit." Dad, who was twenty-three when he became a father to my older sister, Deborah, operated from this mentality. If Mum didn't have Dad's dinner ready the moment Dad stepped through the door, all hell would break loose, and he would pin her up against the cooker by her neck. That was his move. His thick hands would grab her by the neck and choke her.

My little heart would beat so fast, and every time it happened, I would sit there trying to muster up the courage to do something about it. I'd tell myself that I was strong. That I could stand up to Dad. I managed a few times to overcome my fear and ran into the kitchen with clenched fists and screamed at the top of my lungs,

"LEAVE MY MUM ALONE!" But it didn't matter how much I screamed; it didn't stop him; this was his house and his rules, so we were subjected to living in his antiquated playbook.

My family never dished out apologies or sincerity—everything became a joke. I asked Mum why Dad always choked her up against the cooker because it felt like the cooker was somehow a part of it. In a classic Mum-like fashion, she said, "He had a fetish," adding, "What kinkiness goes on in your house? Ohhhh, I liked to be held by the throat up against the cooker."

While the choking was a regular thing, I only know of Dad really beating my mother once. I was two or three. It was just after they had gotten married. I don't remember it, but Mum tells me it was so bad that Dad called the police himself. Mum held her head over the bath so as not to get blood all over the new beige carpet before getting carted off in an ambulance. The police arrived at our flat, but Dad was let off because he had been the one to call them. That's how it was, you could beat your wife so badly that she goes to the hospital, but because you've done the "decent thing" of calling the police, they let you go.

Mum threatened to leave a few times; one night she even packed a suitcase, and I threw myself inside it. If she was leaving, then I was going with her, but every time Mum threatened to leave, Dad always threatened her right back. "You ain't fucking taking my kids. You try and take them, watch what happens," he'd say. If he'd been paying attention, he would have seen that Mum wasn't taking me—that I was willingly going—but I didn't understand then that it wasn't about us kids; it was about control. The things my dad would say to my mum behind closed doors were as bad as the beating he gave her: insults and stuff to undermine her like, "Why do I need a dog when I've got you? Bark for me, Amber." And here's the thing, it was always behind closed doors. In public, Dad was a saint. Everyone loved him. People wondered how Dad put up with Mum—because Mum was a whole different story when she was out of the house and in front of people. At home I saw a side of my mother that was quiet and timid, anxiously hovering over the stove, worried about setting Dad off, but in public, when Dad was playing the part of The Saint and unable to control her, she was a crude, shocking, and hilarious woman who wanted to make everyone laugh with her profanity.

My parents lived for the weekend. Some people grew up going to church on Sundays; I grew up going to the pub. Dad was as atheist as an atheist can be. He believed God didn't exist, the church was corrupt, and priests were creepy old men you shouldn't trust around your children. (This latter part turned out to be true on many counts.) His religion was getting drunk with friends—a religion I would inherit and overdo.

When we would go out to said pub, Dad would nurse a beer with the husbands while Mum would get pissed with the wives, and before you knew it, she'd be on top of the table, pulling her shirt up and flashing her tits.

Mum was the complete opposite of Dad. Dad didn't talk, and Mum didn't shut up. Once you got her going, that was it, and after a couple of drinks, she was wild. When I was eight or nine, she drunkenly walked down the street pretending to be a donkey in front of all of her and my father's friends. I'd never been so embarrassed as I was when watching my mother walk down the street pissed out of her mind, cocking her leg to the side, and screaming to strangers as they walked on by, "Look at me. I'm a donkey. Hee-haw, hee-haw!!"

In the safety of others, it was always Mum's moment to give Dad shit. At home he ruled, but she was the queen in public, and mockery was her form of punishment. That's when she would refer to him as a "short, bald bastard" or a "tosser," and he would laugh through gritted teeth. She'd pay for it when we got home, but at that moment she would enjoy her freedom and revenge.

From a particularly young age I wanted out of family life. I was fed up. Sick of being chased up the stairs by Dad and whacked with the meter stick. Or coming home from school to see Dad and Deborah had tied my teddy bear Edward from the ceiling by string to make it look like he'd hung himself. One evening, I decided enough was enough. I packed a bag with my teddy bear, Edward, my journal, and some snacks I'd stolen from the kitchen and declared I was leaving.

"Where are you going?" Dad said, with a smug grin across his face.

I had no idea where I was going; I hadn't thought that far ahead. I was following my compulsion to get out of there. I racked my brain and came up with "Spain." Because it was sunny and the only place I knew that was far away from them.

I didn't get very far on my voyage. In fact, I didn't make it past the front gate. Once I got outside, I was suddenly so terrified of what might be out there in the world that I hid around the side of the house behind the trash can, or what we in the UK call a wheelie bin. I sat there for hours, stewing in anger that I was trapped in this family and that there was nothing I could do about it. I planned to sleep outside until I could come up with a real plan, but Mum came out and screamed so loud the whole neighborhood could hear, "KEELEY REBECCA, GET INSIDE NOW!"

You knew it was serious when my middle name was involved.

I went in reluctantly and was greeted by Dad and Deborah, who were sitting on the sofa watching television. "Oh, I thought we'd lost ya," Dad said, placing his hand over his chest, feigning being hurt.

"How was Spain?" said Deborah. "That was a short trip." They both started laughing.

"Must have been *wheelie* good," Dad said.

"I bet it was *wheelie* fun," Deborah said. They went on and on cracking jokes.

I looked at Mum and rolled my eyes. She started laughing, "Sorry," she said, trying to stop herself. "You've got to admit it's pretty funny."

"*Wheelie* funny, you guys are just a bunch of comedians. HA-HA-HA-HA," I said sarcastically as I made my way to my room. I was fluent in sarcasm and jest; those were my default buttons. I had learned the family ritual of turning everything into a joke, but honestly, I'd hit my limit. I'd seen the movie *Matilda*, and that little genius—who was the spitting image of me—got adopted at the end by a kind, loving teacher, and I wanted to be adopted by a kind, loving teacher who would read books to me. If Matilda got to ditch her family, then why did I have to keep mine?

Hollywood movies are partly to blame for putting grand, unrealistic ideas into my head. These kinds of movies sell you lies, and when you're a kid, you don't know they're made up. You grow up believing that a fat white man who lives in the North Pole flew on a reindeer and then came down your chimney and delivered you gifts. When your tooth falls out, you're told that a fairy came down to collect it and left you money. You are fed lies from the moment you are born, and then you watch movies where kids have these magical happy endings and can't fully discern between what's real and what's fantasy.

I was a sucker for a lie. I believed in magic. Despite being miserable at home, despite everything I saw, I held on to this idealistic hope that things were going to get better. That's when my susceptible ears overheard the rumors. *Oh, the rumors.* Nothing greater had ever happened to me than when I overheard Dad quizzing Mum as to whether or not I was his child.

"Are you sure she's mine?" Dad asked.

My eyes lit up.

As the story goes, people around town had started talking when I came out with jet-black hair and looked, as my parents nicknamed me, like an Eskimo. Given Dad had white-blond hair (when he had hair) and bright blue eyes, the usual crap spread around town that I had to be the milkman's, the postman's or some other man's that Mum was apparently having it off with.

As rumors go, this was a pretty dumb one. All you had to do was take one look at my mother's jet-black hair and figure out where that came from. Still, it fascinated me. I clung to the rumor like it was a winning lottery ticket. Because if I wasn't my father's daughter, that meant I had a father out there, one who might love me unconditionally, one who might read to me at night, one who might make me feel like I belonged...one who might be... *David Beckham!* It didn't occur to me that David Beckham would have only been eleven when I was born. The moment the thought crossed my mind that David Beckham could be my father, I was overwhelmed with joy. Home life seemed tolerable with the fantasy that one day David Beckham would come and knock on my front door and reveal his true identity as my father. I dined out on this fantasy for years, yelling at Mum every time Dad pissed me off that my real father was David Beckham. "Oh, shut up, you mug! You aren't that lucky; stop living in fantasyland and accept that Roy is your father," she'd snap. I despised her for this, so when David started dating Victoria, I decided she was going to be replaced. A football player was going to be my father, and a Spice Girl would be my mother. And could they hurry up and collect me so I could see my mother perform "2 Become 1" on tour?

Mum was always the bearer of bad news. It became a joke between Deborah and me when we were older that somehow Mum would tell us stories about people we didn't know, and at the end of the story, they were dead or dying of cancer. When I was eleven, she decided to ruin my life by telling me I was going to have a little baby sister. "But I don't want one!" I said when she told me. "Send her back!" I'd been trying to abandon the family; I didn't want it to expand, and then along came my little sister, G, to shake up the family dynamic.

Before my little sister arrived, I spent most of my time with

Mum; I was Mummy's little soldier who followed her everywhere like a shadow. When G arrived, Mum had to look after a newborn, so she palmed me off on Dad. At first I was unhappy about this arrangement, but over time I started to enjoy it.

What's tricky growing up with a father like mine is that you can hate them for being abusive, you can fantasize about having a different father, but you can still really love them and enjoy spending time with them. It's a complete mindfuck. One that will take you twenty years of therapy to unpack. Spending time with Dad when it was just the two of us and his moods were stable was a blast; I can't even deny it. He would take me to play mini golf and to McDonald's. He taught me how to shoot a pellet gun; we would line up cans in the garden and shoot them. On the weekends, he would take me to work with him. He worked as a window fitter and let me ride on the side of his van. There was a rail screwed on the side for carrying glass, and he would let me hold on to it as he drove down the street. We could go to the DIY stores and the dump—where we would bring all the rubbish at the end of the day. I *loved* going to the DIY stores and the dump. The smell of a DIY store? I mean, come on, the only thing better than that was the gas station.

I was thirteen when my parents separated. Dad became a walking cliché and had an affair with a woman half his age. Deborah uncovered the affair by going through his work phone and finding messages from someone called Jason. Dad didn't have any friends called Jason, and the messages didn't sound like they were from a man, so she called the number and a woman answered.

Julie, a twenty-three-year-old blonde woman who worked the reception at the window fitting company Dad worked for. Deborah told Mum in dismay, and they were both distraught.

After Deborah told Mum and then me—Mum confronted him.

"Oi, you short, bald bastard. I found this in your van," she said, holding up the jewelry box. She'd done her investigating by then and found a gift-boxed pair of earrings that was clearly not for any of us. That's when Dad left. He didn't want to talk about it. Didn't apologize. He even let her get away with calling him a short, bald bastard—which was rare. Dad just got off the sofa, gathered some things, and left.

Nothing was more bittersweet than the moment he walked out the door. I never knew I could be so happy and sad. Everyone around us believed that the breakdown of the nuclear family was one of the worst things that could happen to a child. They place so much emphasis on staying together for the children. Let me tell you, there is nothing worse than growing up in an abusive, chaotic, toxic household with parents who hate each other's guts. I wish they'd broken up sooner.

After Dad left, I saw him briefly every other weekend when he came to pick up G and sometimes when he stopped by on a Wednesday evening. Even though he'd stopped living with us, he still managed to assert himself. On one of his Wednesday visits, when I refused to stay in the living room, as I was walking up the stairs to my bedroom, he leaped up from the sofa, grabbed me by the hair, whipped me backward, and dragged me back down them. "I told you not to go up them stairs," Dad said, as I refrained from crying. The back of my head was killing me, but I pretended, like I always did, that it didn't hurt.

I went from seeing Dad every other weekend and on the occasional Wednesday to every morning. It was an arrangement my parents came up with when Mum was being prosecuted for my lack of attendance at school. They devised a plan to get me there to stop her from being sentenced. Dad was tasked with picking me up and dropping me off at the gate. His white van would pull up each morning, I would jump in, and we would ride the whole way in silence. He never spoke about the affair or his leaving; he never asked me about school or my life. He was like an Uber driver; he picked me up, dropped me off, and then went about his day.

If there is one thing I've learned to appreciate about my father in my adult years, it is that he has developed a sense of self-awareness and emotional maturity he didn't have when he was younger. On being a dad, he has accepted that he was, perhaps, not the greatest. "Look, they make you take a test to drive a car. No one makes you take a test to be a parent," he said. And while it felt like an excuse, it also felt like one of the smartest things he's ever said. As a kid, Dad blamed everyone else for his actions; he accepted no responsibility. Abusing Mum was always because of something she had said or done, but the older Dad has gotten, the more he can look at himself and attest to his character defects and even admit that "It's much easier to blame others than to take responsibility." The older he gets, he's more open and willing to talk. He shows a depth that wasn't present when I was younger. He's said many things that have given me pause. He has acknowledged that he's unable to control his emotions, and I quote that he's "not very nice to women." He admitted that he doesn't automatically consider how his actions make other people feel, which, I'm not going to lie, raised some alarm bells. But lately he's been making an effort to understand their impact.

"I've often wondered if you girls have turned out the way you have because of me," he said to me sometime in my thirties over dinner. Hearing Dad ask such a question made me want to cry while simultaneously saying, "No shit, Sherlock." But instead, I got curious and asked him what he meant.

"Well, I don't know. You girls' taste in men for a start..." he said, commenting on some of the terrible men my sisters and I had dated.

"If you're asking why we all date assholes," I replied with a smirk, "we've all got daddy issues." Dad and I laughed. I took a sip of wine and decided now was the time to break the family tradition of deflecting with humor and launch into attachment theories. I explained, as my therapists had explained to me, that unconsciously, humans are wired to re-create how they felt in their homes of origin, how you experienced love as a child can determine whom you seek as partners, so that could explain why "we've" dated men that have abused us, because that's what we witnessed growing up. That's what was familiar. That's what I was subconsciously trying to re-create so I could redo it in the hopes that this time I could get my needs met. (Shocker— I never did.)

Dad seemed intrigued, so I continued, so very excited to talk about one of my favorite topics: *the brain.* I spoke about the psychological impact of abuse and trauma and what happens to the nervous system and the amygdala. "The what?" Dad said, like I was suddenly speaking French. I explained that the amygdala, which is sometimes referred to as "the lizard brain," is located at the back of the brain and is responsible for processing emotions, but halfway through my lecture, I decided it was best if I didn't get too overly excited and try to conduct a neuroscience lesson and perhaps just say what I wanted to say in plain terms.

"Look, the way you were as a parent growing up and who you are as an individual is a by-product of a certain number of factors. One of those factors is your upbringing. What did your childhood look like? Were both of your parents present? What was their relationship like? How emotionally mature were they? How did they treat you? Did you feel seen? Did you feel loved? Do you have unmet wants and needs? All of that contributes to who you are, what lens you view the world through, and how you show up."

"Oh, right," Dad said, squinting as if he was thinking about what I said or deciding whether I was crazy.

We ended the dinner with me drunkenly ordering Dad a copy of the book I was currently reading on Amazon, *What Happened to You? Conversations on Trauma, Resilience, and Healing*, by Oprah Winfrey and Dr. Bruce Perry, which is a funny way to end an evening with a parent—buying them a book that's title implicitly implies that they fucked you up. I'd been completely sincere in the moment, but I found this funnier the next morning when I'd sobered up, realizing that perhaps buying a man who'd never been taught how to read or write as a child and had only read one book in his adult life—which was a book on green juicing or something related to eating healthy that he read during the pandemic—was maybe not the best way for me to get him to look further inward to understand why he turned out the way he did.

But still, I tried.

I tried because it was this relationship that had fucked me up the most. And while I understood all the reasons it had fucked me up and I could write a detailed essay on it, along with a detailed psychological analysis of Dad's character defects, potential personality disorders, limitations and capabilities, social conditioning, and biases, none of that eradicates the psychological imprint and trauma. It didn't change its impact. It's all well and good knowing these things, but knowing them is half the problem. I can intellectually understand that I can feel hate toward my father because he used violence to control my mother and sisters, but it didn't stop me from confusing love with physical attraction, hate, fear, addiction, and a whole bunch of other things it's not. It didn't stop me from confusing dependability with affection. Emotional abuse with fondness. Intimacy with intensity. Sex with closeness. It takes years and years of work to uncover these things and make the unconscious *conscious*, and yet you can still be romantically involved with a man you know is a version of your father and be unable to do anything about it. You'll lie in bed next to him at night begging yourself to leave him—you'll read everything you can on love and sex addiction, but it will take him destroying your life for you to do it. And even then, sometimes he'll destroy your life, and it will take *him* leaving *you* for you to be done with it. The relationship you did or didn't have with your parents will get to ya one way or another, even if you think it won't.

I'm not sure whether Dad ever got around to reading the book I drunkenly sent him, but when I mentioned to Mum that I'd ordered him a book without naming the title, she said with the utmost jealousy, "Oh, so you've ordered your dad a book? Didn't order me one, then." So I got on Amazon and mailed her a copy. It felt poetic, really—I had daddy issues because Mum had me with a man who abused her, and she ended up with a man who abused her because she grew up with a shitty and absent father. And also a shitty and semi-absent mother, who also had a shitty father, but if you get me started on this train, then I'm afraid it will just keep on going and going and going.

My Name Is Kevin

The year was 1990, and all I wanted for Christmas was the coolest toy I'd ever seen—a *Ghostbusters* backpack. This thing was epic! A backpack with a gun attached and a trap that opens up when you catch a ghost. I watched the movie and became obsessed. I couldn't stop talking about it. I was going to catch ghosts and then release them in my sister's bed. My best friend, Max, wanted it, too, and that made total sense because Max and I were practically twins. We liked all the same stuff: guns, cars, slime, climbing trees, and *Teenage Mutant Ninja Turtles*. But there's one small snag, one tiny detail I haven't accounted for: Max was a boy, and I was, quite definitively, in the eyes of the world, not.

The adults around us are quick to point out this glaring difference. Max could want the *Ghostbusters* backpack. But me? I was told to ask for a doll.

Now, I was four, so I wasn't fully prepared for this kind of life-altering realization. But there it was—clear as day—toys were segregated! There were boys' toys, like guns and cars and slime—basically all the fun stuff—and then there were girls' toys. So. Many. Dolls. Dolls that were short, dolls that were tall, dolls that looked like cabbages (seriously, why?), dolls that looked like babies, and dolls that looked like women with perfect blonde hair and impossibly tiny waists. There was even this one doll that peed and pooped, and you were given the fun task of changing its nappy. But all I wanted was that *Ghostbusters* backpack.

"I want a *Ghostbusters* backpack," I said, practically vibrating with excitement. It's the only thing on my mind. Aunt Anne, who clearly was not paying attention to my wishes, looked at me and said, "You don't want that! That's a boy toy... Why don't you ask for a doll?"

I looked at her with all the disgust I could muster. Like, really, Anne? No, I don't want to cradle a doll, give it a bottle, and pretend to be a mum, thanks. I want to climb a tree and kill ghosts.

But it wasn't just Aunt Anne. Everywhere I went, I was told the same thing. My mum's friends' daughters would sit in a circle and pass the dolls around as if they were real babies, and I was supposed to join in. "Come sit with the girls," they'd say, but all I wanted was to be outside with the boys, having gunfights and rolling around in the dirt.

So I decided to take matters into my own hands. If the only path to being afforded the freedom of being a boy and getting my *Ghostbusters* backpack was to become a boy, then that's what I was going to do. Dad seemed to have it better anyway. So when Mum took me for my next haircut, I told the hairdresser to cut my hair like the Australian pop star Jason Donovan. And they did it. Mum couldn't say anything because she had short hair. Next, I refused to wear dresses. Even at four, I was so strong-minded and stubborn; it would drive my mum nuts. She'd smack me, and I'd still refuse to put a dress on. And in the final act of defiance, I changed my name to Kevin. That's right, *Kevin*.

Every time someone would call me Keeley, I would yell, "MY NAME IS KEVIN!"

And for six glorious months, I didn't go by any other name. I was Kevin, a boy who could ask for a *Ghostbusters* backpack without anyone batting an eye. I hung out with Max and played with all the toys I liked, and just like my dad, I got to sit on my arse with my legs sprawled and watch television while Mum cooked me dinner.

Of course, it didn't last forever. Max moved, and I became friends with two girls who loved wearing dresses. *Yuck.* Eventually I went back to being Keeley, which turned out to be quite fateful in the grand scheme of things, but I never really let go of that first sharp lesson about the world: Life is different for girls and boys. Life is *very* different.

You've Made Your Bed, Now Lie in It

Back in 1961, long before the women's movement came to shake things up, before women could have credit cards in their names, before they could obtain mortgages, before marital rape was considered a crime, at a time when traditional gender roles were deeply ingrained in society, it was hardly a blessing in life to be a woman—even worse, a pregnant, poor, working-class woman out of wedlock who has no desire to be a mother. Nothing was more shameful and faced more social stigma than having sex outside of marriage and getting yourself knocked up.

Enter my grandmother, Dorian, a factory worker who hid her pregnancy like a goddamn Russian spy because not only would this information destroy her reputation but could also have cost her her job. Yep, you could get fired for being pregnant, and without a husband, you were shunned from society. What fun times.

In a state of panic, and with abortion being illegal, she told no one she was pregnant and lied about her name when she gave birth to my mother—her only child. Written on my mother's birth certificate is the last name "Levitt," the name of a solicitor's firm Dorian had driven past on the way to give birth, along with "father unknown." But this was not the truth. Dorian—a woman I've met approximately three times because she worked in the petrol station up the road from my school—knew who my mother's father was: an Irish immigrant window cleaner. When my great-grandparents eventually found out, they were mortified that she had a baby outside of wedlock and forced her to marry the Irish immigrant window cleaner as quickly as possible. That's how you fixed reputations back then: shotgun weddings. My grandparents' marriage didn't last long (shocker). When they split, my mother, just a little girl, got shipped off to live with her Irish grandmother by the seaside. Dorian didn't stick around. And as for the window cleaner? He stuck around just long enough to find a new wife and start a new family—and acted like my mother never existed.

Reluctantly, my great-grandmother—who somehow lived to one hundred and one despite a diet of mostly cake—took in my mother. She raised her until around the age of ten, when my mother decided she'd had enough of the seaside and called up Dorian to ask if she could live with her in London. Dorian agreed—not out of love but out of duty. She strongly lived by the motto "You made your bed, now lie in it." So my mother moved to South East London to live with a woman who had no maternal instincts and, by all accounts, even less patience. Her childhood wasn't just tough—it was full-on misery memoir material. She didn't get a real pet, but she took in two mice that she left on the windowsill one Christmas, and they froze to death. Mum had thought her Irish grandmother was strict and cold, but that was nothing compared to Dorian. Abuse, neglect, and a general absence of love were daily realities.

Dorian hadn't wanted to be a mother at a time when she had no choice. And yet, instead of giving my mother up for adoption to people who may have loved and cared for her, she stuck out raising a child she didn't want because she had been raised to believe when you made your bed, you must lie in it.

This motto seemed to be a generational anthem for the women in my life who came before me, reinforcing the idea that they had to accept the consequences of choices they barely had the freedom to make in the first place.

My mother had the kind of beauty that could have been her ticket out of poverty. She could have been a model. In her youth she was outrageously beautiful, with a symmetrical face that lent itself to the societal beauty standards of fashion models. She has high cheekbones, curly hair, light hazel-green eyes, and naturally full lips. They were so big she was often called Rubber Lips, which, somehow, back in the day, was an insult. Now you can't scroll through Instagram without seeing dozens of girls who've paid surgeons good money to look the same.

She's tall, too, the tallest in the family—easily four inches taller than Dad. When they stood next to each other, she looked like a skyscraper and he looked like a charming cottage, and she's all legs. Long, slim legs.

A few people tried to talk her into modeling. She even got scouted once by a big agency, but she didn't follow through. She had no interest. To be a model meant having your photo taken, and she hated it. If you so much as point a camera at her, she'll pick up the nearest item and hide behind it or pull a face. In most of the photos I have of my mother on my phone, she has a teapot in front of her face or this awkward look like she's a five-year-old child who's just been caught peeing on the carpet.

She also never viewed herself as beautiful, and maybe that's why she never saw her beauty as a commodity or a privilege, or perhaps she didn't like the unwanted attention that it rendered.

In my twenties, I used to think that my mother rejected the conventional "packaging" of women's beauty of her era as an act of rebellion, but now I think it was to draw less attention to her physique for fear of what would happen. Beauty can leave a woman vulnerable, visible, unsafe—all the things modeling left me.

It's telling that now that she's in her sixties and the world has stopped paying as much attention, she seems to care more about her appearance than she ever did when she was young and could have capitalized on it. She goes to the hair salon and wears foundation. Growing up, the only makeup I ever saw her wear was lipstick, and that was rare.

"I can't understand them mothers who put makeup on to drop their kids off at school!" she would say as we walked past women who looked like they were on a photo shoot, foundation caked on, painted nails, tight feminine clothing, and not a hair out of place. Mother was the opposite. She didn't conform to the expectations of soft, feminine beauty but instead seemed to lean into a more androgynous aesthetic. She always looked stylish, don't get me wrong, and if there was any vanity in her character, it was all in how she dressed, but it wasn't about looking sexy or enhancing her figure. It was all in the name of fashion. She wore trousers and men's shoes with her short pixie haircut and looked like she stepped out of an avant-garde fashion magazine.

From the exterior she appeared to be rebelling against the ideals of what it meant to be a woman, but in reality she was a total traditionalist.

What she wanted—more than beauty or success—was love, which, in her naïveté, she equated with a classic domestic ideal. To her, love was an image: a polished partnership, a boyfriend on paper who would love her unconditionally. But it was just that—*an image*, polished and pretty but lacking emotional depth. Having only known love marked by neglect, cruelty, and rejection, she clung to the idea of love without the emotional maturity to see beyond its surface. Love was punishment; love was hate.

Enter my father.

My parents met in one of the most romantic ways back then: at a bus stop. Dad was engaged to a woman named Kay, whom Mother knew and was loosely friends with. She introduced them. "Kay was the love of your father's life," Mother said when telling me the story. "*Blonde*," she added with a look. I was eight. I didn't know what she meant by this comment, except that blonde hair seemed superior to my dark brown, almost black hair.

Dad got carted off to prison for a few months for reasons I still don't fully know, but I think it involved stealing and crashing a stolen car under the influence. (Apparently, Dad was great at stealing cars. I didn't inherit that skill, but I would later learn I was great at setting them on fire.) When he got out, Kay called off the engagement and my parents became friends. I'm not sure how long they were friends before they started dating, but when they started, it was only three months into their relationship that Mother fell pregnant with Deborah. She was twenty-one, and my father was twenty-three.

A few years later, I was born, and a few years after that, they married in a registry office in Lewisham because Dad refused to step foot inside a church.

Dorian disapproved of Mother's marriage. In her eyes, Dad was a waste of space—a good-for-nothing loser who'd been to prison and wasn't going to treat her right. Just before Mother signed the paperwork, Dorian turned to her and said, "It's never too late to back out. Marrying that man will be the biggest mistake of your life." My mother took the pen, looked at Dorian, and signed, partly, I think, in spite, partly for love (if that's what you can call it), but mostly for money. More accurately, the saving of money in the form of tax credits. By legally binding yourself to an individual of the opposite sex, you saved money—and money improved one's fortunes. And since my parents were dead broke and sharing children already, they might as well get hitched and save some cash. God knows we needed it.

Dorian didn't attend the wedding, causing *quite* a stir, and that was the end of their relationship. She walked out of my mother's life for the unforgivable act of marrying my "good-for-nothing" father while I enjoyed the party and made my first public appearance... topless.

"You ran around the whole night with your top off!" I've been told by nearly all who attended. I was two and a half and meant to be dressed in a polka-dot two-piece that Mother picked up from a market stall, but I took my top off and refused to put it back on—clearly a sign of what the future would hold.

Of course, Dorian was right about Dad. He treated her like shit. And Mother saw Dorian once more after the wedding. A few months later was the incident when Dad beat her so badly that he called the police as Mother held her head over the bath so she didn't get blood on the beige carpet.

Dorian showed up at the hospital and found Mother in a hospital bed. Mother begged Dorian for money, begged for her to take her home with her to get her away from this man, but she wouldn't. Instead, she busted out that famous motto of hers. "You've made your bed, now you must lie in it," she said. And with that, Dorian walked out of the hospital, leaving Mother to come back home to our council flat to deal with the misfortunes of her choices.

Mother inherited this motto, adopted it in fact, and tried to make the most of the bed she had made, which just happened to be in a council flat in Catford, a stone's throw away from Lewisham.

We lived there until I was about five, then moved around the corner to the Excalibur Estate. The word "estate" conjures up images of expansive country land with a large mansion in the middle and horses with names like Betsy, Doubtlet, and Sanction. The Excalibur Estate was nothing like that, though I'm sure there was a resident called Betsy—about seventy years old and with a cigarette dangling from her mouth at all times.

The estates you found in the country were for rich people. And council estates were for poor people. It was government-funded housing that had the same reputation and trappings as the projects.

The Excalibur Estate wasn't any old council estate; for a start, it looked nothing like other council estates in London. It consisted of 187 prefabs and one tin-roofed church. These cheaply made, quickly assembled houses were churned out post–World War II to solve England's housing crisis. They were prefabricated in warehouses, shipped to Catford in flat packs, and assembled by German and Italian prisoners of war. The walls were resin-bonded plywood, painted in ivory, with felt-covered flat roofs and single-pane timber windows. It looked more like a trailer park in South Carolina than anything else—so wildly out of place like you'd been transported to another time entirely.

The prefabs weren't expected to last ten years. Forty years later, when we lived there, their ivory paint had faded to streaky off-white, mold clung to the walls, and blackberry bushes overtook the lawns. The interiors weren't much better—outdated and far past acceptable living standards. Dad spent weekends stripping walls and replacing tiles, pouring time and money we didn't have into a government-owned property. It was baffling to me to decorate a home we didn't own, but the government wasn't in any rush to fix it. They thought we should be grateful that they'd transformed the slums at all. What more did we want? A working toilet to shit on?

Mother had limited options in the bed she had made. Financially, leaving Dad was an impossibility, not to mention unsafe. Who knew what hell Dad would put her through, and quite honestly, *society*. This was the time of "you've got to stay together for the kids no matter what."

In light of her choices, she decided she wanted to become a homeowner—to stick it to Dorian and prove she'd "made it." Living on a council estate was a source of shame. Renting carried a stigma. But being a homeowner, *now that* was a badge of honor.

Margaret Thatcher had introduced the Right to Buy scheme, which allowed council tenants to buy their homes at discounted rates. It was a way for people like us, who couldn't afford non-government-funded housing, to get on the property ladder. But our prefab in Catford was excluded—which made sense because it was planned to be demolished decades ago. Determined, Mother listed our prefab on the council's home exchange list, hoping to swap it for something eligible for Dad to purchase since he was the only one who could get a mortgage.

Trading a prefab for a real house felt like swapping our beat-up Ford Escort for a new Mercedes. Why would anyone in their right mind do that? Mother was certain it was never going to happen. "Luck has never been my friend," she said. But still, she put an ad in the local paper.

At the time, a TV show featured a girl with a magical fifty-pence coin that granted wishes when she rubbed the queen's nose. I begged Mum for a fifty-pence coin and rubbed the queen's nose like my life depended on it. I wished for a house for us and end-less chocolate for me, and a week later, we got a reply from an older couple. The woman was in a wheelchair, and they needed a house without stairs—exactly what we had. Mum couldn't believe our luck. And I couldn't believe my wishing had worked. Now all I had to do was wait for my chocolate.

I swear, the day Dad finished renovating the prefab was the day we moved. Everything we owned was shoved into boxes and loaded into Dad's work van. I was beyond excited when we arrived at our new home. I had no idea what it looked like until moving day. I was shocked to see it was a house—an actual house made of brick and not plywood. This was the greatest day of our lives. Mum fumbled with the key. Deborah and I shoved each other, arguing over who would go in first. She won, but when Deborah stepped in, it was clear she hadn't really won. The house was so grotesque, I started dry-heaving. I tried to bolt back outside, but Dad's sharp tone stopped me: "Don't you fucking make a scene."

Nose pinched, I turned back in. I don't know if I smelled dog shit, dead people, or both. I headed upstairs to escape the smell, Deborah trailing behind me. We explored the three small bedrooms in less than a minute—cobwebs, stained walls, dirty red carpets everywhere complete with black dog hair. The place looked like a derelict crack den. Our prefab wasn't exactly a palace but at least it didn't look or smell like a sewer.

"I'm getting the biggest room because I'm the eldest," Deborah announced.

"Shut up, Veruca Salt," I shot back, too nauseated to argue properly, running downstairs. I found Mum. "I hate it here. Can we please go back to the prefab?" I begged. It felt so unfair. Why did all of her bad choices have to affect me? She tried to reassure me. "It'll be amazing when we're finished. You'll get to pick your bedroom colors." I stuck out my bottom lip.

"You can have the bigger room," she whispered. I perked up slightly but still wanted to burn the place down. The penny— or the fifty pence—had dropped. No wonder the old couple was desperate to swap. If I were them, I'd have swapped for a tent.

I was supposed to help carry the boxes from the van, but instead I found myself holding my nose and looking at the toilet in a tiny room off the kitchen.

"An old man died on the toilet, you know," Deborah said, peering over my shoulder as I looked at the filthy toilet bowl, wondering if I would get sick by simply sitting on the thing.

"Didn't Elvis die on the toilet?" I asked.

"He died eating a hamburger," she said definitively.

"I thought he died on the toilet?"

"He died eating a hamburger *on* the toilet," she said, her eyes narrowing as if it might happen to me.

I looked at her, not knowing if she was telling the truth, and then I looked back at the toilet. I was about to make a lame joke about being "all shook up," but I started to get emotional, so I tried to stuff it down.

"We have stairs," I said as if it had just occurred to me. "We have stairs now." Just then, a loud clackety-clack echoed through the house as earthquake-like vibrations rippled through my body, making everything shake. Deborah and I ran to the kitchen window only to see a train fly by.

"We live on a train track!" she yelled, both exhilarated and terrified.

Dad managed to get a mortgage and purchase our house from the government for twenty thousand pounds. At the time, it seemed like so much money, but Mum said it was worth every penny to be homeowners and no longer council tenants. Dad started renovating, ripping the house apart. I lived on a blowup mattress in my parents' room for months while he decorated my bedroom.

Two years after we moved in, he painted my room mint green

and baby pink—then ran off with twenty-three-year-old Julie, leaving the rest of the house in shambles.

After his departure, nothing in the house changed. No improvements were made. All the work just stopped. Mid-refurbishment. Stopped. Paused. And it never resumed. It was like everything got stripped in preproduction for a makeover that never quite happened.

There was a half-built wall in the garden, a half-built archway in the kitchen, plasterboard and tools, bare floorboards, and walls without wallpaper that ended up getting littered with graffiti—the hallway and garden had so many building items in them that our house looked like a home improvement store on its best days and a junkyard on its worst.

Mum gave everything to be the perfect wife and mother, doing all of the domestic duties, and even waitressing in the evenings. All she had wanted was love and a home, and Dad had left her with three kids, no money, and a half-decorated piece of shit. So much for "you've made your bed, now lie in it."

Rightly so, she was angry. Mum had stuck out this terrible marriage with a man who abused her only to be left in this mess.

So she did what all women do when they're in a crisis. *She cut her hair off.*

Over the years, she had grown it out, and now she had cut it all off into the shape of a mushroom. A dark black mushroom. She got a Winnie-the-Pooh and Piglet tattoo on her shoulder. And she was losing weight by the minute. Every day she was getting skinnier and skinnier until she looked like someone had eaten her and all they had left were bones.

I found her in the kitchen a month after Dad left, on her

knees at the bottom cabinet, pulling china plates out and smashing them onto the floor. "YOU KIDS! I'M SICK OF LIVING IN THIS HOUSE WITH A BUNCH OF SLOBS! TIDYING UP AFTER YOU! YOU'RE ALL A BUNCH OF PISS-TAKERS! I DO THE WASHING UP…" She threw another plate on the floor. The white porcelain cracked and shot across the floor into tiny pieces. "THE CLEANING WHILE YOU LOT SIT ON YOUR ARSES, WHY DON'T YOU!"

I stood there and watched her in bewildered amusement. Mum clocked me standing by the half-built wooden frame and hurled a plate in my direction, so I backed off.

I'll tell you what, the trains were good for one thing—in the middle of Mother's yelling, they would muffle the sound of her voice, and I'd miss all of her insults.

"You Keeley, I've had ENOUGH OF YOU…(train passing)…that's it now!"

Her anger seemed to be a product of history repeating itself. Playing in a loop. Dorian stayed in a life she didn't want because she thought she had no choice. Mother did the same. And now here I was—standing in a half-finished house, dodging flying plates, wondering if this was just the family tradition.

I went back upstairs to my room, terrified. I sat on my floor, and I prayed that I would never end up in this mess. That I would never end up trapped like my mother.

Differences

When we lived in the prefab in Catford, a library bus would stop near our estate once a week. It was exactly what it sounded like—a bus that had been turned into a library. I was always so thrilled when it arrived. "The bus is here!" I'd scream with excitement and run around the corner, jump on, and check out the latest books. No one in my family read, but learning was one of my favorite things. I was such a nerd. I loved books. I loved school. I had high grades and was friends with the smartest kids in my class. I desperately wanted a pair of glasses because every smart person wore them, so I pretended I couldn't see during my eye test.

"Can you tell me what that letter is?" the eye examiner asked.

"F," I'd said, knowing full well that it was a G.

I had my eyes examined three times because the doctor couldn't determine whether I was starting to go blind. Eventually, he realized I had perfect vision and gave me a fake pair of glasses to wear.

When we moved to Grove Park, I was eleven, and that fall, I

started high school. I got into a school in Bromley, a neighborhood close by but vastly different. Grove Park, like Catford, was urban. Bromley was suburban. Grove Park was racially diverse. Bromley was a sea of white. Grove Park was considered rough. Bromley was what we called "posh." It had a rich history of being middle- to upper-class. Our house in Grove Park was a part of the Downham housing estate, filled with working-class people. The residents of Bromley were so appalled by the likes of my people that they once built a wall to keep us out.

I did well in my first year. Despite being dyslexic, I was mostly in the top sets, with all the smartest kids. The teachers were always confused. They would say, "She keeps writing 'coming' instead of 'going' and gets her Ds and Bs mixed up, but she just got an A on this science test. We don't understand it. Is she cheating?"

I didn't know if I was coming or going. I felt completely misunderstood by everything and everyone, but I applied myself, worked hard, and genuinely loved learning.

I was one of two children in the school to be chosen to perform in a play that started at the local theater and then went on to have a few runs at the Royal Opera House.

During a talent competition I'd entered, they asked me what I would do if given ten thousand pounds. "Save it to go to university," I said. I wanted to be the first person in my family to go to university, but then I became a teenager. And teenagers, as we know, are not normal or nice. Hormones were pumping through me, and something embarrassing seemed to always be happening to me. My period arrived in a swimming pool. In the same pool, my bikini top popped off in front of one of the boys in my year. He saw my left tit, told everyone, and I never wanted to go to school again. An older boy was always tripping me up on the stairs. And if he wasn't, I was somehow always falling over like I had two left feet. Mr. Gardener, the most horrendous teacher, entered my life, and he disliked me greatly. Very quickly I stopped wanting to go to university because I realized that it was filled with teachers, and my teachers were knobs, and there would be nothing worse than ending up like them.

Being a teenager was an overwhelming, chaotic experience, highlighting how unfair everything was and how mean people were to those different from them. My only recourse was to rebel.

If you met me at twelve, and then thirteen, it was like I'd had a complete personality transplant. I was not the same person. I went from having good grades to getting kicked out of half my classes. I was always in trouble. Always in detention. I spent more time in Mr. Gardener's office than in any classroom. "You're a disgrace to this school," he said, leaning over his desk. "Your life is going to amount to nothing."

"Well, great," I replied. "If my life is going to amount to nothing, then I don't need to come to school." And that was it. I walked out and stopped going.

I Have a Confession

My name is Keeley Hazell. I just turned thirteen and I have a confession. Okay, this is going to sound a little nuts. I'm mentally okay, well, I guess that's up for debate because once I confess, you'll probably think I'm batshit and should be committed. Personally, I would argue that I'm just creative and curious. That's right—not crazy, but *curious*. I'm so curious, so curious, that when someone offered me to smoke cocaine from a can the other day, I jumped at the chance. I'd never tried cocaine, and how can I know if I like it if I've never tried it? I sucked it through a straw out of the side of a Coke can and felt like I'd eaten a pack of paints and gotten on a roller coaster that goes upside down and immediately decided that I hate cocaine, which I guess turned out to actually not be cocaine but *crack*. An ever-so-slight difference that the guy who offered it to me failed to mention. Anyway, that isn't the confession. The confession is that I've discovered fire. I didn't "discover" it. Obviously, it's been around for years, but I got myself a lighter and discovered how to create fires, and man, fire is sooooo cool. I used to think that the Ghost-busters were cool, but have you ever lit a match and put a piece of paper on the flames? It's amazing. The orange, the warmth. I was sold. I'd always loved science. I liked knowing what compounds contracted heat and which didn't. I'm actually top of my science class. And maths. I'm just obsessed with knowing things. I used to have this science book that had a record in it, you know, one of those things they had before tapes and CDs. Anyway, it explained how you scratch the record with the metal needle; it moves through the grooves on a record, vibrates, and these vibrations are then converted into electrical signals, which turn into sound. I mean, what? MIND BLOWN. It's all just so fascinating. So, I was playing around with fire and thought I would try a science experiment and see what things caught alight. Leaves, they did not. Plastic bottles—they're lame. They just sort of melt. Don't ever burn plastic bottles. They're dumb and boring. Paper goes up really quickly, but not all paper, weirdly. Next, I put gasoline into the mix. I found an abandoned petrol can. I don't know if you know this, but gasoline and fire are like star-crossed lovers. Wow. Sparks are flying between those two. They're like Romeo and Juliet. So I started pouring gasoline onto things and watching what happened. I was blown away. It was magic. I was in love, but I needed something bigger to burn so I could see fire on a larger scale. I wanted something I could make explode. I went into the woods. But I couldn't find anything, until I came out of the woods and noticed the abandoned car. This thing had been sitting there for months, rusting, with flat tires. It was ugly as hell, and it was stolen. Deborah's friend Kirsty had stolen it and left it abandoned on our street, which was very offensive because she didn't leave it on her own street. No, the residents of our road had to look at the ugly thing. And it was a two-door car. Who in their right mind steals a two-door car? If you're gonna steal a car, make sure it has at least four doors! Plus, it was left unlocked, so really, it had it coming. And really, I was doing Kirsty a favor because if the police ever found this thing, I bet they'd have found her fingerprints all over it. I popped the boot, poured gasoline over the back seats, set a bit of newspaper on fire with my lighter, and threw it in. I thought it was going to be like the movies: that it was gonna explode into a fire bomb. But it was so anticlimactic. Nothing went up in flames, not even the paper. My science experiment was a failure. So much so that I actually walked away. The car was parked next to a park, so I went in there and tested my lighter on the swings. The metal heated up but didn't catch fire, which was interesting because cars are largely made of metal. When I turned back around, well, let's just say it was lucky that the fire station was about a hundred meters away because there was orange all right, and thick black smoke. The car had gone up in flames, and I was like, *What the fuck have I done?! Fire is the scariest thing on the planet! Why did I do this? What is wrong with me? Why can't I control my brain sometimes?* It's like when someone puts a cookie in front of me and says, "Don't eat it." And I can't control myself and put it in my mouth.

I threw my lighter into a bush to discard the evidence and ran to the fire station. "Help! Help! A car is on fire! Some stupid kid did it, and he ran away!" They put it out, and then I felt so bad. Oh, my days, I felt so guilty. I don't think I've ever done something as stupid as this before. Well, that's up for debate. I did... I'm gonna save that for another confession. I felt so bad that the firefighters had to come out and guilty that Kirsty had gone to all this trouble to steal this ugly two-door car and I'd burned it to the ground. *And I did burn it to the ground.* By the time they put it out, it was a black frame. So, to make amends, I went to the petrol station and I stole some flowers and left them on Kirsty's doorstep along with a note, "I'm sorry for setting your car on fire. I hope you get a new one with four doors."

The Class Ceiling

My mother used to say, "I couldn't leave your father because I was dependent on him financially." Even with a job, she couldn't afford to build a life for us without him. That dependency became her prison. We were poor before he left, but after, we were poor on a whole different level. It's one thing to be poor, it's another to feel it.

We couldn't afford to have the heating on during the winter, so Mum had it on a timer to come on for a few hours a night so we didn't freeze to death. The hot water was conserved for two hours a day for baths. All the lights had to be turned off, and anything electrical plugged in and not being used had to be turned off by the switch. The gas and electricity were both on card meters, and sometimes they would just run out, and everything would switch off like a power outage. Before Dad's departure, we had the luxury of MTV and Nickelodeon, but now we didn't even have those. And Mum would kill us if we tried to make any calls from the landline. She switched it off at one point so that you couldn't make any outgoing calls, period.

We were on any form of welfare we could get. The only reason I could eat in school was because of the government. They paid for my school uniform. And I got a meal ticket at lunch. I had to line up to get my £1.50 voucher and endure teasing from other kids. "Your family is so poor you have to get a meal ticket!" a boy said, laughing in my face, so I walked over to where they kept the salt packets, picked up three or four, opened them, tipped them into his hair, and laughed while saying, "Ahhhh, you're so poor your mum can't afford to buy you Head and Shoulders for your dandruff!"

Mum kept filling out forms and applying for any benefits she could get, but it never seemed to be enough. After school, I would search the coin return in phone boxes, trying to scrape together £1.99 to buy chicken and chips. Some days I'd get lucky; some days I'd have to wait until the chicken shop was closing, and Raj, who ran the joint, would give me the throwaway scraps for free. Times were rough. Money was scarce. Mum was in full survival mode, trying to keep up the mortgage payments so she didn't lose the house. She was constantly worried about how to put food on the table. Not that we had a table for her to put it on. Most of the time I was in trouble and Mum was yelling, "Keeley Rebecca, I'm gonna fucking kill you if you don't start behaving!" She would try to ground me, and I'd jump out of the window. It didn't matter how high or dangerous it was. I'd risk breaking my leg to be out of that house. Home for me during that time was a nightmare. It was the last place on earth I wanted to be. And school was very much the same. I hated it. Being poor was a source of shame. The teasing, the meal tickets, the ruthless authoritarian teachers with illogical rules.

The only place that offered some sort of ease from the dissatisfaction of life was the streets. They were my happy place. Filled with chaos and mayhem but the good kind. This is why so many kids end up getting into gangs, because they give you a sense of belonging and of family when you feel like you don't have one.

My crew all gathered at a wall in Grove Park. It was a crumbling brick wall next to the fish and chip shop, and we'd hang out there for hours. We'd plot ways to make money or just shoot the shit, like we did on this one afternoon.

"So, I've heard if you steal clothes and shit from M&S and return it without a receipt, they give you a gift voucher, and then you sell the gift voucher for half the price and keep the cash," Zadie said.

"Really? Shall we try it?" Tracey said.

"You should try it. I'm gonna get myself back down the job center," Zadie said. They were both sixteen and had already left school but couldn't find jobs.

"Cheryl?" Tracey said, turning to face her. Cheryl was fifteen and beautiful. The two boys I fancied, Rattie and Skattie, both fancied her.

"Na, I got barred 'cuz of that fight, remember? I can't go in there, or I'll get arrested." Tracey kissed her teeth. "Oh, yeah. Christian? Trek?" she said, looking at Christian and Trek. Most of the boys had street names or graffiti names they went by.

"W'at, you think I'm gonna go nick some women's bras or something? 'Llow that, Tracey," Trek said, laughing.

"I'm good," said Christian, who was fourteen and the nicest

kid in the crew. Him and Trek always made me feel safe, like if trouble was brewing they'd have my back. They'd stuck up for us girls when random men started fights and called us names.

"I'll try it," I said. I was thirteen, the baby of the crew. But I was always eager to try new things and prove myself.

I'd become friends with the Grove Park crew because Tracey and I always saw each other in the chicken shop. Even when I was scared shitless, I made it my mission to never take shit from people, so when Emma McKay, who'd just been released from prison for stabbing someone, called my sister Deborah a slag, I punched her in the face. Tracey thought that was funny, and we became friends.

The next day, Tracey met me after school, and we went to M&S and shoved things into our bags. We walked out of the store and waited an hour before hitting the returns department and exchanging our stolen items. "Sorry, my mum asked me to do a return for her, but I must have lost the receipt," I said to the cashier. My nervousness was coming off as upset for my perceived mistake.

"I can't give you a refund, but I can give you a store credit for the items," she said. It wasn't quite a gift voucher, but I took it. Tracey was doing the same on another counter. We met each other outside and couldn't believe it. It felt like the best scam around. Steal stuff, return it, and make money selling the store credit. It was the golden heyday of shoplifting. I searched for two days for a buyer. Eventually, a lady who lived down the street took it from me for half the price. I took the cash and went to see Raj in the chicken and chip shop. "The usual," I said, putting down a five-pound note. He raised an eyebrow, impressed—he'd only ever seen me with coins.

Tracey and I started stealing all the time. We would go into the Gap, try stuff on in the changing rooms, and then just walk out of the store wearing it. We put makeup in our bags as we walked around the drugstores. We went to the Disney store and stole Winnie-the-Pooh socks, which I would wear pulled up over my tracksuit bottoms. I just stole all the things the other girls in my school had that I couldn't afford. I was a pro at stealing. Security guards would be on me as soon as I went into a store, but I was so good they couldn't catch me. While I could steal, I couldn't sell water in the desert, and it's no good being able to steal if you can't sell the goods.

Tracey wasn't any better. "We can see if the Ghetto Boys know anyone," she said, kicking her legs into the wall.

"Bruv, *as if* I'm seeing if the Ghetto Boys want to help us sell M&S vouchers and some eyeliners from Boots. That is the dumbest shit I've ever heard." The Ghetto Boys were a local gang. I knew some of them, but they weren't dealing with petty crimes like this.

"Wagwan Bredren," Christian said, which is street slang for "what's going on, friend."

"Tracey wants to see if the Ghetto Boys want to sell our Winnie-the-Pooh socks," I said, mocking her. Christian laughed, knowing how ridiculous it was.

"You come up with a better idea, then," she said, angered.

*   *   *

We decided to change tactics. Zadie still couldn't find a job after tirelessly searching, and Cheryl was up for making some money, so we decided to rob one of the perverted cabdrivers who was always hitting on us. The girls had a word for it: "puts." Which meant robbing a man, typically one who deserves it.

"The plan is this. When he starts wanking himself off or whatever, you grab his wallet and run. He always leaves his wallet by the gearstick. I'll be waiting outside the car," Cheryl said, explaining what I was going to do. The other girls were sitting on our wall, shooting the shit. I'd agreed to be the girl in the car because, technically, Cheryl and I were the only girls out that night who were underage; everyone else was sixteen, and that was the legal age of consent. And while we didn't need consent to rob the man, his willingly accepting some sort of sexual interaction with a thirteen-year-old gave us the justification for it.

I'd never seen a grown man's penis before, and now I was going to sit in a car with a fifty-something-year-old overweight minicab driver and wait for him to pull his cock out before grabbing his wallet and running. Cheryl sat with me in the car for a while, and we flirted with the guy. "My friend Francesca wants to give you a blowjob," she said. "Why don't you get it nice and hard for her."

I nodded, pretending that what she said was true. I'd literally only learned the meaning of the word "blowjob" a year earlier and thought if this man put his dick anywhere near my mouth, I was going to bite it. The man was in the driver's seat. He undid his belt, unzipped his trousers, put his hands down his boxers, and began touching himself while making noises.

"You want my dick, huh?" he said.

Cheryl and I were in the passenger seat.

"Francesca really wants it," she said seductively. His black leather wallet was in between us by the gear stick where Cheryl said it would be. I kept looking at it out of the corner of my eye.

"I'll leave you guys alone," she said, stepping out of the car. When she closed the door, my heart skipped a beat. I was so panicked that maybe he would lock the doors and that I would be trapped in this car with this man, and there'd be no way out.

Once Cheryl left, he pulled his ugly semi-hard dick out of his boxers. I took one glimpse of it; it was girthy and large, and I was instantly repulsed and even more terrified. I was supposed to wait until it was fully out and hard, but I couldn't stand the sight of it. I grabbed his wallet, opened the car door, and threw it to Cheryl, who was waiting outside. She began running and then threw it to Zadie, who threw it to Tracey. The man opened his car door and started yelling, "Stop her! She's stolen my wallet! Somebody stop her!" He began pulling his trousers up as I sprinted around the corner. I saw a bus pull up at the stop. I ran to the doors, but the driver saw me coming and closed them. Bus drivers did this all the time. They'd see us kids coming and would close the doors and drive off. It drove me nuts. I continued running down the street to my house, stopped halfway there and lay on the pavement breathless.

I found Cheryl and the rest of our crew thirty minutes later. We each made a tenner, and while I wanted to save it to eat for the week, I had no other choice but to spend it all on alcohol and cigarettes to drown out the memory of the man's dick. I was still a virgin, and now I'd seen a pervert's penis. I didn't care about the money. I was never doing that again.

Most boys my age weren't into me romantically, but there was a man who traveled through Grove Park on his way to work who took a liking to me. He must have been the same age as my dad, midforties. Every day on his way back from work, he would search the shops for me to see if I was alone. "Some fucking nonce keeps trying to talk to me," I told the Grove Park crew when I got to our wall.

The girls told me to ignore him, and Trek offered to punch his lights out, which I declined but respected.

The last time I'd seen the man, he came over to talk to me as Christian was walking toward me, so I gave him a look to indicate I needed saving. He came and put his arm around me and said, "Is this man bothering you?" The man suddenly looked terrified—a feeling I wanted him to have, so he would leave me alone.

Truth is, people who traveled through Grove Park on their way to central London typically avoided me. Middle-class commuters called me a chav—a new and inventive word for white trash—and crossed the street. Everything about me, my attire, my accent, where I lived, who I hung out with, made me a certain kind of person they wanted to avoid, but then you would get the odd older guy who didn't see any of that and instead saw a weak young girl he might be able to take advantage of.

The next time the older man got off the train after work, he came up from the train station and started looking for me. I pointed him out. "That's him," I said to Tracey.

"Wait here," she said, going over to the man. I thought she was going to tell him to fuck off, but she brought him back with her.

"You know my friend Keeley," she said.

"Yes," he said eagerly, sweating. I gave Tracey daggers for revealing my real name to some old creep. "Well, she's having to move out of town and needs some money. If you could help her out."

I pretended I was foreign. "Me homeless. I have no money," I said, pretending to be devastated. He put his hand in his wallet, pulled out a ten-pound note, and gave it to me. "Thank you so much," I said.

The man looked pleased with himself. "I have to go, but I'll come and find you tomorrow," he said, walking off.

Tracey turned to me, kissed her teeth, and said, "I bet that fucking pervert is going home to his wife."

I felt so creeped out, I spent the man's money on booze, and for months after that, I purposely hid behind the wall to avoid him every time he came out of the train station and looked for me.

"He wrote you a letter!" Tracey said to me one day, waving it around in my face. She'd been collecting money from the guy whenever she saw him, writing him letters on "my behalf," saying that I'd moved back home to Poland and could he please send me money. I grabbed the letter from her hands and read it. He said how much he missed seeing me and would like to kiss my lips.

"I'm gonna throw up. This is sooooooo messed up. How much did he give you?" She waved a twenty-pound note in my face. "I'll give you a fiver," she said.

"You made a score off some pedophile who's after me, and you're not giving me half?" I said, shocked.

"I did all the fucking work! I'm the one writing the letters. That took some real creativity, you know. I had to say how much you wanted to bang him and wished that you didn't have to leave," she said. I told her to keep the money but to give me a cigarette.

Dad had taught me to be tough and I always felt like I could stick up for myself, but that wasn't going to help me with a man twice my size. And Christian and Trek weren't always around, so I decided to learn how to protect myself better. The keys between my fingers weren't going to cut it—I needed to learn how to use nunchucks.

I knew this guy Ronnie who lived a few miles up the street who knew a thing or two about the martial arts weapon, so I spent the night at his house learning how to use them. I thought it would be a cool skill to have. Instead of punching some creep, I could whip my nunchucks out from my back pocket and show him what's up.

It was pretty late when I hopped on a bus back to Grove Park. It was only a few stops—if that. I jumped off the bus at the stop located at the top of my road, and as I came out of the back doors, I saw that part of the road was closed off. I spotted Trek and Zadie. They were standing about a hundred feet away, hugging each other and crying hysterically. I ran over to them, extremely concerned and uncomfortable because people don't cry where I'm from. Crying was a sign of weakness, especially for men, and Trek was wailing, so something crazy must have happened. I went to ask what was going on when Zadie screamed, *"Christian's dead! He's been killed!!!!"*

My whole body had chills. He'd been shot or stabbed or beaten to death, I thought. Fuck me.

I asked what had happened, waiting for the gruesome details. I'd seen endless fights, and just the week before, I was hanging out on the Flower House Estate when someone came by with a gun and started shooting it, and I was forced to flee.

"We were running for the bus," Trek said, playing it out in his mind. "And...and...Christian put his arm out and tapped on the window...He put...he...put...his arm out so the bus driver would stop! Ya know? HE JUST PUT HIS FUCKING ARM OUT!" Trek put his arm out in a confused reenactment.

"We wanted to get on the bus, he tapped on the window... and, the bus driver wouldn't stop...and the bus took him...it took him under the bus, and it ran over his fucking head...His head EXPLODED! And the bus driver just drove off down the road because he didn't FUCKING CARE!"

At this point, Trek was angry and hysterical. Zadie was sobbing and walking around in circles. "HE DROVE OFF DOWN THE FUCKING ROAD!!! THE BUS DRIVER DIDN'T EVEN FUCKING STOP!!" Trek looked up to the sky and softened. "No one cares about people like us around here, man..." He tried to compose himself, but he couldn't. I was trying to make sense of what had happened, that he'd been killed by a bus and not a gang member, by one of the bus drivers that always refused to stop for us. Tears welled up inside of me, and I did everything possible to appear strong and hold them back.

"Where did it happen?" I said, my voice cracking. Trek and Zadie pointed across the road to the bus stop.

"It was over there," said Zadie, disgusted. I looked over to where they had pointed and saw police tape blocking off the road. I noticed a few of our crew were sitting on our wall outside the fish and chip shop—even from across the road, nobody was talking; everyone was traumatized.

Christian's body had been taken by the time I arrived, but his brain, well, parts of it, were still splattered all over the road—small chunks of flesh and blood. I wanted to vomit. I had seen guts and gore, but let me tell you, that does not prepare you to see what Trek told me were the remains of Christian's head. I'm not sure what running over a body feels like with a double-decker bus, but the bus driver drove over it, and yet he was still too scared to stop.

I stood there catatonic.

I had seen Christian that afternoon, and now he was dead?!? It didn't make any sense; he had his whole life ahead of him, and it was gone?

Trek put his hands to his face, tears dripping down. "All he wanted was a job in JD Sports. That was his dream! To get a job in JD Sports." He kept repeating it over and over again, like if he said it enough times, Christian would come back, and all would resume as planned.

When I remember the tragic event, I remember Trek saying these words the most. I looked at the blood on the road.

Zadie had a sudden realization that someone had to go and tell Christian's mother. We were all far too young and inexperienced to know that the police would probably do that. She grabbed Trek's arm. "We have to go and tell his mum," she said. "She needs to know." Zadie looked at me and gestured for me to come with them.

"No. You guys should go. You were here when it happened," I said.

"Oh fuck," Trek said, pulling himself together. He wiped his hands over his eyes, getting rid of the tears, and straightened himself up.

When they left, I stared at the bloodstains in the road for ten minutes straight, Trek's words looping in my head: *"All he wanted was a job in JD Sports. That was his dream."* I couldn't quite grasp why that hit so hard, why it mattered so much.

It came to me later, when my grieving turned into understanding. When I saw the truth for what it was. We didn't have bright futures to look forward to. Most of us were just looking down the barrel of the gun at our parents' lives, destined to repeat it. Another generation lost to poverty, welfare, crime, and minimum-paying jobs...if we could get them. And that's the thing—could we get them?

Tracey still couldn't find work. Neither could Zadie. Mum spent three years applying for a job in the same supermarket before they let her in—three *years* not as a manager, but to pack other people's groceries. *Three years of rejected applications until she got an interview and was hired.*

Meanwhile, rich kids were dreaming about gap years in Bali, being CEOs, scientists, and movie stars.

I grew up, like you probably did, hearing *"You could get hit by a bus tomorrow."* A reminder that life is short, that you should live while you can. But as I stood in that street that night, staring at the blood in the road, the words took on a different meaning. It wasn't just *you never know when your time is up.* It was *you never know if you'll get the chance to live at all.* Life had a cap; life had a ceiling.

My Boyfriend and His Pregnant Girlfriend

made the executive decision to lose my virginity. I was done with being a virgin. I was fourteen, about to turn fifteen, and ready to be an adult. I wanted to know what sex was like. But figuring out how or when to lose my virginity was tricky terrain. My parents taught me nothing about sex. Hollywood movies, meaning the best movie of the time, *Cruel Intentions*, taught me that you could be cool like Sarah Michelle Gellar's character and be obsessed with sex, but men would never want to be with you, or you could be a sad and boring virgin like Reese Witherspoon's character, and have the lead character fall in love with you. I aspired to be Sarah Michelle Gellar's character because she was a rebel and had the coolest necklace where she secretly stored drugs. The incoming mixed messages I received at school were: If you lost your virginity too soon and you weren't in a committed romantic relationship, you were a big, fat slut. If you lost your virginity too late, you were frigid, and being frigid was the same as having six toes. Either way, you were going to be shamed for your experience or inexperience, so you had to pick which one you preferred to be shamed for. Boys were taught to lose it as quickly as possible, and if they hadn't by eighteen, they were better off lying about it.

By these standards, all the girls I hung out with on the streets were sluts, and I didn't care if losing my virginity outside of a committed relationship made me a slut because I wanted to join them. I saw losing my virginity as the new roller coaster at the theme park that I hadn't tried, but everyone else had. Nothing would stop me from getting on that ride and having the time of my life like Sarah Michelle Gellar in *Cruel Intentions*. Sure, it would have been nice to have a boyfriend to take the ride with, but that might involve feelings, and after my dad had cheated on my mum and left us for a woman half his age, I was so terrified of catching those. I wanted to avoid any form of intimacy or vulnerability. I just wanted to have emotionless sex.

My friend Verity, who I met on the Ferrier Estate one night, was seventeen. I liked having older friends so I could learn things about the world. Verity knew a thing or two about sex. She'd already had lots of sexual partners—twenty in fact; she counted them all in front of me. I told her about my desire to lose mine, and together we picked out who I'd have sex with.

I set my eyes on a boy named Joe. He stood out because he could do wheelies on his moped. He'd pull up to the curb on his black 50cc, take off his helmet, and put his hand through his dark brown hair like it was some sexy cologne ad, and all the girls would melt. He was sixteen with blue eyes and a beautiful face full of acne. He was one of the coolest guys around. I picked him out one evening while we were on the streets hanging out, like *you. You're the one. You're taking my virginity, pal.* I'd figured out that was how it worked. Boys were so desperate to have sex, according to this American movie I'd watched, they'd literally have sex with a pie.

For the boys in my neighborhood, it was all about upping their numbers so they could brag about it because, to them, nothing was more impressive than sleeping with as many women as possible.

Verity told Joe I wanted to have sex with him, and we made our way to his house along with his brother Will. Their parents were never around. I left Verity and Will downstairs, and Joe took me upstairs to his room and I took the plunge in his baby-blue bedroom. It was one of the worst nights of my life. Honestly, I felt cheated after, as I lay on his bed in a pool of blood and smoked a cigarette to numb the pain. I had been sold this belief that sex was supposed to be wonderful and fun. When, in fact, there was nothing wonderful or fun about it. I felt like I'd been attacked by a power drill. It was so painful. And Joe was in his own world. Focused solely on himself. He barely looked at me, let alone gave me a compliment.

To make matters worse, after this horrific experience, I felt a strange sense of attachment to Joe. I'd suddenly gone from a girl who wanted to have emotionless sex to a girl who was desperate and needy. I felt like I was worthless if he didn't want to be with me romantically. It felt like the only thing to do was ask him to be my boyfriend. He said yes, and we committed to an exclusive relationship. I feel so juvenile thinking about how excited that made me. In truth, I think I enjoyed telling everyone I had a boyfriend much more than I enjoyed having one. Having a boyfriend meant I was mature, and I'd ticked a box in the societal test of life. I was desired and chosen. Someone—Joe, the cool boy with the moped—wanted to be with me. He didn't want to just have sex with me; he wanted to be my boyfriend. Though all that really meant was we had sex and smoked weed together.

Everyone told me that I needed to try sex a few more times as it would improve. I hate to use such a lame comparison, but I also got told the same thing about coffee; if I kept drinking it, I would grow to enjoy it and love the taste. Sex and coffee are two things that people rave about, with a guarantee that everyone on the planet will enjoy. I tried drinking coffee for years and years, and I know I am in the minority here, as every street corner reminds me, but it never did improve and I never did grow to love the taste. Sex with Joe was the same. It never did improve, and without having to spare you all the details of this horrendous love affair, neither did our relationship. Because I found out he was cheating on me.

Don't ask me how. Okay, I'll tell you. I stalked him. What else was I supposed to do? This was the old days of stalking, when you had to put the work into it and do it in person. I knew something was up; I'd heard rumors, so Verity and I waited on the corner of his block, and I saw him come out of his house with another girl, who I recognized as his "ex-girlfriend." I looked at her round belly while he kissed her on the lips. He was not just cheating on me—he had another girlfriend, and she was pregnant with his kid. I felt like I was in a bad episode of *The Jerry Springer Show*, even more so when the pregnant girlfriend left, and I bowled over there screaming and shouting so loud that his friend came out of his house to see what was going on.

"You said you broke up but you're still together and she's fucking pregnant?"

I was so pissed. I felt so betrayed. It wasn't exactly like he'd treated me very well, but the least he could do was be honest with me. I lost my virginity to the guy!

It was confirmed after the confrontation by Joe's friend that he'd been with the girl the whole time and gotten her pregnant before we got together. He was going to be a father, and he didn't even have the decency to tell me. I was having unprotected sex with a man for six months who was sleeping with God knows how many other women (I had no evidence there were any more women, but I made the assumption that there could be) and now he'd lied I would never know if he was telling the truth and I'd have to get tested for STDs.

I screamed all of this at Joe, who was so dismissive—so I kept on at him. You should have seen me. I was pissed, and I wasn't backing down. I demanded answers.

"I DON'T WANT TO TALK ABOUT IT!" he yelled.

"Well, I don't care what *you* want. I want to talk about this!" I got close to his face, "I told you…" And that's when he clenched his fist and *wham*, he punched me. It was so painful. Oh my God, my left eye felt swollen. I'm not even gonna front. The pain was unreal, but I was never going to let him know that. Verity was shouting at him that he was a prick. His friend even told him he'd taken it too far. Hitting a woman was a low blow. Men still slapped women about a bit, and emotionally abused them to no end, but you were still a piece of shit if you actually punched a woman. But no doubt it was my fault. No doubt I'd be painted as the crazy one who deserved it. Because even though men who hit women were a piece of shit, it always ended up being the woman's fault. What did YOU do to make him hit you? would be the question.

My piece of shit boyfriend might have cheated on me and just punched me in the face, but the motherfucker was never going to take me down. I looked him dead in the eye, and I said, "You punch like a fucking pussy!"

He didn't like that. In fact, it angered him so much, he lunged forward to hit me again. His friend jumped in and held him back. As he stopped him from coming near me, Verity and I walked off down the street, sticking our middle fingers up at him.

Jailbird

There is a photograph of Dad cradling me as a baby. I'm in his arms as if he is going to feed me a bottle. Instead, a pint glass is up to my mouth, and I'm drinking beer. I look unbelievably happy. Out of all the photos of me as a baby, this is one of the happiest. I don't remember it at all, but Mum tells me that I used to throw my dummy into Dad's pint glass or that they would take it out of my mouth, dip it into his beer, and give it to me to stop my crying. *This*, we say, explains it. *This*, we say, is when I developed my taste for alcohol. *This*, I say, was when I entered the family religion.

The first time I actually remember tasting alcohol, I was eleven. My family and I were away on our yearly caravan summer holiday in Clacton-on-Sea with some of their friends. We were in the holiday park clubhouse for the nightly entertainment. It was '80s night, and "Like a Virgin" played while an array of colored lights darted around the room. Parents got drunk and danced on the sticky dance floor while their kids played in the arcades next door. Deborah, who was nearly fourteen at the time, was told that she was allowed to have her first alcoholic beverage. She chose Hooch—a drink popularized in the mid-1990s for its sweet taste and low alcohol content. She sat in a red-backed banquet chair in her Morgan dress and Tammy Girl jean jacket, stroking her mousy hair with one hand and nursing her Hooch with the other, so desperate to be an adult.

My parents believed that if they gave Deborah and me a little alcohol in our early teens, as people in other European countries did, then we wouldn't go mad for alcohol the older we got. This works in countries like France, Spain, and Italy, where they drink wine with their dinner, but it doesn't work so well in a country like Britain, known for its binge-drinking culture and where parents neck a gin and tonic with their dinner and not a glass of cabernet sauvignon.

(I can now say with absolute certainty that their theory was wrong and that their approach with my younger sister G—not giving her any alcohol until a legal age—worked far better.) But because of this lenient theory and the fact I knew that Deborah had started smoking (and my parents didn't), I told her that if she didn't let me take a sip of her Hooch, I was going to grass her up. She handed me the bottle. I took a sip and spat it out with a look of confusion. Alcohol was disgusting. *Why was I ever going to want to drink this?*

A few years later, when I turned thirteen, I tried alcohol again. This time it was a White Lightning, a cheap cider that came in a blue bottle. It was the most revolting drink I've ever tasted in my life, much worse than a Hooch; even now, when I think about the taste, I feel like I'm going to gag; it was that disgusting. But

I decided to stick it out. After all, my parents swore by drinking, and after a few more mouthfuls, I was drunk.

The buzz of getting drunk is great, the lightness, the giggles, the sense of carelessness, and the feeling like you can do or be anything. Drinking became my jam, my hobby, my kryptonite. I took to getting drunk like some people my age took to chat rooms on the internet. The problem with drinking and the internet is that sometimes it can be fun, but sometimes it can get dark and go wrong, and I learned about it going wrong on the night I got arrested.

It was Sunday, 24 March 2002. I know it was Sunday, 24 March 2002 because it says it on my criminal record. I was with two girls from school. We stood outside the Euro Supermarket in Grove Park as I asked every passerby if they would kindly go into the store and buy a bottle of Aftershock on our behalf. It didn't take long until a guy agreed to get it for us.

The man reemerged from the store. "Enjoy," he said, handing over the bottle of Aftershock and the small amount of change. After giving up on illegal ways of making money, I got myself a Saturday job in a hair salon in Eltham, so I had a little bit of money. We'd all chipped in for the bottle. None of us could afford it on our own, and none of us should have been left to drink it on our own since it is 30 percent alcohol and meant to be taken as a single shot, but that's what happened. We all took some shots and spun around, deluded by the myth that spinning around when drinking somehow got you drunk quicker.

Soon after, I was making a tit of myself by pretending to be a bird; about ten minutes later, the girls decided in tandem that the aftershock you got from the drink (whose name so clearly described what it did to you) wasn't for them, and it was now looking like a terrible idea to get completely wasted the night before school. It was getting late, and they wanted to go home to their families. I would have gone home to mine, but who was I going home to? Deborah had moved out and was living in a bedsit somewhere. Dad was living with his friend in Croydon. I had no idea where since I'd never visited him. Mum had gotten herself a boyfriend and spent the weekends at his house. And G was either with Mum or Dad. Weekends were just me on my own. If I went home, I'd be returning to an empty, half-decorated, cold house with no cable, no computer, no internet. Not even a landline phone to make calls. So when the girls departed and headed to their abodes, with their blessing, I made the decision—albeit a rather dumb one—to finish the rest of the bottle. I backed the rest of blue liquor before hurling the empty bottle onto the street and watching it smash into pieces. Glass shattered everywhere. I loved smashing glass, maybe more than I loved setting things on fire. There was something so chaotically joyous about it: the sound, the suddenness of it all. The destruction.

Since no one from my crew in Grove Park was out, and I didn't want to be alone, I walked the short distance to Burnt Ash, a town about a mile away, to see if anybody was there. Back then, I hung out on the streets all day, every day, and so did everyone else. There was no texting to see what people were up to. Even though I had a pay-as-you-go mobile phone, I never had enough credit to text someone, and why waste it when I could just walk to the park or the row of shops in whatever area the people I wanted to hang out with were in and see who was out. I'd even knock for people. Like show up on their doorstep and see if they were home.

When I got to Burnt Ash, I was devastated to learn that nobody was there. All the shops were closed; even the kebab shop that was always open had retired for the evening. I loitered outside Waitrose for a moment. I was so drunk that I'd gone past the fun, chatty, loosened inhibitions stage and was in the incoherent, I'm so upset and angry, and I hate everything and everyone stage. The depressed, bad-drunk stage. It's the final stage of drunkenness, where you've lost all grasp on reality, and you're just so mad that you've decided to start World War III with a parked car.

That is the last full memory I have. After that, there's a flash of glass, *lots of glass*, a window shattering maybe. Then there is nothing—a complete lapse of consciousness. Boom. Total blackout drunk. The next flash, flicker of the night, is of being handcuffed and put in the back of a police car and of my face pushed up against the glass window and being told to sit upright, and trying but not wanting to. I have no recollection of the rest of the journey to the police station.

I resurfaced from my blackout when I reached the station. I was dragged out of the car, stripped of my belongings, and pushed into a cell so hard by a male officer that I landed face-first on the dirty blue plastic mattress on the floor. The cell was grim. It had a metal toilet in the corner that smelled like it had never been cleaned. The walls were off-white with black scuffs all over them. I imagined that the scuffs got there from people before me fighting for their freedom. (Or there had been a guy in here before me rubbing his shoe up against the wall. Which one was hard to tell.)

I put my head down the toilet and vomited a few times before lying down on the dirty blue plastic mattress, shivering.

I lay in that cell, boxed in by those four walls, and stared at the revolving ceiling. I was still drunk, but I was aware now—aware of my surroundings, aware that the room was spinning, aware that I'd been arrested, but with absolutely zero idea *why*, and still so drunk that I didn't care, but feeling this overwhelming depth of sadness.

I read somewhere or heard it in a musical that when words can no longer suffice: sing. And that's how I came to blurt out Mariah Carey. I started with "Hero." *It's a long road... when you face the world alone...*

Followed by "Love Takes Time." I went through all of Mariah Carey's oeuvre at the top of my lungs in the middle of a jail cell. I sang, and I sang, circling through albums and mixing them together like a bad Mariah Carey tribute DJ. I was halfway through her album when I noticed an intercom near the metal door of the cell. I stood up. The room was still spinning, but I managed to walk over and push it.

"Hellloooooooooo," I said.

"Yes?" I heard someone reply.

"Oh, you can hear me!"

"Yes, what's up?"

And with that, I held the intercom button down and made the ears of the officers bleed while I belted out Mariah Carey songs to them. I sang like I was the star of a West End musical. I put my all into it. I sang until I couldn't sing, and then I must have passed out.

I've got to say before Mariah cornered the Christmas market, she really nailed sad-white-girl music.

*   *   *

The next morning, I was rudely awakened by a banging and a man telling me to move it. I was horrified when I opened my eyes to see my surroundings and learned that I was face down on the dirtiest blue mat. For a split second, I had no idea where I was or what was happening; I rolled over sharply, my back aching, my head pounding, and my mouth feeling like it had sand in it. I looked up at the ceiling and gasped. Panic—or was it *shock*—overtook me as I realized I was in a police cell and I had so very clearly been arrested.

Fuccccckkkkkkkkkkkkkkk.

Fuccccckkkkkkkkkkkkkkkkkkkkkkkkkkkkkk.

Fuck.

I was flooded with the memory of singing Mariah Carey songs, but I couldn't remember anything else. If my mouth wasn't so dry and my head in so much pain, I might have sat upright and screamed. I'd been arrested, but *why? What did I do?* I went through all the crimes I could remember that could have caught up with me. The car I set on fire. The stolen car I'd been in that had crashed into someone's garden wall. The umbrella I'd stolen from the Disney store. All the hoodies I'd stolen from Gap. The list went on. There were a lot of things I could have been arrested for. A male officer was standing by the cell door waiting for me to get up, so I composed myself shamefully and followed him. I was sure he was about to take me in front of a judge and have me sentenced—if not for the crime that had escaped my memory but for the singing I'd subjected the station to. He walked me down a hallway and told me I'd been released on bail, a relief. I opened my mouth to ask what exactly I was being charged for but thought better of it. I was so embarrassed that I couldn't remember, and I was so hungover, I thought I might die before my sentencing anyway. The officer walked in front of me and opened another door to what looked like the front of a police station. There was another officer behind a raised desk. The first officer told me that I would have to attend court for my prosecution and then handed me over to the officer behind the desk. He put what looked like a contract in front of me and told me to sign it. I picked up the pen next to it and looked at the document suspiciously, wondering if it was some sort of trap. The officer picked up on this and said, "It's just to say we've given you your belongings back." He held up a plastic ziplock sandwich bag with my stuff, which was basically just my Nokia 3310 with a dead battery. I signed the document, and he handed me the ziplock sandwich bag. Then he handed me a paper document with my court hearing date on it. I stood there awkwardly, not knowing what to do, where I was located, or why I'd started my morning in a grim police cell in the first place.

"Can you...?" I said, trying to find the words.

"Someone's come to pick you up," he said. I wondered who that might be. Praying that maybe now was the moment David Beckham would reveal himself as my father and pick me up on a motorcycle.

The officer motioned his head to the right, pointing out the exit. I turned around slowly; the left side of my head, right above my eye, was throbbing. I so desperately wanted an ice pack, some paracetamol, and for someone to explain everything. I looked at the exit and around the station and knew I was inside a police station somewhere, but where that station was located, I didn't know.

"Remember to show up in court in a few days," the officer yelled while my back was turned. I walked outside with my zip-lock sandwich bag, and the light of day hit my face as I squinted and shaded my eyes with my hand, looking for who'd come to pick me up. I noticed a white van waiting right out front, a van I knew, and then I noticed who was sitting inside it. *Oh God*, I thought. *Oh, God, they didn't tell me Darth Vader had come to pick me up.* I tried to walk back into the station and ask the officers to keep me there. I had almost turned my back when Dad rolled the window down and said through gritted teeth, "Get in the car now." The police had obviously alerted him. He'd gone inside the station to sign me out, but they said it wasn't needed, so he went and sat in the van. I held my breath, opened the passenger door, and climbed up. *Well, this is going to be fun*, I thought, *as fun as a fucking funeral.*

He started the engine, and we drove off. I wondered how painful it would be to jump out of a moving vehicle and concluded it might be less painful than this car journey.

I'd never worn a seat belt in Dad's van, but I was so unnerved that I thought about putting it on and buckling up for the ride. I couldn't hack the silence. I wanted him to snap so we could get it over with. It was so annoying that Mum didn't have a car because if she'd picked me up, I knew what would happen. She was predictable; she wasn't soft. She would have punished me for my actions and wouldn't hide how she felt. I knew exactly what she would say and do. She would look at me like I was a bit of shit on the bottom of her shoe and say, "You're a fucking dis-grace. You need to sort your bleeding life out, I tell you. You're a fricking mug." She'd continue on about how I was grounded and needed to stop drinking and hanging out with my muggy lowlife mates, and that would be it. I could handle my mother, but Dad was unpredictable. He might laugh or drag me out of the van by my hair.

I had no idea what was coming. I tried to brace for whatever it was by grabbing on to the side of my seat. I dug my nails in.

"So...you have to go to court?" Dad said calmly.

"Yes?" I said sheepishly.

He nodded.

"For assault," he said.

I looked at the gear stick as Dad shifted from third to fourth, trying to read between the lines and understand whether that was a question he had asked me or a statement.

"I guess?" I said, searching my mind for what the heck had happened. I couldn't remember jack shit. It was actually quite worrying how the brain could black out like that.

"Whatcha mean 'I guess'? That's what they said on the phone to me," Dad said.

"Who?" I said.

"The cops."

"Oh. The pigs," I said. I realized this was my opportunity to find out what else Dad knew secretly. "What else did they say?" I asked.

His voice was stern as he spoke, reprimanding, "They said that two officers had kindly offered to take you home because you were drunk. They told me you were like a wild fucking banshee! You decked one of them in the face and kicked the other one in the balls and then threw up—"

I had to stop myself from laughing. *I'd done what?* Then all

I kept thinking was: *This is the coolest thing I've ever heard!* I was going to be a legend for this, my street cred is gonna go through the roof. I beat up 5-0. I punched a pig in the face. I can't wait to tell everyone!

"*That's it?*" I said, wanting to know if I'd smashed up their car or something.

"Whatcha mean—'that's it?' You hit two police officers." His voice was raised.

"I mean, that's all I'm being charged for?" I said, backtracking and trying to make out whether I was being charged for anything else.

"Yes?" Dad said, not understanding. He seemed annoyed by my question, so I started picking at my bottom lip anxiously.

"How much did you drink?" he said.

"Well…about eighty percent of a bottle of Aftershock," I said. He was in a lane, stuck behind a car that wasn't moving, and started yelling at the car. "What's this person doing? Come on, move out of the way. I bet it's a fucking woman driving." He managed to pull out from behind the car and into the next lane and looked into the car window to confirm that it was a woman. "Shouldn't be allowed on the road, I tell ya." I dug my nails further into the seat; I started feeling carsick.

"You and your sister need to slow it down with the booze. The pair of you can't handle yourselves." I rolled my eyes and looked out the window; I had a sudden urge to be boastful and say I'd drunk nearly a whole bottle of Aftershock, and I was still standing. Most people would have ended up in the hospital having their stomachs pumped.

Dad told me that the police had received a phone call from a resident to report two boys dragging a girl down the street; worried for the girl's safety and hoping to stop the girl from being raped, the woman immediately called the police. It turns out I was the girl, and the two boys were two of the Burnt Ash boys. The Burnt Ash boys were a part of the crew that lived and hung out in Burnt Ash.

They'd been on their way home when they found me shitfaced, wandering down the high street, destroying everything in sight. Being decent friends, they offered to escort me home. In their words, not mine, I told them to "fuck off." Not wanting to leave me on the streets in case I actually got raped, they both grabbed an arm and began walking me home. As the story has been told, that's when they heard a police siren—and a police car pulled up next to us. Two officers stepped out of the vehicle— a man and a woman. They saw how drunk I was and offered to take over and drop me home. It's unclear whether it was my distrust for the police that prompted my behavior, whether it was because I thought I was being arrested, or whether I just really needed to throw up and I was trying to get them off me—we don't know and never will because I can't remember the incident, and I've tried many times. Either way, I'm told that the male officer grabbed my arm and tried to move me to the police car, so I lifted my right leg and kicked him straight in the balls. The female officer came in for me, so I punched her in the face and tried to get away, but my attempt failed because I vomited everywhere. Apparently, I was so sick that the spaghetti hoops I'd had for dinner came out of my nose. One of the Burnt Ash boys told me this part of the story with much laughter. The image of me sitting in the middle of the road after vomiting, wiping sick from my face, and picking a spaghetti hoop out of my nostril before being handcuffed is one he couldn't forget.

It was midmorning when Dad dropped me home. I caught sight of myself in the wing mirror, and I looked like I'd been hit by a truck and then dragged through a hedge backward. I think it was because of this that I managed to bypass a scolding. At least, that's what I told myself at the time. Dad told me to go and think about my actions. I'd never been so grateful not to be in trouble. I was in trouble, *of course*, and I would get punished for this, but he surprised me and waited for the moment I thought I'd gotten away with it. Right now he was letting my hangover and self-pity pass so he could really home in on me. I jumped out of Dad's van and prepared mentally to see Mum. Then I remembered she wasn't home. She was never home. I watched Dad drive off; his van faded into the distance. He was on his way to fix a smashed shop window. Some hooligan had broken it, apparently. As I went to get my door key out of my ziplock bag, I wondered who that hooligan could be. I looked down at my left hand and noticed it was red and swollen, and then, like a bad dream, a flashing image of shattered glass came back to me. *Oh fuck.* I smashed a shop window.

Part Two

Girl

Birthday Boobs

Ms. Rowe was teaching us how to make vaginas. Well, technically, she was showing us how to re-create *The Furry Cup*, the surrealist art piece that we all knew was a euphemism for a vagina, though none of us had heard of the word "euphemism" then. We just thought it was hilarious, as fifteen-year-olds inevitably do when a teacher discusses anything remotely sexual. I was at the back of the classroom, giggling and making jokes about drinking from "The Furry Cup," which was probably the most I'd contributed to a class all year. I was so rarely in school that when I did make an appearance, people were shocked to see me—it was almost like the mayor had come to visit. Students wanted to know where I'd been and what I'd been up to (usually hanging out in someone's house taking ecstasy or sitting in the park on my own so I could have peace for once in my life), and teachers seized the opportunity to lecture me, which Ms. Rowe did when she noticed me holding a piece of fur inappropriately. She went on and on about my lack of attendance and bleak-looking future.

"If you want a well-paying job, you need an education. Otherwise, you'll be cleaning toilets for the rest of your life," she said, assuring me it was the only job I was going to have.

I was about to say, "I'd rather make money scrubbing shit than listening to *you*," but I wanted to make a point, and it didn't feel like it proved much. So, instead, I said with a smug grin to stop myself from laughing, "I'll just become a Page 3 model. I don't need an education for that." It was completely absurd. I'd said it because Page 3 models didn't even need to know how to spell their own names (which was great because my second middle name "Margaret" was always such a pain in the arse to spell).

The class was snickering, but Ms. Rowe, who, unlike my other teachers, I actually liked, decided to take it one step further. "That's ridiculous!" she said, loud enough for everyone to hear. "Your boobs are far too small."

I would have come up with a witty response, but the whole class and I couldn't stop laughing. She was right. I was as flat-chested as an ironing board.

Not long after Ms. Rowe roasted me, I left school for good. I'd spent years dreaming of the day I could walk out of that hellhole and never look back, but when it finally came, I was terrified. I had no qualifications. No plan. And as soon as I walked out those gates, Mum said, "Right, you. If you want any money, you better get yourself a job, 'cuz you're an adult now." I was sixteen. I couldn't even vote; I wouldn't have exactly called myself an adult. And since Dad left, she hadn't handed me so much as a penny. In fact, I'd been fending for myself since I was thirteen. I told her as much, and she held out her hand and said, "Great. Cough up and pay me my housekeeping then." I think they called it tough love, and Mum called it "tough shit" when I complained that everyone else from my school got to enjoy their summer holidays while I had to look for a job. I don't know why I was complaining; I was desperate for a job. I *needed* money. And more than needing money, I yearned for a way out.

Twenty-four hours after leaving school, I walked down Bromley High Street and went from retail shop to retail shop and then restaurant to restaurant, asking if they were hiring. I even tried JD Sports, where Christian had dreamed of working. I found the manager and asked her if they had any jobs going.

"We do. You have a CV?" she asked. I handed it over nervously. She barely looked at it before saying, "Mmmm, you're gonna need some experience to be hired here." The catch-22: I needed retail experience to get a job, but no one would hire me without it.

"How am I supposed to get experience if no one will hire me?" I asked, genuinely confused. She just shrugged and walked away. That's all I kept hearing after. *You need experience to be hired here. You need experience.* I legit couldn't get a job folding hoodies at JD Sports, and I didn't know whether to laugh or cry.

Luckily, I had experience working in a hair salon, and after dropping into every one, I was offered a full-time position in a small salon in Beckenham—a predominantly white middle-class neighborhood a few miles away. The hours were long, and the pay was very little, but it was a job no less, one that would keep me going until I figured out how to become rich—like swimming-pool-in-my-house rich.

Six months into washing random people's hair and answering phones at the salon, no opportunity for wealth had presented itself. It was another day of asking, "Would you like a cup of tea or coffee?" and pretending I cared if the client got layers or started covering their grays. The salon hadn't opened yet, so I indulged in one of my favorite rituals: flicking through the new batch of magazines at reception. I was obsessed with fashion magazines— *i-D*, *POP*, *AnOther*, and *Vogue*. I studied the photos like I was in an art museum. But first I turned to the not-so-high-fashion magazines to check my horoscope. I flicked to the back of *Cosmo* and started reading Virgo. I couldn't resist searching for a sign— any hint of how I'd finally make my millions and leave this place behind.

Though they didn't offer much hope—three different magazines, three different horoscopes, and not a single mention of money or success. But Lyn, the stylist I was training under, did have something to say.

"A client of mine who's a model is coming in..." She tapped her finger on the paper calendar in front of me and found her name. I didn't recognize it, but I did recognize a name on the calendar for the following week: *Ms. Rowe*. It was just my luck that I worked at the very salon she went to get her roots touched up. My small tits and I were always tasked with washing her hair and making her a black coffee, as her words would repeat in my head: "You'll be cleaning toilets for the rest of your life."

"Who does she model for?" I asked.

"She does loads of stuff—catalogs, commercials, that sort of thing. She was the model on *This Morning* the other day. You wouldn't know who she is, but she makes a killing!" Lyn squealed, like she had just discovered stacks of gold. "You could do that kind of stuff."

I looked up at her. "What? Model?" I snorted, glancing at my reflection in one of the salon mirrors, thinking it was shocking how I sometimes left the house.

"Yes! I can't believe I didn't think of this before!" she exclaimed with her hands out as if she were entering into a jazz routine.

"*As if.* The only modeling I could do is for the blind," I said, dismissing the idea. I mean, I was flattered, sure, but I'd just seen myself in a mirror, and it wasn't a pretty sight.

"What you talking about? You're gorgeous," Lyn said, which is exactly the sort of thing people say when they think you're ugly but are trying to be nice. "Why wash people's hair for no money when you could get your photo taken for a lot?" she said seriously. I didn't know if Lyn was deluded or blind or if I was better looking than I thought, or if this was just one big windup.

A few minutes later, the model showed up for her appointment. She pulled up in a brand-new silver Mercedes SL and strolled into the salon dressed immaculately with a Dior handbag draped over her arm. I sized her up by awkwardly standing beside her as I put her gown on, trying to see if we looked alike. We were about the same height and looked the same—if I stopped dying my hair black, making my eyebrows pencil-thin, and I were a few years older. I couldn't tell if this meant I could be a model. All I knew was I was ready to sell my soul if I could buy a Dior saddle bag and a Mercedes. I walked over to Lyn and whispered, "If you're being serious, sign me the fuck up."

Lyn was serious all right, and by the end of the day she had secured me a session with a local photographer to shoot some "test shots." I was so excited that I just nodded when she told me how much it would cost. I couldn't bring myself to tell her I couldn't afford it.

After work I called my wife for life, my sister from another mister, my bestie: Patsy. We met in school. And no greater moment has ever happened to me than when Ms. Rowe seated us next to each other in math class, and Patsy turned to me and asked if I liked Eminem before singing "I'm a Criminal." I joined in, and an overhead fluorescent tube light burst, and glass sprinkled down on our desk and we couldn't stop laughing.

"How much?" Patsy asked, her cheery voice coming through my speaker.

"Three hundred pounds," I said.

"Whoa," she said.

"Who has that kind of money?" I sighed, thinking three hundred pounds was three weeks' wages. I could afford it if I saved for three weeks, but I needed to eat, buy phone credit, and give Mum housekeeping money. Realistically, it would take me a month and a half to save, and she had booked me with the photographer for the following week.

"Why don't you ask Jamie for the money? He just loaned me some. You have to pay him back with interest, though," Patsy said with a hesitation in her voice.

Jamie was a drug dealer and a loan shark. If you didn't pay Jamie back, he would shoot you with a Taser gun until you pissed yourself. I knew who he was. I'd met him at Patsy's house about a year earlier—he was good friends with her older brothers. From the moment I saw him, I was drawn to him. He wasn't physically attractive, but he had a certain toughness that I found appealing.

One he would tease me about much later as I would help him count cash and weigh cocaine before putting it into packets. "You just want to live a life of crime and be married to a gangster," he'd say. And I'd think, *Honey, I don't want to marry a gangster. I want to* be *the gangster.*

After our first encounter, I would go over to Patsy's house just to see if I could see him, but I was always too shy to talk and would turn beetroot every time he spoke to me. I saw him a few times before his house got raided. The police found a stack of cash, a list of names, and twenty-nine cannabis plants growing in his bedroom, and he was sentenced to twelve months in a youth detention prison. Once he got sent down, I begged Patsy to tell him I fancied him and to see if he liked me back. It felt safe with him behind bars because if he rejected me, like most boys I fancied did, then at least I had no chance of running into him.

Jamie played it cool and didn't say if he liked me romantically or not, but he did ask for my address so he could write me a letter. I waited for the mail to arrive each day like a wife whose husband was at war. Finally, a letter with my name on it arrived from Feltham Prison. I tore it open and sat on the stairs by the door to read it eagerly. It felt so romantic, like we were from a previous era. Pen pals sending each other love letters. I imagined him showing up on my doorstep after his release, declaring he wanted to be with me. Instead, when he got out, I never heard from him again.

That evening, I walked up to the pay phone to call the man who had ghosted me. I picked up the receiver, put in a twenty-pence coin, and with sweaty hands, I dialed Jamie's number. I was so nervous when he answered.

"'Ello," he said in his deep, raspy voice.

"Hey," I said nervously.

"Who's dis?"

"It's Keeley."

"What's up?" he said.

I went silent until I plucked up the courage to speak. I hated asking for money. I hated asking for someone to help me, but I also wanted this opportunity so badly that I would have sold my grandmother.

"Well...I was wondering...obviously feel free to say no... but I was wondering...if you could borrow me three hundred pounds? I'll pay you back and everything—with interest. I just need it to pay a photographer for some test photos."

"You mean lend?" he said, correcting me.

I rolled my eyes. "You know what I meant."

"Rar, what...you going into modeling now?" he asked.

"I don't know...A girl at my work thinks I should get them taken and send them to some agencies," I said, embarrassed. Expressing that I was pursuing modeling made it seem like I thought highly of myself or deemed myself more attractive than I actually was. I hated appearing arrogant and egotistical unless in jest.

Jamie made a half "Ohhhh" and laugh sound simultaneously. It was a sound he often made and reminded me of a bird. "Keeley, the little model," he added mockingly. I switched the receiver to the other ear.

"Shut up," I said playfully. I wanted him so bad. "So...can I *lend* the money or what?"

"The rules are—you pay me back with twenty percent on top. So I give you three hundred pounds, and you give me back three hundred and sixty pounds, got it?"

"Got it." I smirked. It was so cold out that I could see my breath, so I held my mouth close to the glass door of the phone box and watched as it steamed up. Then I drew a heart with my finger.

"Where's you?" he asked.

"In Grove Park by the chicken shop—not Chicken Cottage, the other one. Why?"

"I'll meet you there in ten minutes."

Giddy with excitement, I put the receiver back and stood inside the phone box, waiting for him for what felt like the longest ten minutes of my life. He pulled up in a car. I got in, and he handed me the cash. I thanked him by kissing him on the cheek. He looked at me smugly. He knew I fancied him, and I hated it. I got out of the car, and when he drove off, I held the money to my nose and smelled it.

The whole salon was cheering me on to be a model, and my boss very kindly gave me a paid day off to have my pictures taken. Everything was still shot on film then, and it meant I had to wait a few days to get the negatives back. I remember being filled with such an urgent unease that if I didn't move fast enough, I'd miss my shot, so I showed up two hours early to collect my contact sheet and select the photos to be printed. The photographer was standing next to me as I looked over the images, trying to see which ones I liked. I've never been a fan of looking at photos of myself, but I did scrub up all right. It's incredible what professional photography and makeup can do. I asked the photographer where he thought I should send the photos. He suggested I go and see some glamour modeling agencies. "*Glamour modeling agencies?*" I repeated, taken aback. He assumed I didn't know what glamour modeling was and said, "Yeah, you know, they look after Page 3 models, that type of thing. They'll love you."

I nearly burst out laughing. Page 3 wasn't exactly what I had in mind when I thought about modeling. I wanted to model for Gucci, walk the runway for Versace, and be on the front cover of all the fashion magazines I loved, and if I couldn't do that, I would happily model for catalogs or high street brands like M&S and Zara. And if I couldn't do that, I was happy to model dog food, Tampax, and the cream you put on around your bum when you had piles. Then there was swimsuit and lingerie. Under that was Page 3, so bottom of the list that it wasn't even on it.

The photographer wrote down some names and addresses of glamour and commercial agencies on a piece of paper. "Send them to these addresses," he said. I just did what I was told and mailed photos of myself, along with a handwritten note with my contact information.

A local newspaper called the *South London Press* was running a modeling competition, trying to find the next big thing, so I entered that as well. I heard back from almost everyone asking me to come in for a meeting, and I was a finalist in the competition. There were ten of us in total, and they sent us all to Storm, one of the biggest fashion modeling agencies in London and the agency to discover Kate Moss. Dad gave me a lift as he was driving through town for work.

"What's this you're going to?" he asked in the van.

"It's an interview for a job," I lied. Lucky Dad wasn't one to probe because I hadn't figured out what it was a job interview for. I just knew I didn't care to hear the potential jokes about how I fell from the ugly tree and hit every branch.

The Storm office was grand and intimidating. I'd never been anywhere like it. A whole wall was covered with photos of models on the front covers of all the high-fashion magazines I loved reading. (Well, let's be honest, I wasn't reading them, but you know what I mean.) I freaked out. The frames looked more expensive than our house. The thought of shooting with those photographers and wearing all these designer clothes. *Oh, the clothes. The Versace dresses. The Gucci horsebit shoes. The Dior bags. The Prada trainers. The Tiffany and Co. silver heart necklace and matching bracelet.* My mouth practically watered thinking about it while some impossibly chic woman took Polaroid photos of me and the other hopefuls. I couldn't help but crave this new life. I wanted it more than I'd ever wanted anything, more than David Beckham being my father, more than a lifetime supply of chocolate. But it wasn't happening. Not now, not ever. Storm signed one girl out of the ten of us, and it wasn't me. She was tall with strawberry-blond hair, wide-set eyes, and freckles all over her face. She looked like a cross between a china doll and an alien. I looked like a hamster had sex with Dumbo, and apparently that look wasn't in.

I met with several agencies in the following weeks, including a commercial modeling agency called IMM Models and Models Plus. They all scanned my photos and said they would be in touch if anything came up. After the meetings, I followed up by calling the offices a few times, but I *have* yet to hear back.

I was so frustrated and confused. I couldn't understand the sorting of my beauty or attractiveness into these societal ideals and fashion standards. I hadn't developed a clear internal sense of self or viewpoint on my looks, and all of a sudden I had people telling me I could model, but then I couldn't get a single modeling agency to return my calls. I had no idea if I was attractive or unattractive, and if either mattered. I just had a strong desire to make it.

A few weeks later, I was back in the salon when I got a phone call from Jamie. I thought he was calling about his money. I was preparing my excuse when he said, "Are you in the newspaper? My mate just called me and said you're in the *Daily Star.*"

"*What?*" I said, suddenly terrified. I went to the shop to obtain a copy of the newspaper, and there I was: participating in the paper's "search for a beach babe" competition. I hadn't entered this one, but one of the photos I'd mailed to the addresses the photographer gave me had found its way in.

Somewhere between that phone call and my being crowned the number one beach babe of the year, Jamie became my boyfriend. It's incredible what being featured in a newspaper can do for one's desirability. I was like the lobster—once the "cockroach of the sea" served to prisoners, now a prized delicacy. It made Jamie want me, and as over the moon I was about getting the man I fancied, I was even more ecstatic that I didn't have to pay him back. My prize for winning was an unpaid lingerie photo shoot in a hotel room. Lucky me.

* * *

In the months leading up to my eighteenth birthday, I was on a mission. I made relentless phone calls—to photographers, agents, and practically anyone who might listen. I thought that if I won, it would lead to paid work or, at the very least, an agency signing me. But it led to nada. By the time my birthday rolled around, I was so defeated that only two things kept me going. The cowboy boots Jamie had bought for me on the King's Road I paired with a jean skirt and white T-shirt so I could look like my new style icon, Sienna Miller. The other was my birthday wish. Wishing felt like the only power I had left. This was my last chance to ask for a way out of my dead-end life.

My family and some friends gathered for lunch in the Toby Carvery to celebrate. My sisters came out with a Colin the Caterpillar cake, and everyone sang "Happy Birthday." They placed the cake in front of me, and someone yelled, "MAKE A WISH!" *This is my moment*, I thought. If birthday wishes come true, then they will definitely come true on my eighteenth birthday. I looked at the candles. I knew exactly what I was wishing for. I got my wish in my head and repeated it as I blew the candles out.

I kept making phone calls, but I realized that I couldn't just sit around waiting for this modeling thing to happen. I needed to make something of my life, and I knew that I didn't want to be a hairdresser, so I went to see a career counselor, who gave me a test that said I should be either a fashion designer or an interior designer. I chose fashion because what the fuck did I know about interiors growing up in a house that resembled a building site?

I took the leap and quit working in the hair salon and applied for a government grant that gave underprivileged adolescents thirty pounds a week to study, and I enrolled in a fashion course at the local college in Lewisham. I was broke, really broke, and thirty pounds a week didn't cover the cost of a textbook. Jamie helped me out by letting me work for him, and as much as I enjoyed counting cash and weighing cocaine before putting it into packets, I didn't want to be dependent on him. I wanted my own money. I was thinking of legal ways to make it that wouldn't take away from my studies when one of the girls from the salon called. "There's a competition in *The Sun* searching for a new Page 3 model. You should enter it," she said. I hadn't been old enough to pose for Page 3 before—and, let's face it, I had tiny tits. But I purchased *The Sun* to read about this "Page 3 Idol" competition—a spin on the TV show *Pop Idol*—and saw that there was a model with small breasts, so it wasn't entirely out of the realm of possibilities.

The problem with modeling for Page 3 is that you had to be topless, and even the thought of showing my tits had my face turning the deepest shade of red and sweat dripping from my armpits, hands, and knees. I could talk a good game, but the moment I was in the company of strangers, God forbid the center of attention, I would have a complete meltdown. And maybe I could get over the embarrassment of showing my tits in *Vogue* magazine, but it was showing them on Page 3 that was the issue. People looked down on Page 3 models. The amount of shit these women got, they were ridiculed as "dumb" and "cheap." I'd have to endure people making fun of me. But I guess the reality was—being a girl who grew up on a council estate, they already did.

It took me weeks to commit to entering. I wanted a way out—out of Grove Park. But Page 3? What would people think? What would *I* think? Could I deal with the shame? The embarrassment? I thought back to Christian and how it had been his dream to work in JD Sports and how I couldn't get hired there. This felt like my only option to better myself, and if I didn't take it now while I was young enough, then would I be poor and trapped forever?

I got Jamie to take some topless photos of me on a disposable camera while I weighed up the public humiliation versus the chance to make real money. "Are you actually gonna enter?" he asked.

"I don't know," I replied. I could tell that he was conflicted. That dating a Page 3 model was both boastful and shameful.

I put the photos in an envelope and wrote the address of the competition on the front; then I hovered over the mailbox. I thought, *You only live once*, and dropped it in, but as soon as I let go, I immediately tried to get it back and got my hand stuck.

Over two thousand girls entered. My photos arrived on the last day and were the very last to go in. One day later, I would have missed the deadline. A few days after that, I got a phone call from a photographer named Sally. "Is that Leelee from Bromley?" she asked.

Okay, okay, soooo I lied a little in my entry, changed my name by two letters and my location by three miles—big deal. I couldn't entirely commit myself to what I was doing. I wanted some sort of identity protection because I hadn't told anyone but Jamie that

I'd entered the competition, and I was hoping that if I appeared in the paper with a different name, no one would know it was me.

Sally invited me to the studio to do a test shoot with her. When I arrived, she asked for my ID to ensure I was eighteen. She looked at my name and said, "Is it Keeley or Leelee?"

"It's...mmmmmm, it's *Keeley*," I replied, almost through a cough as panic set in. "My boyfriend submitted my pictures, and he calls me Leelee." She handed my ID back. *Fuck, fuck, fuck*, I thought.

"We've not had a Keeley in the paper before," she said, thrilled. I, however, was catatonic. There was no way I could let my real name appear in the paper, but I couldn't bring myself to say it outright for fear she would know I was ashamed. Around me, other girls were practically ripping their shirts off the moment they walked through the door, so excited at the prospect of being the newest Page 3 girl.

Sally handed me a G-string and a pair of high-heeled shoes and gestured toward a changing room. I got changed and stood there almost in a daze as she took my photo.

Sally said that the girls who made it into the first round of the contest would have their photos published in *The Sun* a few days later. On the morning of publication, I snuck out of the house before Mum could spot me and headed to the local newsagent's. The nerves were hitting hard, and I kept thinking I might shit myself. Who knew if I'd make the cut, and if I did, how I'd feel?

The newspapers were on a stand outside. I scanned for a copy of *The Sun*, and then I froze. *Forget shitting myself. Nope, I'm about to puke right here on the pavement.* There was a picture of me on the FRONT PAGE of the newspaper. I reached out, picked up a copy, and looked at my face with a sense of sickness and enjoyment before quickly scrambling through to find the images, and there I was—with a bunch of other hopefuls, all with our tits out.

Any joy I had about making the first round of the competition was quickly replaced by repulsion and shame. I hated the photo. My head was leaning down as far as it could go, and I had this creepy smile on my face. Honestly, I looked like a witch in an advertisement for Halloween. There was a caption underneath saying, "Keeley, 18, from Bromley," followed by "Vote For Keeley on this number." My jaw literally dropped. I couldn't get over it. I was so embarrassed, I thought I might die. I was topless in a national newspaper. Not just any newspaper but the biggest-selling newspaper in the UK. *Why the fuck didn't I push harder for Leelee?* I asked myself. *Now I'm in the paper as Keeley, 18, from Bromley. I have an uncommon Irish name and went to school in Bromley!* It's not exactly like this was a hard puzzle to piece together; people were going to know it was me.

I was standing outside the newsagent's staring at my tits and mentally berating myself and simultaneously wondering if I needed to flee the country to escape the public humiliation I already felt, and that's when I noticed the increased size of my breasts. I pulled the paper closer. For a split second, I stared at the photo, wondering if they were actually my tits. I held the newspaper in one hand and started touching my left tit with the other. Then it hit me: My birthday wish had come true.

Holy shit, my birthday wish!

Feeling like it was the one thing holding me back, the one thing that would make my career, I had wished...Okay, I know it's really shallow, and I'm ashamed to admit it, but I had wished for *bigger boobs*. And it seemed like whoever it was that granted these things, the universe? The genie? The tooth fairy? The doctor who put me on birth control? I didn't know, but I had tits the same size as my head! It was wild.

Looking back, I should've noticed the change sooner. I mean, going from a 32B/C to a 32E isn't exactly subtle. My bras had been fitting funny for weeks, but I just assumed I'd screwed up the back size and that I was probably a 36C and not a 32.

As I tried to make sense of my birthday wish coming true and my tits being in *The Sun*, I felt my phone buzzing in my pocket. I pulled it out. It was a text from my mother. *Is that u in the paper?*

Noooooooooooooooooooooooooo! No! No! This can't be happening!

Next Dad called. I thought about ignoring it, but Dad *never* called, so I wondered if he had seen me in the paper or if someone had died. I answered, hoping it was the latter.

"You think you're funny?" Dad said sarcastically.

"What on earth are you talking about?"

"Yeahhhhhh, you know," he replied.

"Yeah, Dad...about that, oh, I have a call waiting. Later." I wasn't lying; I did have a call waiting.

It was Deborah. "Where'd you get money for breast implants?" she said.

I had to laugh. My boobs were insane. It was not normal how much they had grown in four weeks. "If I had that kinda money, which I don't, I definitely wouldn't have spent it on breast implants," I said.

"Well, how do you explain those boobs, then? Last time I looked, they were the same size as an ironing board. Bloody hell, your boobs have grown overnight. Yesterday you were flat-chested!"

I couldn't think of a way to explain that I'd wished for them for my birthday, and my wish had come true. It sounded ridiculous, and woo-woo, and scientifically impossible.

My phone blew up all day. It didn't stop. And I didn't answer. I was overwhelmed and embarrassed.

I arrived home in the evening to be immediately greeted by my little sister G. She was six and the cutest thing you've ever seen. When I opened the door, she was on me like a hawk. "You have your boobs out in the paper!" she screamed.

I wanted to die. *Oh God*, I thought, *what have I done?*

The panic set in hard. What if I didn't win this competition? What if all I got out of this was endless humiliation—teased to death for getting my tits out in *The Sun*? Desperate to avoid that fate, Deborah and I went to the pay phone and stuffed twenty pounds' worth of coins into it, making call after call to the voting hotline.

A few days later, Jamie and I went to the pub to wait for the results. It was a Sunday. December 19, Mum's birthday, and we were tucked into plates of roast beef and Yorkshire puddings when my phone rang. My heart jolted as I answered. It was a photo editor from *The Sun*, Sally the photographer's husband.

"Congratulations! You've won!" he announced, his voice booming like a game show host.

"I've won!" I said, mimicking his enthusiasm and trying to sound like an over-the-top contestant. But the excitement didn't feel real. My life had just drastically changed, and yet inside I didn't know what I was feeling.

Jamie congratulated me as I hung up. "That's amazing," he said through a forced smile. I knew he was wrestling with his own feelings about my winning and that it had created a distance between us, one that felt like I'd taken a tunnel to an island by myself. It was confirmed ten days later when he dumped me. *Yes, my drug dealer boyfriend dumped me!* He said it was because I was taking Mum on a trip to Tobago with me as part of my prize for winning and not him. But I knew the truth. It was because he couldn't deal with my new job. The idea of me being a model was one thing, but the actuality of me being a Page 3 model was another. He couldn't hack the embarrassment or the teasing he got from his friends who relentlessly took the piss out of him for dating a girl with her tits out in the paper.

What had started out as a joke to my teacher had ironically ended up with me becoming the punchline. And I didn't know how to reconcile that. All I had wanted was a way out, and now I had it. I was Keeley, 18, from Bromley. The topless girl who everyone was now allowed to make fun of.

The Glamorous Life

"Hi! It's sooooo nice to meet you. I'm Nicola, but everyone calls me Nic T—there's another Nicola in the paper," Nic T says, handing me a gift bag as I get inside the black town car. I'm so embarrassed that this fancy car is parked on my council estate, and I want to get moving before someone I know tries to nick it. "I got you a little something for winning," she adds enthusiastically. This is the first time I'm meeting another Page 3 model, and I've never received a gift from someone I've just met—especially someone whose photo I've seen in the paper. I've seen her boobs before meeting her. Is that weird?

"Thanks," I mumble as I clutch the gift bag awkwardly, unsure if I should open it now. Or wait? Put a seat belt on? Do people wear seat belts in the back of these cars? The town car gets moving. We're on our way to have lunch at a fancy restaurant with one of *The Sun* editors to celebrate my win. The editor thought it would be nice if Nic T joined us to "show me the ropes." She won the same competition, Page 3 Idol, two years ago, leaving her job in asset management to capitalize on her *other* assets.

"Open it," she encourages me in a similar but slightly refined version of my South London accent. She's from Croydon, where Kate Moss is from. I know this because I read it in the paper. Dad used to live there when he left us. Everyone goes to Croydon for Ikea. I feel instantly bonded to her because she's a fellow South Londoner. But I also feel intimidated. She's so glamorous. She has beautifully blow-dried brown hair and a flawless French manicure to match her perfect makeup and expensive Louis Vuitton handbag. She looks like a WAG. I don't look like a WAG. I've never had a manicure, and even though I used to work in a hair salon, I've never blow-dried my hair. I used to straighten it with an iron, though. Does that count?

I open the gift bag and pull out a black leather-bound calendar with 2005 engraved on the front in shiny gold. "This is the most important thing you're going to own," she tells me, her tone suddenly serious. I flick it open and run my fingers over the smooth, empty pages. I have my trip for winning coming up but I wonder where the rest of 2005 will take me?

Nic T chats the whole ride. She's bubbly and friendly and talks to me like we're old friends. I like her a lot. I don't know what I expected Page 3 models to be like. But I was scared that they would be stuck-up mean bitches that hated me. Nic T is the opposite, and I'm relieved.

~ MONDAY 3 JANUARY

4:00 p.m. Arrived in Tobago! It's hot and sunny. The hotel is unreal—it has one of those pools with a swim-up bar like in luxury magazines. I could've cried. It's always been my dream to sit at one of those swim-up bars. I'm definitely going to sit there and get myself a piña colada!

~ TUESDAY 4 JANUARY

6:30 a.m. Did a shoot on the beach while Mum snoozed. I had to be careful taking my top off because it's illegal in Tobago to be topless on the beach. I could be arrested. Imagine if I went to jail for showing my baps on the beach.

~ WEDNESDAY 5 JANUARY

6:30 a.m. I'm up again to catch the morning sunlight! It's still dark when I wake up, but I have to get my hair and makeup done, which takes forever. Mum had been against the idea of me modeling for Page 3 because of all the stigma, but she came around soon enough with a free stay in a five-star hotel, bloody cheeky bitch! She even wanted to join us on the beach after lunch, but I told her no way. She moaned, bottom lip pouting, "But why?" Sometimes I think I'm the adult, and she's my daughter. I told her that I don't go topless on the beach in general, and the thought of her watching me model makes me want to run into the sea and never come back out. This is how it starts, you see. Mum watches me topless on the beach, and before you know it, we're one of those families that walk around naked together. No, thank you. It's bad enough that she's seen me topless in the newspaper.

* * *

8:00 p.m. At dinner, Alan, the photographer, said to Mum, "She's got a big future beyond Page 3." I have no idea what he means, but I like the sound of it. He comments on different parts of my body all day long. "You are just beautiful. You have the most perfect breasts and great legs…" and something about the gap in between my thighs being the best because my legs don't touch, blah, blah, blah. I wanna tell him to shut up, but instead, I pretend he's talking about someone else.

~ THURSDAY 6 JANUARY

Modeling, I've come to realize, is a lot of standing around like a lemon trying to keep your eyes open. The highlight of the day was lunch. We ate in the middle of a rainforest! You'd never find it unless you knew about it. No menu, just fresh food cooked that morning. Seemed cool until the plate arrived, and I realized I had no idea what I was eating. The meat didn't look or taste like chicken or beef, and I had a horrible moment when I thought I might've just eaten a squirrel or something. Not sure if that's a thing here. I don't want to insult the wonderful people of Tobago, but I hope it's not. But I couldn't stop thinking about it on the drive back. Made me feel really sick.

~ FRIDAY 7 JANUARY

After I finished shooting, my makeup artist, Emma, did my mum's makeup, and we went all out—full-blown drag queen style. Huge, thick eyebrows, dramatic eyeshadow—the works. It was absolutely hilarious. Honestly, we couldn't stop laughing.

She looked like a completely different person. It's incredible what makeup can do—transforming someone so much that it felt like we were hanging out with a totally different person. Every time she caught her reflection, we'd all crack up again. It's mad that I have a makeup artist. Life is strange.

~ SATURDAY 8 JANUARY

Alan mentioned he bought my domain name because "the internet is where everything is going." I didn't even know what a domain name was, but apparently, it's my name as a web address. I have no money to buy it myself, so I guess it's fine? Also, I don't have a computer or the internet. He said he'd look after it for me and help me build a website. Then he suggested we shoot some "extra" photos to sell later. No thanks, mate. But, of course, I nodded like a total idiot because I wanted to please him.

~ SUNDAY 9 JANUARY

Oh God. Oh God. Oh God. Oh God. Oh God. Oh God. Oh God. I was meant to go back to college when I returned from my trip because even though I've won this competition, I don't want to quit college. But *The Sun* published a story that my college has banned the newspaper because of me. Apparently, everyone went wild on campus knowing that I attended Lewisham College, so they banned the paper! I'm so embarrassed. What should I do? I can't go back. I'll never be able to face them. I'm turning red as I write this.

~ MONDAY 10 JANUARY

Back to London! The flight was horrendous. Thought we were gonna die from turbulence. Then I thought I was going to die from sickness. I filled up two sick bags. I'm not a great traveler. Any movement, and I vomit—cars, planes, and boats. Christ, you get me on a boat for twenty seconds, and I'm spewing everywhere. My stomach is not cut out for this lifestyle! I'm so happy that Nic T got me this calendar thing because my month is filling up with shoots!

Everyone's Seen My Tits

stumbled off the plane from Tobago to the news that there was a Page 3 photo of me taped to the staff room wall of my old school. Ms. Rowe had told someone in the salon, and a few friends who still attended had confirmed this with amused horror. I couldn't help but visualize my former teachers standing around the staff room, cups of coffee in hand, all taking a good look at my youthful tits—acknowledging that this is where studying with them had gotten me. I got a kick out of it. My grand "fuck you" I'd been waiting to stick to them for so long. But I guess my grand old "fuck you" wasn't as simple as getting a provocative rise out of the authority figures that taunted and despised me for being "cocky and opinionated." I couldn't just isolate my tits to this one topless photo in the staff room in an act of teenage rebellion, simply because, in a matter of months, my tits were everywhere. You couldn't open a men's magazine or *The Sun* newspaper without seeing me semi-naked.

My boobs had gone national.

And I was mortified.

As I sat on the train, I saw a man looking at my tits in a copy of *The Sun*, and I turned shades of red I didn't even know existed. It was horrifying, the thought of people around the country doing their morning routines, drinking tea, eating slices of toast, and casually flicking through the newspaper and seeing my tits. (I wasn't sure tits and tea went together all that well, but I didn't get paid to make those kinds of decisions.) A friend told me an ex-boyfriend had my topless poster on his bedroom wall. I walked past his house and saw it through the window. *Like, what the fuck, Chris? You've seen me naked already!*

Seemingly overnight, my body became public property. People I hadn't spoken to in years called my landline out of the blue.

"Are you *the* Keeley in the paper?" one girl asked.

"I guess so?" I replied, blushing.

"Wow," she said. "That's mental. You're, like, famous."

It was beyond mental; it was insane, completely nuts. Unfathomable. I didn't even have a surname. People were referring to me as *THE* Keeley—not just Keeley, but *THE* Keeley. Like I was the fucking Pope or something.

Admittedly, I wasn't equipped on a multitude of levels to handle people I knew—and people I didn't—seeing me semi-naked. I was too young and self-conscious. I hated how I looked. I hated the attention it rendered. I was neither psychologically nor emotionally developed enough. I had the "temperament of an inhibited tweenie," as one journalist wrote about me, which was clearly his polite way of saying I had the emotional maturity of an orange.

The other models I met were so proud to call themselves Page 3 models. Empowered, even. I couldn't relate. In fact, very quickly I started lying about my job and introducing myself as Francesca.

But you know what I did enjoy? You know what I was equipped to deal with? Money.

I'd always believed that money would solve all my problems and fulfill all my desires, and I was right; it did.

I loved being rich. I excelled at it.

When my first paycheck arrived, it was for a thousand pounds, and I was so ecstatic, I nearly did cartwheels down the street to the bank. I mean, obviously this wasn't enough money to support a family, but I was eighteen and still living at home. I had £1.63 in my account at the time, and I thought they might investigate where my money had come from because my balance had never been so high.

Everyone had seen my tits, but money was the one thing that made me forget about it.

Money meant I could afford to eat at the one restaurant I had longed to eat at for so many years: PizzaExpress. Oh, how I had longed to eat there. I would walk past the glass windows and watch the chef in his striped T-shirt toss around the pizza dough and then toss it in the oven. Customers sat drinking wine on marble-topped tables. It screamed sophistication. It was the taste of Italy in London. *It was Italy.* No one wanted to eat anywhere as much as I wanted to eat at PizzaExpress. People will rat on it and tell you that it's just a fast-food pizza chain, a posher version of Pizza Hut, but for me, it was *the one and only* pizza restaurant, and I was like a kid in a candy store when I walked through those glass doors, sat down at a marble-topped table, and dug into a pizza with an egg in the middle. Patsy and I sat at a table at the back of the restaurant, eating dough balls and pizzas like kings. We even had a cigarette after to celebrate. You could still smoke inside then. It was everything I'd hoped it would be, and the dessert, well, you should have seen the smile on my face when I tucked into the chocolate fudge cake. I felt like I'd won the lottery.

Money opened up so many culinary boundaries, and the changes in my diet became more extreme: I ate *sushi*. I grew up on McDonald's and Chicken Cottage. I didn't even know what sushi was. Six months into my new life, I booked a job and flew to New York to work with this big fashion photographer. I was so stoked that I could afford to eat at PizzaExpress, but raw fish on a bed of rice in New York City?!? That was next level. I had no idea what I was doing—which was apparent when I choked on an edamame skin in front of thirty people because I thought you were supposed to eat the whole thing. And don't even get me started on the chopsticks; the only time I'd seen those was in the '90s as a hair accessory.

Speaking of the '90s, I started meeting people I never thought I would meet, including my "parents," David and Victoria Beckham.

Out of all the things that changed straight off the bat—my photos being in the paper, meeting my "real parents," people knowing my name, eating foreign food, my grand "fuck you" to my teachers—it was having money that was the thing I noticed and cared about the most. It was the thing that transformed my life. But it wasn't about the money. It was what money did—it gave me access. One of the things we didn't have growing up was a computer. It was the first item I purchased. I hit the shopping mall like Julia Roberts in *Pretty Woman* to buy the one item I'd dreamed about owning, and boy, did it feel good setting up my chunky black desktop PC in my bedroom right next to my punching bag.

Here's the thing: Middle-class kids my age had had computers at home for years. They'd grown up on them. Their parents would take them to PizzaExpress after school for a cheap meal, and then they would type up their homework in Times New Roman font and surf the internet while I was out roaming the streets and trying to make money. We couldn't afford to make calls from the landline. A computer? That was out of the question. Modeling meant I could afford to bring myself into the twenty-first century and also meant I could sign up for . . . *the internet.*

I had AOL dial-up internet installed, and I sat in my chair staring at my screen as it sounded like it was dialing a number, and then this horrible screeching sound came out, and then poof, I was online—on the internet, baby. The motherfucking internet. It was 2005, and I finally got MSN Messenger and an AOL email address, which felt like all of my Christmases had come at once. I had arrived. I was eating PizzaExpress seven days a week and messaging people on MSN left, right, and center to make up for lost time. It was one of the greatest times of my life. Money allowed me to do more things I'd always dreamed of doing. I got to see my first-ever gig, and I had enough money to get a taxi home on a freezing-cold night instead of waiting for the bus. I got to learn. I signed up to take acting classes at Rose Bruford College and adult evening classes in subjects I could barely understand, like social psychology and law. I took a course in buying real estate. Why? Because I could. I had the money to do these things now. And that course gave me the knowledge to buy investment properties and make passive income.

Money doesn't just give you access; it gives you freedom. It equals choice and opportunity. My mother was trapped without it. She couldn't leave my father because she didn't have any, and she couldn't even divorce him—not because she couldn't afford the divorce but she couldn't afford the *filing fee*. Imagine having to stay married to someone not because you can't decide how to split the assets but because you can't afford the paperwork.

In England, no matter what politicians claim, opportunity is largely dictated by what womb you come out of. Industries like entertainment and media aren't meritocracies; they're dominated by nepotism. Almost all the top jobs in the UK go to those who attended a handful of elite schools, speak with the "right" accents, and have the "right" familial connections. Privilege has always prevailed, and the options for social mobility are limited.

There's an old East London saying: The only way out of the ghetto is boxing, singing, or crime.

For me, it was my tits.

Which brings me back to the mortification.

I was loving my life being hood rich and chowing down on new foods and surfing the internet, but my actual feelings about my job remained the same. Every time I posed topless for *The Sun* or one of the cheaper weekly magazines, I felt so deeply embarrassed in my core sense of being. I was filled with shame. I kept trying to talk myself out of my feelings by saying, *Christ, it's only a pair of tits. I don't know what you're so uptight about—it's not like you've grown up religious. Girls would kill to be in your position and have huge tits. And let's not forget, you were the one who wished for them! C'mon, you once got a man to pull his dick out so you could rob him.* The thing about that last one is that up until now, no one knew about it but the Grove Park crew and the man we robbed, so I couldn't be embarrassed or ashamed by that. With Page 3, my photos were everywhere, and I couldn't deal with what this said about me. And the stigma. *Oh, the stigma.* Being a Page 3 and glamour model meant you were looked down upon. Designers wouldn't touch Page 3 models with a barge pole. And the public had their own opinions that weren't particularly favorable. I tested this when a guy approached me one day and asked if I was "the Keeley."

"Who?" I said.

"Keeley, she's a Page 3 model," he said.

"My name is Francesca," I said. "Did you just compare me to a Page 3 model?" My voice went up, as if I were really offended. He apologized until he was blue in the face, saying that I seemed far too classy to be a Page 3 model and that he didn't mean to offend me by comparing me to a dumb topless model.

My feelings weren't unfounded, as I learned when I shot with the big British fashion photographer Rankin. He shot for all the art house magazines I loved—the magazines I wanted to be in—and that week, he was shooting me for *Zoo* magazine. It was an odd magazine for Rankin to shoot for because it was a low-scale weekly men's magazine that was considered beneath the celebrity photographer who'd once shot photos of the queen.

I stood in the shooting area in a pair of black boots and black knickers, holding two freezing-cold glass Coke bottles on my nipples, trying to make them hard, when Anthony, the editor for the magazine group who owned *Zoo*, among other titles like *FHM* and *Arena*, came over to check in on me. He was overseeing my shoots. He wanted to make me into the next big thing.

"It's great that we've got Rankin shooting for *Zoo*," I said.

"Oh, yeah, it's great. We're not putting his name on it, though. We've paid him a shit ton of money, but we're not allowed to put his name on the photos," Anthony said.

I suddenly felt like I wanted to cry into the Coke bottles. Why was he so embarrassed by me? Why was I so embarrassed by myself? Anthony must have noticed because he added, "He doesn't want to be associated with *Zoo* magazine." I think that was supposed to make me feel better, but it made me feel so worthless.

Of course, I intellectually understood Rankin's desire not to have his name printed in the magazine; both Page 3 models and *Zoo* magazine carried stigma. And Rankin's work was artistic, and this was England, the country that invented snobbery and the class system—association was everything. But the whole thing just felt so...*humiliating*.

The images we shot were the same, whether they ended up on the cover of *Vogue*—a magazine Rankin had recently shot for—or *Zoo*.

But if the same set of images had been published in *Vogue* magazine, my perceived value as a model and how the world viewed me would dramatically shift. It was the exact same set of photos, but change the title of the publication, and it has the power to change people's perspectives. Like an optical illusion.

By association, my perceived value as a model and, therefore, my perceived worth as an individual was categorized by the media platform that published my images. And I had zero control over my image or what images were published. That's what was so dumb about the whole thing. I was defined and judged by an image and, furthermore, a voice I had no control over.

This was before the boom of social media. MySpace and Facebook were bubbling away in the background, but it would be a few more years before they hit the mainstream and people could claim their voices and create their own personas.

There I was, standing with two Coke bottles on my tits at a time when the mainstream media had complete control over the narrative. Back then the newspapers controlled everything. And there was no way of accessing the general public without going through one of the media outlets. To understand this paradigm more astutely, *The Sun* newspaper was so powerful that the prime minister's first call in the morning was to the editor. *The Sun* could make or break an election or make or break your career. That's how much power they had, and the only way you could stop them from ruining your life was if *you* had power. Then you might be able to get that story of you sleeping with a bunch of hookers and blowing cocaine up their assholes put into "the vault" if you traded them something.

I learned of "the vault" on my first trip to *The Sun* office; one of the editors had told me about it. "We've got some great stories on people and photos," he said, mentioning someone I'd never heard of and how they had photos of him leaving a hotel room with a woman who wasn't his wife. He then told me how a famous politician's daughter had tried to commit suicide and how all the newspapers came together and agreed not to print the story. "I was really proud of us for that," he said.

As I walked around *The Sun* office, hearing stories about famous figures—mostly men—who had managed to cultivate a clean image and shape public opinion through deceit, I imagined what it would be like to have the power to negotiate with these people—to sit across from them as an equal, instead of having them control my image, my life, and print whatever they liked. I doubted I would ever know or be given the opportunity. And that fact really irritated me. I got myself worked up thinking that the whole setup was completely unfair and unjust. I only ended up on Page 3 because I didn't have any money, and now my tits were everywhere and people were judging me and making fun of me. I entered full self-loathing mode, wondering why I had to put up with this bullshit. I would have spiraled all night. But then I remembered: I had PizzaExpress and MSN Messenger waiting for me.

The September Issue

~ SEPTEMBER 2005

Holy macaroni! As Patsy likes to say. I'm on the front cover of *FHM* magazine!!!! It says, "Keeley—Only 18 and already perfect." This is soooo funny. I mean, "Perfect?" Bet they wouldn't have said that if they'd seen me with my head down the toilet the other morning. I looked a right state. (Note to self: Do not drink any more sambuca shots!) My agent has told me that this cover is a big deal. The magazine has moved away from featuring models and focusing more on celebrities. You will never guess who was on the front cover a few months back. *Mariah Carey!! Mariah fucking Carey!!!* I'm on the same front cover as the woman whose lyrics I sang while locked up in a police cell. And guess who else was on it this year? Destiny's Child! I LOVE Destiny's Child.

Apparently, putting me on the cover is a big risk, which is why they didn't pay me. The plan is to get some exposure and then book some campaigns. I wanna be in the Pirelli Calendar so bad. I wanna work with Katie Grand. She's so fucking cool. I'm trying to be really *strategic*. Only do high-end front covers and shoot with the best fashion photographers; then I'll step away from Page 3, and I'll only do topless stuff for the fashion magazines.

Scarface

The song blaring through the car speaker was unbearable—one of those soulless techno tracks with no lyrics and a fist-pumping *dun-dun-dun* that vibrates through your body aggressively. I couldn't fathom how anyone could listen to a song like this unless they were in a nightclub high on ecstasy, and even then, you needed to be deaf to enjoy it. I was drunk, and it was driving me nuts. All I wanted was a kebab—a nice late-night doner with a bit of spicy sauce—but I didn't want to be terrorized on my way to get it.

"This song is making my head want to explode! Play something fun!" I yelled from the back seat at Sarah's older brother, Frankie, our designated driver, who was subjecting us to his awful taste in music.

"Yeah, play something fun!" Sarah echoed, holding on to the door handle as we whizzed around the streets at sixty miles per hour. Frankie was still in his boy racer phase, and it caused Sarah and me to be flung about a bit.

Sarah was one of my best friends from school. Back then, when I wasn't with Patsy, I was cheating on her with Sarah and Hayley. We were a trio: Sarah, Hayley, and me—but I hadn't seen either of them in a while, so I came to meet them in their local pub in Beckenham.

Hayley had ditched us outside the pub after giving me her cardigan to wear because it was mid-September and freezing. She headed in one direction, and Sarah and I jumped into the back of her brother's car, who'd also been in the pub, and Sarah's boyfriend had hopped into the passenger seat. I was ready to sing along to a bit of George Michael and soak up the alcohol I'd drunk with a greasy doner, which, let's be honest, I shouldn't have been eating at midnight when I had a photo shoot in two days, but late-night food was my weakness. I loved a kebab or a twenty-four-hour McDonald's.

Frankie went to push eject on the CD player, and bang, the next thing I knew, I'd all but forgotten about the kebab, and I was eating copper coins. Thousands and thousands of them were stuffed into my mouth, and I could hardly breathe.

It all happened so fast. I was in the back of the car one minute, and then I was no longer in the car and couldn't remember being in one. All I knew was I was on my back, but I couldn't tell where... *Wait*, in the middle of the road? My eyesight was blurry and wavering. Then it slid into focus. I could see the night sky and houses and a figure standing over me—a woman. Her mouth was moving; I looked at her lips, trying to make sense of what she was saying, "You uuuuuuuuuuuuuu'vvvveeeeeeeeeeeee beeeeeeeeeeeeennnnnnnnnnnnnnn in a crrrrrrrrrrr," she said as if it were in slow motion.

That's when I got hit with a sudden rush of pain. I tried to scream "fuccckkkkkkk" as the nasty copper coins shot up out of my mouth and into the air and back into my mouth again, muffling the sound of my voice. Then it hit me...Copper coins taste like—*blood. Blood tastes like copper coins.* My mouth isn't filled with copper coins. *It's filled with blood, dummy.*

The woman said something and disappeared out of view. My face was pounding in pain. I felt like a herd of elephants had stamped on it. My legs felt paralyzed. It was the scariest moment of my life. Was I dying? Had this woman tried to kill me? Why was there blood all over my face? I thought. I was disoriented and didn't know what to do. I could feel something digging into my leg. I reached my hand into my jeans pocket and pulled it out. It was my Nokia. I looked at the screen. It was all blurry and out of focus, and I thought maybe I should call someone. I dialed the first number that came to mind, my hands shaking as I managed to speak through the muffled sound of the blood in my mouth. "You need to come and get me...It's an emergency. You need to come and get me," I said, panicked but holding back the tears. If this was my last moment, I needed people to know I was a fighter.

The woman appeared over me again; she placed what looked like a flannel on my face and said something like, "Here, we need to add pressure to stop the bleeding until the ambulance arrives," in an erratic high pitch. *Did she just say "ambulance"?* I thought. *This has to be a dream.* The phone dropped from my hand. I heard the woman talking and kept trying to keep my eyes open, but I couldn't. They were heavy, and I felt the sensation of rushing through my whole body, and everything suddenly became real loud, and time was moving faster than I'd ever experienced before. That's the last thing I remember.

* * *

The next time I opened my eyes, I was in a bright, white room in a hospital bed wearing a blue gown with ECG pads all over my chest, an IV stuck in my arm, and another needle in my hand. My arm had pinprick marks all over it, and I must have been high on something because usually the sight of needles would make me freak out, and I just stared at them blankly. My eyes felt swollen, and I could see that there was this white shit stuck over my nose, but I couldn't tell what exactly. The pain was something to be remembered. I looked around the room to collect my bearings, only to see a man I vaguely recognized sitting in a chair in the corner. Then I realized who it was: *Dad.* I flicked my eyes open a couple of times and stared at him. He shook his head in a way that portrayed disapproval but also relief. It was the most concern I ever saw him show. It should have been a gratifying moment, but I was so unused to him showing any signs of worry that it made me uncomfortable, and I forced myself to look away.

Neither of us spoke for what felt like forever, and it only dawned on me then that I wasn't wearing anything under the hideous hospital gown, so in a sort of shaky, appalled whisper, I asked Dad where my clothes had gone. He frowned. "The doctors had to cut them off. They thought you were going to die," he said, his words sharp and cold. I totally disregarded the fact that he said, "thought you were going to die," and before I realized how much it hurt to talk, I blurted out, "Shit, Hayley's cardigan!"

"You won't be worrying about a posy cardigan when you see your face," Dad said.

My face.

There it was, *my face.*

Yikes, my face. I tried to move my arm to touch it, but wires were all over me, and I couldn't get them out of the way.

"Is it bad?" I asked, panicked. He moved his head around and let out a sigh as if to say it was more than "bad."

"The woman on the phone told me you were in a car crash," Dad said sternly, looking off to the side. "How are you gonna go to work looking like that?"

I wasn't in the mood to be berated; I was tired and out of it and had no idea what I looked like. I was suddenly confused as to why he'd been the person I had called in this crisis. When I was ten, I flipped over the handlebars of my bike—did a midair somersault before crashing onto the pavement with such force that I cut my right knee open through my jeans, exposing my bone, and whacked my head so hard that my brand-new helmet my dad had just gotten me, and I was wearing for the first and only time, broke in half. I hobbled in the front door with blood dripping everywhere and found Dad sitting on the sofa, eating a sandwich. The whole bottom of my jeans was stained crimson, and my knee was still bleeding. Dad looked at my knee, and a loud giggle erupted straight from his stomach; he took a bite of his sandwich and continued watching the television. The man *laughed* at me, so I went and found the first aid kit and bandaged up my knee. I still have a scar to this day.

Dad was clearly incapable of offering comfort, so why had I called him? Had I wanted him to see me like this? Was I testing him to see if he loved me? Did I think he could save me? I'd placed the call to Dad—no one else but me had done that. I could have called Mum, Deborah, or the hot guy in a band I was dating, but I didn't. Heck, I could have called the emergency services instead of my father, but I didn't.

"Yeah, it was a car crash," I said weakly. "It looks like I'll have to call in sick at work. I wonder if I'll get sick pay." I closed my eyes so I didn't have to talk further.

Sometime later, Sarah appeared at my hospital bed. Her boyfriend, Jimmy, who was in his midtwenties and much more mature than us teenagers, stood by her side.

"OH MY GOD, Key, are you okay? OH MY GOD, your face!"

There it was again, *my face*.

"I feel like I've been beaten up. I think my nose might be on my chin. Is it sexy to have two noses?" I said. Sarah said something funny, and I wish I could remember it. I just remember that it hurt my stomach to laugh, but I needed the laughter. It was the only emotion that could stop me from falling to pieces. Otherwise, I'd have to accept that I could have lost my life and that my career might be over, and I wasn't ready to face those realities just yet.

Jimmy told us that Frankie was fine but had been arrested. "When he went to change the CD, he drove straight into a parked car. The impact of it caused the car to flip over. It was proper scary," he said, his voice cracking, shaken by the whole thing. Dad asked if Sarah's brother was drunk or just an idiot because only an idiot would drive into a parked car.

"I don't know. I couldn't tell," Sarah said, which made me laugh because it sounded like she couldn't tell whether her brother was an idiot or not.

We all looked at Jimmy, "I'm not sure how much he drank. He seemed fine to me."

"What happened to you guys?" I asked. "When I woke up, all I saw was a woman."

"I don't remember any of it. I blacked out," said Sarah.

"My airbag went off. I was all right, and so was Frankie, but there was tons of smoke coming from the engine. When I looked in the back, Sarah was on top of you, and you were both passed out, so I had to drag you both out of the car unconscious," Jimmy said. He had dark circles under his eyes and was completely shaken up. I thought about how I'd been told you should never move someone in a car crash if they're unconscious because if they have an injury in their neck, it could kill them. That you should only do it if there's immediate danger. I knew then that the car looked like it would explode, and I let my mind imagine for one second what could have happened, how it could have all been much worse than it had been. Chills went through my body, and my eyes started welling up. Sarah and I spent inconceivable amounts of time together, and to think that in one split second she could have been gone. Any of us could. I could have died and the last thing I would have heard was that god-awful techno song.

"Who was the woman?" I asked.

"She was from one of the houses. A few people came out. The crash must have been so loud it woke them up," Jimmy said. Dad was just sitting in the chair, not saying anything.

"Or they were woken up by Frankie's terrible taste in music," I said, trying to lighten the mood. That made Sarah laugh.

I spent the night in the hospital. Dad stayed by my side. The following day, still out of it and weak, I decided to get up and go to the bathroom to see my face. I needed to see the damage. I slowly got out of bed. I was hunched over, as this was the only position that felt comfortable, and I slowly pulled my IV drip into the restroom. I locked the door and immediately went to the mirror above the sink. I was so mortified by my reflection. I had no idea who was staring back at me; I couldn't recognize myself. It was so terrifying that I laughed (seemingly my only reaction to distress). It wasn't a *HA HA HA; this is sooooo funny laugh.* It was an *OH MY GOD, I look like I've been smashed in the face repeatedly with a sledgehammer.* My nose was broken in half—legit broken into two. The skin had been ripped apart, and the bone had split right in the middle. The doctor had stitched the skin back together, but the way my nose had broken had caused the bottom half to bend to the right. In the middle, where the break took place, the bone was sticking out. So where the stitches were, there was now a bump that was the cartilage. There was dry blood all over my face. My eyes were swollen and bruised. My lips looked amazing, though. Apart from the cut on top of them, they were all pumped up from the swelling and looked like I'd had lip fillers. Honestly, I've never seen them look better.

"Keeley, only eighteen and already perfect," I said, my voice croaky and weak.

I stared at myself for longer than I should have. I couldn't get over the fact that I looked like a disfigured, chubby panda with full lips.

When I returned to my hospital bed, the emergency doctor who had stitched my nose up told me that I should expect scars and that I'd need to rest for the next couple of weeks. I'd be out of work for a while if the crash didn't wreck my face so bad that

I never worked again. I had no idea what these scars would look like or how my broken nose would heal. I knew my career wasn't contingent on my nose—no one looked at my face. I'm surprised they even knew I had one, but it was unclear what would happen. I'd never seen a broken-nosed, scar-faced female model, even in the glamour world.

Mother didn't visit me in the hospital. When I finally returned home, she took one look at me and said, "Oh my God, look at the state of you."

I said nothing, so she continued. "Something like this would only happen to you. I bet no one else was injured, were they?"

"Clearly bad things happen to me," I said, annoyed. I was the only person in the car who had a career based on my looks, and I was the one that had a fucked-up face. I just had an innate ability to do that. She examined my face with an expression of disgust. "Can you stop looking at me!" I cried.

It felt so wildly unfair that had it been Jimmy or Frankie who'd ended up breaking their noses in the accident, it would have added character and made them even sexier. But no one wanted to see a broken nose on a woman's face. No one wanted to see any form of impurity. Scars, stretch marks, cellulite, birthmarks, or even lines of aging were not tolerated on a woman. Women had to be blemish-free and youthful, but the same rules didn't apply to men. Many years later, I would date a male model who had a massive scar across his stomach and salt-and-pepper hair. His scar was a sex symbol that added to his appeal. Photographers wanted to photograph it. If the same scar had been on a woman, it would have been treated very differently. She'd only be photographed as part of an article meant to empower women by celebrating their "imperfections." She'd be labeled "brave," and the interviewer would ask her how she came to accept this obvious imperfection of hers.

I stayed in bed for two weeks straight. Mum would bring me food and water. Every morning, as soon as I opened my eyes, I would get up and stare at myself in the mirror, examining my reflection. I watched as my nose began healing. The stitches dissolved, and a deep scar formed right above my lip and across my nose, making it look like I'd slept face down with sunglasses on, and they'd left a heavy indent.

Sally, the photographer, and her editor husband were incredibly supportive. They told me to return to Page 3 when I felt ready and that we would "figure this out." However, I felt like they were protecting me, shielding me from the reality that my career was over. A girl had once been fired from Page 3 because she didn't have her roots done. I now had an entirely different nose.

Those two weeks were brutal, consumed by self-pity and overthinking. Each time I looked in that mirror, I winced, horrified by my own reflection. Then I would put the mirror down, despising myself for my vanity and shallowness. Then I'd pick it back up, thinking it was only a matter of time before Rebekah Brooks, the head of the newspaper, saw me, and I'd be fired.

"I'm sorry I'm not there to look after you, but can I see you as soon as I get back from this part of the tour?" the hot guy from the band I was dating asked me on the phone a few days after the crash.

"I'm not sure," I said, getting out of bed and looking in the mirror. I wanted to see him, but I didn't want him to see me. He would never love me looking like this, so I broke up with him.

When I hung up, I berated myself. *Why did you have to get in the car to get a kebab, you greedy bitch? Why didn't you walk? Why did you ask Frankie to change the song? WHY? FUCKING, WHY DIDN'T YOU PUT YOUR SEAT BELT ON?*

(I do with regret what Catholics do with guilt.)

When I eventually returned to Page 3, in an act to save me, the photographer, Alan, erased the scars and photoshopped my nose straight until I could "get it fixed."

"Everyone's had work done. It's no biggie these days," he said, dismissing the idea that people still looked down on plastic surgery and that it didn't carry the same cultural stigma.

This seemed to contradict the fact he always pointed out in a dismissive tone when a woman had work done and would comment, "Her boobs are fake. Fake arse. Fake lips," adding, "Not like you, who's all natural." The comparison was meant to make me feel like I was better, and it did make me feel that way. It gave me a sense of smugness and a disgusting moral superiority wrapped up in the illusion of pride that I used to fill up my self-esteem before I knocked it down whenever I looked at myself in the mirror.

To have cosmetic surgery or not felt like a confusing box to navigate. Alan and others around me seemed to be saying, "You should be beautiful, pretty, and sexy, but you should be born with it. And if you're not born with it, you should try to obtain it secretly but will be heavily judged and have your beauty discredited if it turns out to be fake."

While my surgery was reconstructive and not cosmetic, I still didn't want to go under the knife because I felt ashamed. I was ashamed of what people would think of me, ashamed and sickened that I was a person driven by vanity. I was internally conflicted. I felt like there were so many more important things in life than my face and that I should feel lucky to be alive, and yet, how I made money was tied up solely in my looks.

I put it off for months, relying on software editing to erase my misfortune. That was until I saw the behind-the-scenes footage from the *Maxim* cover I was shooting, and I couldn't bear to look at myself. I was disgusted. My face repulsed me. I couldn't live like this any longer. I had to go and see Robert.

Robert was a veteran plastic surgeon in his sixties on Harley Street. I sat in the waiting room and flicked through endless folders of before and after photos of women, my heart racing like I was highly caffeinated. Nose after nose. Boobs after boobs. Tummy after tummy. Face after face of procedures I'd never heard of. I was suddenly overcome with a desire to change everything about myself—my ears, my butt, my stomach, my cheekbones. The notion of physical perfection leaped off the page and seeped through my oversized pores. I closed one of the folders in a panic and waited to be called into Robert's office.

"You've got a deviated septum and a twisted cartilage. I can't fix the twist—the bone's set—but I can shave down the bump here and refine the tip," Robert said casually as he touched the bridge of my nose with a small silver measuring device as if he were a tailor and my nose were a pair of pants he was hemming.

"What about the scars?"

"Can't do anything about those, I'm afraid. But if I refine the tip, it will make a difference."

I didn't care about the scar above my lip, but the scar across my nose was hideous. I might have been able to tolerate it if it had been located somewhere else, but it looked like a sunglasses mark, for Christ's sake. It was ridiculous. I looked like a clown.

"Why can't you do anything to the scar?"

"Scars aren't my specialty. But it's too deep." He started talking about the formation of the tissue, and I stopped listening because I didn't want to hear it. I wanted a solution. And the only one offered was the refinement to the tip of my nose.

I didn't know I had a problem with the tip, but now all I kept wondering was if the slightly upturned tip was ugly and I was a fool for not noticing. I started touching it self-consciously. Robert noticed.

"It won't be dramatic. It will just look a little better on the eye," he reassured me. *Better on the eye? What does it look like now, a pig's nose?*

I immediately signed up for the surgery.

My manager picked me up after the operation, and I stayed at his house with his wife and children until I recovered. I didn't tell any of my family or friends about the procedure for fear a rumor would spread that I'd had a nose job. I couldn't have people put me down like I'd seen them do to others by saying, "Her nose is fake."

When it was time to take the bandages off, I stood in front of the mirror, so excited to see my new nose. At this point I'd convinced myself that it would be better than *before* the crash, that maybe the crash happened so I'd have a nose job and dominate the fashion world. When I looked in the mirror, it was apparent that it was clearly not the case. It would be an understatement to say I was seething. I hated it. The bump beneath it had gone; that bit I enjoyed, but the tip was different and looked less pronounced, my nostrils looked uneven, and the scar—well, now that the bump was gone, the scar was larger than life. It seemed to be the only thing noticeable on my face. I didn't have a face anymore; I just had a scar.

I would have been devastated even without my career, but my job aspirations made it a thousand times worse. Beauty or attractiveness was a currency—one that could be placed on the free market to measure its value. I'd been turned into a monetizable commodity, and I couldn't quite wrap my head around that.

Being attractive was a single entity. There was a separation between the "inside" and "outside."

How I'd operated in the world before modeling, how I had made friends, or the attention I had rendered had been based on other aspects of myself. In the real world, I was a whole person with an "inside" (personality, character, bad jokes) and an "outside" (appearance), and it was the "inside," the intrinsic part of me, that was front and center. Patsy was my best friend because we made each other laugh and had similarities and similar ideologies on life. She didn't care what size my tits were. Yet I had suddenly found myself building a life and career around one "outside" aspect of myself, "being attractive." As someone who grew up not being prized for my looks, residing more in what was viewed as "masculine," wearing one earring and having the same haircut as Jason Donovan, it felt intoxicating to gain so much attention for my physicality. I was deeply grateful for it. I loved feeling desired, especially by men who'd often ignored me, but in the same breath, I cared more about having fun than my appearance. I craved knowledge, understanding, and experiences.

Though I cared more about my "inside" life, the message I received over and over was that my appearance was the most important aspect of myself. The only thing that had value. I SHOULD CARE ABOUT HOW I LOOK. I SHOULD STRIVE FOR PERFECTION. I SHOULD GET RID OF MY SCAR. I felt that pressure every day as the little voice in my head told me I should go to the gym, stop eating crap, and invest more in beauty products and procedures.

It's hard not to be resentful when the world values superficiality above everything else. But fame isn't about you. It's about what other people think of you. You might ask, Who was I now that I had to prioritize the exterior for money? And I'll tell you. I was: a person obsessed with a scar who hated herself for being a person obsessed with a scar. I spent hours of my life staring at myself in the mirror. No one should spend this much time looking at themselves, even if they make mirrors for a living. I rubbed bio-oil and various other gels and creams on it. I'd gone back to work two weeks after the surgery but spent the next ten years googling procedures. I spent thousands of pounds having microneedling and laser and fillers stuck in it. Then I wouldn't wash my face for three days and eat the greasy junk food in an act of rebellion.

My scar tormented me to no end and made me feel like my self-worth and self-esteem had been thrown into a washing machine and then hurled off a cliff. I often wonder if it would have helped if someone had explained to me that under a patri-archal capitalist society, the beauty industry and the media set unattainable beauty standards that make women feel inferior and not enough in order for them to sell products. In light of this, there are two options: Conform or reject these ideals, but you'll be judged regardless. I honestly don't think that knowing how the world operated would have mattered. There's no use telling a prisoner that she's in prison.

I'd love to inform you that this is a story about acceptance—that, like all women who have "imperfections," I overcame the scar in the middle of my face. But I didn't. I still hate it. I still hate what Robert did to my nose as much now as I did then. So, if this isn't a story about acceptance, what is it? Well, dear reader, this is a cautionary tale of why you should never drive under the influence of techno music.

Celebrity Crushed

There was no one in the world I had a bigger celebrity crush on than J.C. I still, to this day, remember the first time I saw him. I was sixteen and lying on the sofa nursing a hangover and mindlessly changing the channels on the television when his face came on the screen. I immediately stopped flipping. I took one glimpse of his blue eyes and sat upright. Who was this man? I had to find out. So I did what you naturally do when you see the man of your dreams: I picked up the landline and called my best friend, Patsy. In a panicked state, knowing time was of the essence, that if she didn't turn to the same channel right now, he might go off-screen and I might never see him again, I yelled at her to call me back because my mum would kill me for running up the phone bill; then, when she did, I told her to turn on Channel Three to look at my future husband. "He's the most handsome man I've ever seen. I'm in love with him," I told her definitively, not knowing his name or anything about him.

Patsy, who was much more up to speed on these things than me, told me he was a football player. The team he played for was a bit wanky, not one I would have chosen to support, but I was willing to throw any loyalty I had out the window for those blue eyes...

I had no way of looking my dream man up online, so I did the next best thing and purchased a calendar of the football team he played for, and Mum, who always kept a calendar on the kitchen wall, decided she wanted to use it to save herself from buying another one. So there it was—a calendar for a football team no one in the house supported hung in the kitchen.

The calendar had photos of different players for each month of the year, and every time a new month would arrive, my mum would change it, and I would change it back to April—the month with a photo of J.C. I couldn't stop staring at him. I tried to use the power of my mind and will him out of the photo and into my kitchen. I started going by K.C. to all my friends, as if we were already married. I'd named our children. I even took a pen to our kitchen wall, which still had no wallpaper and looked like the inside of a bathroom stall because my family (mostly me) had scribbled all over it. I found an empty space and wrote in big capital letters with a permanent marker: I LOVE J.C.! And K.C 4 J.C., followed by IDST (if destroyed, still true).

I still hadn't gotten over my J.C. crush a year later, when, aged seventeen, I entered my first modeling competition, and the newspaper asked me, "What would you like to do if you win?" and I said, "Meet J.C."

What did I have to lose? It was my dream, my destiny. There was nothing else I wanted in this world but to meet J.C. and marry him. It was all I thought about. And I manifested the shit out of him.

*   *   *

After I won Page 3 Idol, Nic T invited me on a night out. It was my first time inside a bougie West End nightclub with a VIP section and bottle service. It felt so awfully posh and grown-up. As soon as I trotted nervously into the VIP section, there was J.C., every five foot nine inches of him. His face was lit up by sparklers coming off champagne bottles, and I couldn't believe my luck. I stood there looking like I'd just seen Jesus rise from the dead. I was unable to speak or look away. *Of all the clubs in London, of all the millions of people in London, I was in the same nightclub—at the same time—as J.C.! If this wasn't fate, then I didn't know what was.*

Not aware of how much I loved this man, Nic T casually introduced me. "Keeley, this is J.C."

He hugged me and said, "All right."

My heart fell from my chest and into my stomach. I started shaking. I thought I would faint. I was so nervous. I couldn't believe I was meeting him. I could barely string together two words, let alone a sentence. What are you supposed to say when you meet your future husband? *Shall we cut this crap and just head to the altar?*

Sadly, I didn't need to think of anything to say because as soon as we walked away, I told Nic T how much I fancied the pants off J.C., and Nic T—being the perfect wingwoman—asked one of J.C.'s friends if he was single, and it turned out that J.C. had a serious girlfriend. "He's probably going to marry her" were his exact words, and I was devastated. How was he going to marry this other woman? He had just met me, and I was his future wife. How did he not know that?!?

The blow was fatal. All the movies I'd watched had led me to believe that the moment I met the man of my dreams, we would look into each other's eyes and just know. Our love was going to be so powerful that he would rather die than not be with me. I hadn't accounted for him having a girlfriend. To be honest, I hadn't accounted for much. I had an inaccurate idea of what love and attraction were—one that would drive me through to my midtwenties. But then, I was just a girl who'd met her ultimate celebrity crush and was on a mission to have him fall in love with me. I devised a plan—the long game. I was going to wait the girlfriend out.

The long game lasted about two weeks.

Another thing I hadn't accounted for was how many hot football players there actually were. I couldn't recognize most of them from their appearance, but you could tell who was a football player and who wasn't from the swagger they had and the number of girls lined up waiting to meet them and take their shot.

I remained committed to J.C. for a whole two weeks like, *There's no one else but J.C. If I can't have him, then I don't want anyone.* Then a few days later, in a nightclub called Funky Buddha, I met J.C.'s teammate—an Icelandic player whose name I couldn't spell, let alone pronounce, but that didn't matter because I was too busy snogging his face off.

Over the next year I started seeing J.C. and the rest of London football teams on the London party circuit a few nights a week. We weren't exactly friends. I didn't know anything about them. But we got drunk, danced, and texted each other about parties and which club they were going to on what night. Wednesdays at Chinawhite, Thursdays at Embassy, etc. I was in my element. I embraced this new life of West End nightclubs easily. I was made for it. One of the Page 3 girls would always have a hookup, and these were the good old days—when I'd be out till five a.m. and somehow still manage to function the next day. I would party with football players and other celebrities alike and pound the booze. Nothing gave me more of a thrill than getting shit-faced and snogging football players. It was one of my hobbies. I was really good at it.

Unless J.C. saw the interview I did before I became a Page 3 model, I'm not sure he knew about my crush on him, which was good because over the year of seeing him out and about, it had started to dwindle. I'd come to realize this new world I found myself in felt like I was visiting an amusement park—thrilling and surreal but not where I belonged. Not my reality. Eventually I moved on and fell in love with Theo, who wasn't a part of this new world at all. He lived around the corner from where I grew up in Grove Park. And that is, of course—since my life was like the Alanis Morissette song—around the time J.C. ended up in my bed.

It was worse than rain on my wedding day.

There he was, J.C., lying *in my bed*. The same single bed I had slept in and fantasized about him in. I looked at his face, the light stubble around his jaw, his very kissable lips. He was so handsome, even with his eyes closed. And that's the thing. His eyes were closed. His eyes were closed because he was asleep. Yes, *asleep!* My celebrity crush had ended up in my bed, completely passed out. Nothing says "dream come true" than having to take off a man's coat and shoes and put him to bed because he is intoxicated.

After I tucked him under the covers, I hung his coat on the wooden doorknob of my wardrobe, put his shoes together, and then slowly crept out of my bedroom, taking one last look at him as I closed my bedroom door and crept downstairs, immediately pulling my Nokia phone out of my pocket and calling Patsy.

"Oh my fucking God, you'll never believe who is in my bed!"

"*Who?*" she said, excited.

"J.C.!"

"Oh my God! Why is he in your bed? What is happening? TELL ME EVERYTHING!"

I explained what had happened, how everyone had left the club to go to a party and how I had been to the bathroom, and by the time I made my way outside, everyone had gone, including Nic T. The only person left was J.C., who was blackout drunk and couldn't stand up or form sentences, so I hailed a taxi, and J.C. jumped in and slurred, "Partttttttyyyyyyyyyy. We?" I tried calling Nic T to find out where everyone had gone, but her phone was switched off. I didn't have anyone else's number, and J.C. had lost his wallet. I said I'd drop him home and kept asking him where he lived, and he kept replying, "England!" The taxi driver started yelling at me to tell him where he was going, and I didn't want to leave J.C. fucked up in the middle of the street on his own. We had the World Cup coming up. I couldn't leave a valuable player in the streets of Mayfair stumbling around while blackout drunk, so I tried to take him to Nic T's West Ham football player boyfriend's apartment, but no one was home. So I did what I thought was the next best thing to do in that scenario, and I mixed my worlds and brought him back to my council estate. I carried my celebrity crush out of the taxi over my arm and made him drink tons of water in the hallway—because I thankfully remembered that "I LOVE J.C." was written all over the wall in the kitchen. I had to make sure he didn't see it, so I walked him up to my bedroom, took off his coat and shoes, and put him to bed.

"You're having me on," she said. "I'm coming over."

Five minutes later, Patsy arrived in a taxi, merry from her own night out, and we were peering through my bedroom door at J.C. like he was some sort of exotic zoo animal. She pulled out her Motorola flip phone and took a photo.

"Patsy! Don't take a photo of him!" I said in a hushed voice.

"I was trying to get a closer look! I've never seen him in person," she said. We looked at the photo. It was blurry and pixelated.

"Delete it," I said, panicking that he might wake up and embarrassingly find us taking photos of him. She huffed and puffed and then deleted it. We were both drunk and giddy with excitement, so we made our way downstairs to the kitchen, leaving J.C. to sleep. My mum wasn't home. Deborah had moved back in, but her door was locked, so I had no idea if she was there or not. I searched the kitchen drawers to find a pen and started scratching out K.C. 4 J.C. so I wouldn't look like a bunny boiler on the off chance he found his name graffitied all over the wall. I couldn't think of anything more embarrassing.

As I tried to change J.C.'s initials into Patsy's, we did what we always did when something completely mad happened: talk about it repeatedly. We went over every moment of the evening. How many shots had J.C. had? *Was it three? Or four? Or fifteen?* Who else had been at the Embassy nightclub? *All of the England football team.* Where had they all gone, and why was J.C. on his own? *To some party or a seedy hotel with women who weren't their wives or girlfriends.* I told her I'd seen a bill for drinks for £600, and she opened her mouth in an O shape. Spending six hundred quid on drinks felt insane; it was more money than I'd made a month as a hairdresser, and these boys threw it around like it was peanuts.

After I finished scratching over my love confessions to J.C., I poured us Jack and Cokes, and we were cheersing when my phone rang.

"Shitttttttttttt," I said, looking at the caller ID.

"Who's that?" Patsy asked.

"It's Theo," I said. "What should I do?"

"Just answer it—innit."

"Yeah, but what am I going to say about J.C. being in my bed?"

"Don't tell him."

I gave Patsy a sideways glance and answered. Theo was my childhood crush, who was now my boyfriend. His car was parked outside my house. His key was inside my house. He had been waiting until I got back to collect it. He wanted to know if I was home. I said yes, and he said he was coming over. I tried quickly to find an excuse for why he should wait until the morning, but all I had was, "Patsy is staying over," and he replied, "Yeah, so?" I told him he couldn't stay but he could collect it.

I hung up the phone, absolutely convinced Theo would think I'd kissed J.C.—or worse, that I'd slept with him.

Before I could mentally untangle myself, he arrived. I kissed him hello, trying to act sane while freaking out on the inside at the very real possibility that J.C. could wake up at any moment, shuffle down the stairs, and, well, ruin my life.

Patsy and I had already agreed, under no circumstances would I mention J.C. There is no simple way to explain why my celebrity crush was upstairs in my single bed. But then Theo asked me about my night, and, well, I found myself wanting to tell him for a variety of reasons.

One, when I started dating Theo, he was well aware of my crush on J.C., and he would always put me down.

"As if J.C. would ever date someone like *you*," he'd say.

(If you're wondering why I dated someone who treated me so poorly, please refer back to the chapter "Daddy Issues.")

While a comment like this was meant to erode my self-esteem, and it did, I tried to turn it into a competition. I wanted to prove that I could date someone like J.C. even if I didn't entirely believe it myself.

Two, the idea of not telling him and him finding out was too much to bear.

Three, I was drunk.

Four, I was incapable of lying, so in a fit of verbal diarrhea, I told him all of the madness of the evening—how J.C. was blackout drunk, how he'd lost his wallet and couldn't remember where he lived and, in a weird turn of events, was upstairs in my bed.

I had started out wanting to prove Theo wrong—that a girl like me was fully capable of getting a guy like J.C., but then I quickly realized that proving that would make this look like something it wasn't. So I backpedaled and reassured Theo that even though he *knew* I used to have the biggest crush on J.C., I no longer had one because I was in love with him and that no funny business had happened between us because I was a great believer in monogamy and furthermore karma, and furthermore, I wasn't into "trying it on" with guys while they're asleep unless, of course, it was Theo, which I said in a sexual tone.

"You're lying," he said like I'd played an April Fools' Day prank on him. "There's no way he's in your bed."

"That's what I thought," said Patsy, "but I went up there, and he's asleep in her bed! So mental." Patsy and I looked at each other and laughed. It still hadn't sunk in. It seemed too bizarre to be true.

My celebrity crush is in my bed.

"I'm going to take a look," said Theo nonchalantly, "just to see if you're telling the truth."

"I'm telling the truth!" I shot back. "Why would I make up such an elaborate lie?"

"I dunno, 'cuz you think it's funny?"

"I mean, it's pretty funny...but I'm not lying," I said, handing Theo his car key. He started walking toward the front door, which just so happened to be next to the stairs.

"Where are you going?" I said, confused.

"I'm just going to have a quick look. I'll be quiet." He put his foot on the first step, so I went and stood in front of him.

"Theo...believe me, I'm not lying," I said tartly. "It's three thirty in the morning! Let the guy sleep."

"I just want to see for myself," he replied. I knew he didn't believe me. I was accustomed to the fact that being a woman meant your words weren't enough; there needed to be evidence. And sometimes even then you wouldn't be believed.

"Fine. Take a look. See that I'm not lying," I said. "Just don't wake him up."

"I promise. I won't," Theo said softly, looking directly into my eyes. My God, he was such a convincing liar. Really and truly, he was one of the best.

"Just be very quiet," I said, letting him pass. He nodded and walked up the stairs.

I walked back into the kitchen.

"I fucking hate it when he thinks I'm lying," I muttered to Patsy, picking up my Jack and Coke and taking a well-needed gulp. It irked me to no end that, in my experience, the biggest liars were always men, yet they were the ones constantly accusing women of dishonesty.

Then, just as I was about to set my glass back down, we both heard a loud bang from upstairs.

We froze. *What the fuck was that?* We heard the sound of a door opening, which set about confusion. Voices followed. I glanced at Patsy. She glanced back at me.

Who else is home? I wondered, and more importantly, *What the hell was that bang?*

I rushed upstairs to investigate, my heart pounding, and suddenly the whole night took a turn for the worse. Micky, Deborah's boyfriend, was standing in the doorway, blocking the entrance to my room like a bouncer at a nightclub. He had his back to me, and he filled up the whole doorframe. Deborah was passed out in her bedroom. I tried to push past Micky, but he stood firm and made it clear he wasn't moving.

"What the fuck is going on?" I said. Micky turned slightly, just enough for me to peek through the gap, and that's when I saw it: Theo on top of J.C., throwing punches at J.C.'s head. J.C.'s arms flailed, trying to shove Theo off, but Theo kept pinning him down, landing punch after punch on his head.

I shoved Micky as hard as I could, but he wouldn't budge. "Let them fight it out like men," he said, enjoying it. He took so much pleasure in it that he started cheering Theo on. "Go on, mate, hit him again! HIT HIM! That's what you get for playing for a scummy team!"

I was mortified. Completely and utterly mortified.

My sister's boyfriend showed his true colors as a football hooligan, and he was having a field day seeing a player from a rival team get beat up. I had to do something. I tried pushing Micky again while yelling, "THEO, STOP!!!!" My voice cracked with panic. "MOVE, MICKY! HE WAS ASLEEP!!!" I yelled and pushed, but Micky didn't flinch.

"Well, he ain't asleep anymore," he snorted, his eyes gleaming with sick amusement.

Inside, J.C. was curled into a ball, his hands shielding his head as Theo circled like a predator, his fists clenched, waiting for him to get up just to knock him down again. "Come on, J.C.! You big man, show me what you've got!" His voice was vengeful.

"MICKY! *Jesus*…don't be a fucking dickhead!!" I screamed, shoving him with everything I had, but there was nothing I could do; he was twice my size, a fact that angered me and pleased him greatly. A smug smile spread across his face. One I had seen many times from men who were so pleased to be stronger than me.

Patsy was behind me; she was catatonic. All of the color had drained from her face; she was pale before, but now she looked translucent. She actually looked like she might disappear entirely.

I continued screaming at Theo to stop, saying he was gonna kill him if he wasn't careful. I was honestly worried for J.C.'s life. This wasn't some scrappy little bar fight. Theo had a punch on him. He was dangerous—once he saw red, that was it. And he was going for it. He was beating the shit out of him. J.C.'s shirt had been ripped off; he was bruised and bleeding.

I had no idea how this horror was going to stop, but then, in a miracle-like fashion, J.C. emerged from his ball and fought back. He hit Theo on the side of the face. Theo swung back and he ducked out of the way. The pair began rumbling around my room, and then, in a move that had turbo speed—a speed that I didn't know was possible—J.C. zoomed through Micky's legs, straight past Patsy and me, and before any of us had moved...he was gone. It was like a magic trick. He disappeared. That is why he was a professional football player, and Theo, who had wanted to be a football player, wasn't. J.C. was fast. He was out of the house in only his trousers, and we had no idea how. The whole thing was a complete mystery.

Theo emerged from my bedroom, his shoulders drawn back, his head held high.

"Why did you do that?" I said, pushing him.

"He's in my girl's bed. Man needs to learn a lesson. You don't sleep in my girl's bed...simple as." He dusted himself off and pointed at me. "And you, Keeley, this was your fault." And with that, he walked out of the front door with his car key in his hand, and I began to panic.

"WHERE ARE YOU GOING?" I yelled after him. He ignored me, jumped in his car, and started the engine. I tried to stop him, but he sped off.

"Fuccccckkkkk, what if Theo's going to find him? We need to do something!" I said to Patsy, who looked severely unwell and like she was having an aneurysm. It wasn't like she hadn't seen a fight before; she had seen plenty. But that was in our world, where violence was commonplace, not in this other world with famous football players.

That world was different.

Micky, who was now bored because the fight was over, said, "I'm going back to bed." He walked into Deborah's room and closed the bedroom door behind him. And I don't know how, but Deborah slept through the whole thing. She was also the kind of person who would wake up with a slice of pizza stuck to her face or a half-eaten Big Mac still in her hand, so maybe that explained it.

Patsy and I had no idea what to do, so we did what most teen-agers do in a crisis: We called her mum. She arrived ten minutes later, ready to head up the search party. We made it our mission to find J.C. We had to. This was South East London. Out there on the streets Theo was the least of J.C.'s problems. At this time of night, I'd seen guys run around with machetes.

Patsy and her mum went one way, and I went the other. We all began searching the streets for a shirtless, shoeless J.C., who had no wallet and no phone—as I had found his phone in his coat pocket, which was still hanging up on my wardrobe doorknob.

As I ran around the streets I grew up on, I called Theo a bunch of times, but he didn't answer. In a panic, I called a football player friend whose mum lived up the road to see if he could help find J.C. He got out of bed, got dressed, and also went out searching for him on the streets. We had a whole search party out there looking for him until 7:00 a.m. When it was clear that he wasn't going to turn up, I eventually headed home and retrieved J.C.'s Nokia phone from his pocket. It didn't have a passcode, so I could call anyone from it, but I didn't know who to call. His mum? His dad? His girlfriend? And say what? "Sorry, your son/boyfriend got blackout drunk and lost his wallet, so I took him back to my house to sleep, and while he was sleeping, my boyfriend went and rudely woke him up by punching him in the face, and then my sister's boyfriend stood around cheering the beating on like he was watching the heavyweight championship final in Vegas. Now he's somewhere around the streets of Grove Park bruised and bloodied without a shirt, shoes, or a wallet—or a phone for that matter, since I'm speaking to you on it. Send help?"

You couldn't make this stuff up.

The following day, after worrying about J.C.'s whereabouts, I found out that he was safe and sound when he appeared on the front page of a tabloid newspaper with a black eye. The tabloids got wind of the story after J.C. had run out of my house. (Oh, it turned out that J.C. had escaped in a miracle-like fashion— through the living room window, which was just a little bigger than the gap between the barriers at the tube station.) He ran as fast as he could to the top of the street and into the local cab office—explained to the cabby that he was England football player J.C. and they drove him home. (I assume he had sobered up enough to remember where he lived at this point.)

The tabloids reported that I had a party at my house with the rest of the England football team. This did make me laugh because I'm not sure why a bunch of millionaires would have traveled all the way to my council estate in South East London, where I lived with my mother, when they could have just as easily partied in a hotel suite. But I was no stranger to false narratives.

What we did know was someone from the cabbie's office looking to make a bit of cash called up the newspaper and sold a version of the story, knowing—as everyone in the area did—that I lived too close to the cab station for it to be a coincidence.

That's when all the craziness happened, and people started showing up at my door.

"Hi. Is Keeley home?" a man said as his eyes scanned the hallway while mine narrowed in suspicion. Was this some kind of trick question? He wasn't in a police uniform, didn't look like he belonged around here, and the fact that he was asking if I was home made it clear we'd never met. Unless, of course, he meant it in the way someone asks, *Is anyone home up there?* In which case, I could have replied, *Nope, just air.*

I had no idea who this man was, but I slowly hid my gold-plated Keeley name necklace and replied, "I'm sorry. She's not home at the moment. Can I take a message?"

"I'm from the *News of the World* and wanted to ask her a few questions. Here's my business card. Can you get her to call me when she gets back?"

"Sure. I'll pass it on." I swiftly shut the door. I stared at the card for a moment, then walked into the kitchen, opened the bin, and tossed it in.

I peeked out the window a few hours later to see that one journalist had turned into many and that now there were paparazzi outside, too. They kept knocking at the door. I hid in the living room. It was suffocating. The whole night had been such a disaster, and I just wanted to be left alone and deal with my mortification in peace. I called Nic T. for advice. She suggested I stay with her and her West Ham football player boyfriend in his penthouse apartment at Canary Wharf until the whole thing blew over.

Her boyfriend could also get J.C.'s phone and jacket back to him, along with an apology. I packed a bag. Putting J.C.'s things in it, I held my breath as I left the house. I was ready for the flash of cameras and for someone to recognize me, but the journalists and the paps didn't recognize me at all. I was so unrecognizable without makeup and fake eyelashes, and of course, my clothes— that I literally walked out of the house and passed them on the way to my car without anyone taking a photo.

It was incredible. I felt like a superhero. Without the whole production, they were clueless.

I thought I was in the clear, but suddenly one of the journalists who'd been studying me as I walked to my car put two and two together. He jumped into his car with someone else and started following me.

Anyone who watches TV or movies knows the scene of the classic car chase. It involves one car in hot pursuit of another, their engines roaring as they weave through traffic. The lead car is desperate, swerving recklessly, cutting corners, and narrowly avoiding collisions with parked cars, lampposts, or pedestrians. That's what I ended up in. I took a corner at fifty miles per hour, and they followed. I ran a red light, only to find them right behind me. I broke all the speed limits on the road, so determined to lose them before I got to Nic T's boyfriend's place. I even pulled a wild turn near a police station—at a speed that would have given a race car driver a heart attack—just to lose them.

* * *

I successfully camped out at Nic T's boyfriend's house and avoided talking to the press, but all my efforts were for nothing because the next morning *The Sun* ran with their own version: ME AND J.C. was the headline, along with a charming topless photo of me, captioned, *Keeley reveals all.*

It was an absolute piss take. Just like the demoralizing "News in Briefs" that they started adding to our photos, where they would say things like, "Keeley was shocked to learn so many immigrants have come to the UK. She said 'To think around a million have rushed here in just two years is staggering. And while most are here to work hard for a better life, we can't have an open door to everyone.'" I was shocked to learn *what* I had learned as I was reading it.

The sad part is that I was becoming used to it—they did it my whole career. Even when I stopped working for the paper, they continued to quote me despite having never spoken to me. And whenever I called them out on it, they said, "Oops, sorry, but we had to run something. Be a good sport. You understand." What I understood was they were fucking me over. They knew how much I could fetch for a story like this, and let me tell you, it was more than I made a year to get my tits out for them. But what was I going to do? Sue them?

A few days later, Theo and I tried to "talk things out." By "talk things out" I mean I spent an hour pulling teeth. He accepted no responsibility for his actions, but that didn't surprise me. It wasn't like Theo was going to raise his hand and say, "Yeah, sorry, I was feeling jealous, disrespected, and insecure. I was fearful you were going to leave me for your celebrity crush. I should have expressed my feelings and concerns directly to you instead of taking them out on a sleeping man. That's on me." Nope. He had been socialized to use violence as a way to avoid vulnerability and assert control. Much like I learned if someone calls your mother a whore, you punch them in the face. Theo learned the same. It's easier to fight than it is to articulate. And that's exactly what Theo did—he fought.

The violence part I understood. It was always the default solution. When diplomacy and dialogue fail, nations resort to war, like, "You insulted my country? Cool. I'm sending in the troops to kill your people." Doesn't mean I agreed with it—it was just what we knew. What the world had taught us.

I retraced my steps and played out the event tirelessly, thinking of all the things I could have done differently to stop this from happening.

"He obviously came back to fuck you," Theo said. "And you— you should have known better and have been savvy enough to realize that." According to Theo, J.C. wasn't in my bed because he was blackout drunk and couldn't remember where he lived. He was there because of sex.

"He wanted to fuck you. That's why he came back. I'm a man. I know how men think."

"Errrr, he has a girlfriend," I said.

"So?" Theo said. "Why would that stop him?"

"Well, I'm pretty sure he wouldn't have been able to get it up even if he tried," I said sarcastically, but also, it was probably true.

"Do you actually think J.C. wants to be your mate? C'mon, you're not that stupid," Theo said.

It was a line I'd tirelessly hear from the men I dated throughout my teens and twenties—not just about J.C., but about any man who showed me attention.

Do you actually think he wants to talk to you? He's only talking to you so he can try to fuck you.

Awww, bless you; you think he wants to be your friend.

I love you, but that other guy—he is just trying to get his end away.

The underlying message of it always being the same: *You have nothing to offer but sex.*

I told Theo I was sorry and shouldn't have brought J.C. back. I should have thought about how that would make him feel. I wouldn't have liked it if *his* celebrity crush was in his bed, though both of us knew the chances of Beyoncé getting blackout drunk and falling asleep in his bed were very slim.

I apologized until I was blue in the face. He said I was in the wrong, and I agreed.

At least the worst of it was over...or so I thought. Then my phone rang with a number I didn't recognize. I answered it because, typically, when it was an unknown number, it was my bank.

"Is this Keeley?" said a deep male voice.

"Yeah, who's dis?"

"Are you listening?"

"Yes?"

"Listen to me loud and clear. If J.C. doesn't get his phone back...I'll cut your fucking tits off."

The phone went dead. I looked at it, completely dumbfounded.

What-the-what? I'd given his phone to Nic T's boyfriend. Had he got it back? This had to be a prank phone call.

But maybe, just maybe, J.C. and I weren't from different worlds after all.

The Cure & the Cause

The first time I met Theo, I was twelve. It was outside a McDonald's on Bromley High Street. I went there after swimming at the leisure center. He was standing outside with a group of people, and when I say "met," I mean I observed him longingly. I knew who he was, but he didn't know me.

Everyone in Bromley knew Theo. He was handsome—tall, with dark curls and golden skin that seemed to glisten when the skies were gray. He wore expensive jeans and the latest Nike trainers. He had a reputation for going out with all the rich girls whose parents picked them up in brand-new Porsche Cayennes and gave them pocket money for designer clothes. I tried to get him to notice me that day, but I wasn't in his orbit. I was invisible to him.

Years later, I heard his name again. Back when I was dating Jamie. He mentioned Theo in passing. I asked how he knew him. "He's one of my best mates and business partners," he said. I wasn't sure what that meant, but since Jamie sold drugs, I figured Theo did, too.

The next time I saw Theo was at Jamie's house. He was outside talking to him, and I ran to the window to get a look. I wanted to see if he was still as handsome as I remembered. He was. More so. Time had done him favors. He stood there, talking, laughing, looking like someone who could have any girl he wanted. I watched, trying to make sense of his connection to Jamie. But I couldn't understand it. I had no idea what business dealings they had or even what their friendship was based on.

When Jamie returned, I asked, "If this guy is one of your 'best mates,' why have I never met him?"

The first and only time I actually met Theo while I was with Jamie was a year into our relationship. We went on a double date: Theo and his girlfriend, me and Jamie. The girlfriend was one of the rich girl types he dated, went to a private school, and grew up in a big house in Kent. She was the kind of rich kid I'd come across now and again who would indulge in a bit of class tourism by hanging out on council estates, putting on a fake accent to sound more working-class while she slipped her diamanté flip phone into her expensive handbag.

We met for dinner at a hotel. Theo sat across from me. He passed me the bread at one point, and when our eyes met, I had to look away. That was it. That was all it took. I knew. I knew if we were ever left alone, something would happen. That there'd be no way to stop it. I fancied him more than I ever fancied Jamie. And I felt awful about it.

A year after Jamie and I broke up and not long after my car crash, I called Patsy one Friday night to see what she was doing.

"Guess who's at this house party I'm at?" she said. Three incorrect guesses later, she told me it was Theo. I got a bolt of excitement, jumped off the sofa, and nervously changed outfits ten times. Who am I kidding? It was more like thirty, and sometime later, after I'd gone to all this effort to make it look like I hadn't been to any effort, I arrived at the house party to find Theo in the kitchen nursing a beer. I put my arms behind my back, folded them, and swung from side to side as we spoke.

"Are you seeing anyone?" I asked him seductively.

"Why? You know someone who's interested?" he said.

I should explain why I went for Theo in the first place when my world had presumably been opened up to a whole football team of men. I admit, it was a strange choice. My manager used to joke he ran a dating agency: "This week the lead singer of M.5 called, he's in London and wants to take you out. Also, a footballer called J.D. and that host off Channel 4." I didn't even have to leave the house—some of the world's most eligible bachelors were queuing up. And I turned them all down. Something I'd later regret when I met the M.5 guy in LA and fancied him. All I can say is that the girl standing in front of Theo wasn't the one in the photos—with her hair done, makeup on, and scar-free, professionally retouched face. That version of me was a fantasy. In real life, I always felt like a bit of a catfish—like people were expecting the poster, only to meet a girl with a horrendously broken nose. I was just an insecure girl, embarrassed by her job, standing in front of a boy who, not long ago, was out of her league. And much like my mother, I was desperate to be loved, but for who I was and not the idea of me.

Excuse the corny metaphor; I was the desert, and Theo was the rain.

"Actually, I do," I replied. "Blonde chick. Well, she's actually a brunette, but she dyes her hair. People say she's attractive, but I don't see it. Although she has a great personality and can open a beer bottle with her mouth." He tilted his head to the side and looked at me with a smile across his face. I took the fresh beer bottle out of his hands and rubbed it along my lips and opened it with my teeth.

Theo and I started "dating," I mean, we committed to being in a relationship after hanging out in a group of people approximately twice. I thought that's how relationships worked: *I like you, you like me; let's be boyfriend and girlfriend.* I had no concept of spending time getting to know the person or going on "dates." While I'd been seeing guys since Jamie and briefly had a thing with a boy in a band, I'd only been on one official date up until this point. It was with a guy who took me out to dinner at an Italian restaurant, and halfway through my eating an overly salty carbonara pasta, he spotted someone outside the restaurant, said, "I'll be right back, sweetheart," then pulled up his shirt to expose what looked like a gun, before chasing the person outside down the street. He returned twenty minutes later, flustered, picked up the check, and we left. I did not see him again. Not because of the gun—but because I was under the belief that when you know, *you know*, and I *knew* he wasn't "the one," I usually knew within seconds of meeting a guy if I fancied him or not.

The first few months of my relationship with Theo were a whirlwind. We spent every day together when I wasn't working. It was sunshine and rainbows and late-night pizza watching movies. Laughter and cuddles. Dancing. Sex on the kitchen table, sex in the car, sex on the bathroom floor. We were both nineteen and blissfully in love or blissfully in lust but unable to distinguish between the two.

We went to Brighton one weekend a few weeks in, and Theo yelled along the beach, "Everyone, listen up! I'm in love with this woman!" He pulled me in close and kissed me.

"Do you really love me?" I asked insecurely.

"Can't you tell how nuts I am about you? I'm more in love with you than anyone in my whole life. You are the most perfect, beautiful girl. I'm gonna marry you one day. I swear to God," he said.

The man love bombed the hell out of me, and of course, at the time, I had no idea what love bombing meant. "Love bombing," "boundaries," "gaslighting," "toxic," "red flags," these were all therapy buzzwords that I hadn't heard yet, and I was in therapy, but we'll come back to that.

I ignored all the signs—the beautiful big red flags that were being waved in my face. When he boastfully told me how he had cheated on the girlfriend that I'd met with another girl and how he used to keep an extra SIM card in his sock, so when one of them would go through his phone, they wouldn't find the texts from the other. Or how he had to go to court because he'd hit a man over the head with an axe. I just thought they were stupid things he'd done in his past, but now that he'd met me—the love of his life—he was a changed man. So I ignored all the warning signs, and instead, I got a henna tattoo of his initials on my left wrist.

A few months into our love affair, Jamie found out that Theo and I were dating. Jamie—like most of us in South East London—operated from a code of conduct that stated dating your ex's best mate is worse than treason. And I knew it wouldn't matter that we had broken up well over a year ago; I was his girl, and Theo was his mate.

I remember feeling so guilty and terrified at the prospect of Jamie finding out. That my loyalty to him felt somehow compromised. But then I would think, what loyalty? He broke up with me!

Theo and I were walking hand in hand into a pub when Jamie saw us together. I'm not sure if "shocked" as a word is going to cut it. He was gobsmacked. Flabbergasted. He was so utterly astounded that the whole entire pub seemed to feel his energy pulsate through them. I turned to Theo, who was gritting his teeth with his mouth open and scrunching up his face, and said in a low tremor, "Babe, I think we should leave."

We backed out of O'Neill's and walked around the corner to the grocery store car park, where Theo had parked his car. We were almost at his car when we heard Jamie from behind us. "Yo, Keeley, you fucking bitch!" I turned around as a glass bottle came flying across the parking lot before hitting me in the face.

My leather jacket flew out of my hands, and thankfully, the bottle bounced off my cheekbone to the ground and shattered. I couldn't believe he'd actually aimed for my face. *And hit me.* I was so startled. Like, dude, I already had my nose fixed and have scars; get the fuck away from my face!

Just then Jamie came running toward me with another glass bottle in his hand. I turned to Theo, and he tossed me his car key, yelling, "GET IN THE CAR NOW! I'LL TAKE CARE OF THIS!" Heart pounding, I bolted for the driver's seat as Jamie closed in.

I started the engine. I had no idea where Theo had gone, but I noted that Jamie wasn't trying to attack him, which really got me started; I was like, first, you broke up with me, and that was a year ago, and he's the one that's your best friend and "business partner." That's the person you should be mad at. But, oh no, you're furious at me because I'm the easy target. 'Cuz you know if you throw a glass bottle at Theo, he'll kill you. I was vexed. I don't think I was scared. I was just so pissed off.

I revved the engine as Jamie jumped in front of the car, daring me to move. He stood firm. I put the car into reverse to try to get away from him and very quickly found out where Theo was when I accidentally ran over his foot.

Theo began rolling around the ground in pain. I continued reversing, then hit the brakes. I switched gears and put the car into drive. Jamie was at a distance but shouting something. I didn't know if I was going to try to run him over or scare him, but I floored the gas pedal, lunging toward him, when a glass bottle came flying out of his hand and straight at the windshield.

I swerved on impact and drove straight into the metal shelter where they kept the shopping carts and watched as the entire windshield of Theo's car smashed.

The airbag blew up in my face. I got out of the car and checked myself for cuts and bruises.

Car alarms started going off. Jamie disappeared into the night as Theo came hobbling toward the car, dragging his leg and cursing.

"Oh, shit. I need to take you to hospital," I said.

"No. I'm fine. *I'm fine*," he said, his face wincing in pain. I felt so guilty. That everything was somehow my fault.

Theo's foot recovered. The car got fixed. And in a bizarre turn of events, Jamie ended up apologizing to me.

He reached out and asked to meet up. I was apprehensive about this, but an apology from a man? I didn't know it was possible. I had to see this.

I called Patsy and roped her in. The four of us—Jamie, Theo, Patsy, and I—met up in a pub, which, looking back, Patsy and I agreed was a terrible idea, but we were so amped up on the apology and the thought that the four of us could all hang out like civilized modern grown-ups that we didn't really think it through.

At the start of the evening, Jamie brought me a drink to say sorry. "I apologize for being a dick," he said. I nearly fell over. It was wonderfully uncomfortable seeing Jamie genuinely try to take accountability.

We were all getting along swimmingly, reminiscing and taking shots. When the pub closed, we moved the party upstairs to one of the hotel rooms.

I opened the window, sat on the windowsill, and lit a cigarette. Jamie sat beside me while Theo and Patsy sorted out the music. He studied my face like a painting. I watched him watching me. "Yes?" I said, eager to know why he was staring at me.

"Did you love me?" he asked earnestly.

I took a pull of my cigarette and nodded toward Theo before saying, "I'm in love with him."

"So, you didn't love me?" he said. I didn't know how to answer; I thought I'd loved him, but it didn't compare to how I felt about Theo. So I wasn't sure. I didn't say anything.

"YOU DIDN'T LOVE ME? YOU DIDN'T FUCKING LOVE ME?" His face turned scarlet. His jaw clenched. The anger rose like I was watching a thermometer rise in temperature.

"I did love you. I'm not in love with you now!" I cried.

That's when he reached for the Smirnoff Ice bottle and lifted it into the air. I flicked my cigarette out the window and covered my face with my hands, but left a crack so I could see what he was going to do. In one clean, terrifying motion, Jamie smashed the bottle over his head. Glass exploded across the room. Vodka poured down his face, and at the top of his lungs, a piercing sound came out of his mouth. "AHAHAHAHAHAHAHAHAHAHAHAHAAAA!!!!"

You know those moments in movies when the actor turns into a werewolf, and suddenly their whole body starts twitching and shaking, and their fists start flying... Well, it was like that. Jamie started pounding his fists on his chest, then flung them at the wall—and suddenly, they were flying toward me. I screamed. Theo jumped in front of me, grabbed Jamie by the wrists, and they started to wrestle. Theo twisted Jamie's arms into a bind, pressing his right shoulder against Jamie's chest to block him.

"Calm down, mate," he said.

"YOU LITTLE FUCKING BITCH! I HATE YOU!" Jamie screamed, tickles of spit spraying onto my cheeks. Patsy tried to reason with him, but he kept his eyes locked on mine, like a lion stalking its prey. I held his gaze and watched as his nostrils flared out at the sides as he made grunting noises. I looked into his eyes as if to say: *You can't hurt me. You can't control me. You wanna hit me, then go for it, watch what happens.* It is this mentality, this standing up to a man who has no problem using violence against me, that has gotten me into trouble over the years. It is why Jamie looked at me with so much contempt. It is why I've been in more physical fights with men than women. It is why Jamie used all his might to push Theo's shoulder out of the way, loosen the grip on his hands, and grab Theo around the throat to get to me. The two of them started battling it out.

Patsy ran to the door. "Key, let's go!" she kept saying. I didn't want to stand down and let him think he could control or silence me with his behavior. But if I stayed, I knew I'd only make things worse. Someone could get hurt—Theo or Patsy. So I ran toward her, and we bolted down the stairs, out of the hotel, and into her car.

While staying with Nic T and her West Ham footballer boyfriend at his penthouse in Canary Wharf, waiting for the J.C. story to blow over, she convinced me to move there, and I purchased my first apartment. It was a somewhat impromptu decision. They were throwing out mortgages back then, and I viewed a luxury new build for all of ten seconds, saw a freestanding shower, and, having never had a shower growing up, said, "I'll take it." I'd hesitated longer at the cash register, deciding whether to buy a pack of gum.

I moved in. When Theo eventually forgave me for his beating up of J.C., I gave him a key, and in return he hid a gun in my underwear drawer.

Guns aren't that common in England; they're harder to get than in the United States, and there are stricter gun laws. At the time, it wasn't the gun that bothered me—it was the potential fourteen-year prison sentence I wasn't particularly keen on. So I lost my shit on him, telling him to get it out of my apartment immediately. He said it was a fake gun. "It's to protect us if someone breaks in."

THE CURE & THE CAUSE

"Well, a fake gun won't do much protecting," I said. He got it out of the apartment, but what came to light was I was changing. As a fourteen-year-old, the life of crime was somewhat glamorous and sexy. But at nineteen, I had less interest in criminality and more interest in pretending to be a tree.

I spent my Friday nights at Rose Bruford, doing acting exercises and breaking down scenes. That's where I was supposed to be when Theo called a few months later.

"Keeley, I need you to come and get me. The police are chasing me. I'm hiding under a car."

As angry as I was by this phone call and as much as I'd told him that he needed to get his act together, I wasn't going to leave the poor bastard to get arrested. He was my boyfriend. I loved him, and I only knew how to be fiercely loyal to the ones I loved—even if they constantly lied to me, which was what he did.

I sped down the motorway to get him. I arrived at his location in the nick of time. I could hear police sirens in the background, searching for him. Theo quickly rolled out from under the car and jumped into the passenger seat.

"Thank you, baby, I love you," he said, trying to kiss me.

"I don't want to know what you did," I snapped, "so don't fucking tell me." I didn't want to be complicit. And to this day, I have no clue why they were chasing him.

I drove in silence, my jaw clenched. And when we got home, I broke up with him. He didn't fight it. He gathered his things and left.

The breakup lasted three months. It was three months of hell. I craved him like a drug. He changed his number so I couldn't reach out, which only made my withdrawal worse. I tried to distract myself by buying furniture, and I purchased the most expensive and uncomfortable sofa on earth. I moped about on it and thought about him on an endless loop. I needed him. Theo was the cause and *the cure*. The cure and the cause. The only person who could make my pain go away—also the one who caused it.

Whenever I hear alcoholics talk about their addiction, I'm like, yeah, same. Theo was my whiskey. So when he reached out three months later, saying all the right things—how he missed me, loved me, that no other girl came close (and he'd slept with half the city since we broke up, so he knew)—I took him back immediately.

He said he'd changed. For me. For himself. He was sorting his life out. Getting his shit together. He'd even rented a house in Kent. Started doing some "real work." If only I could be patient. If only I could trust him. He would never hurt me. NEVER.

My career was thriving. I was achieving all my goals. I was booking jobs that no other model of my caliber was booking. My official calendar sold thirty thousand copies in its first few days of release, and the month Theo and I got back together, it topped the Amazon bestseller list. I was doing campaigns for Lynx (Axe) and getting offers from lingerie brands, but I was waiting for the right one. I was invited to fancy fashion events with fancy people, where I wore fancy designer clothes. I got offered to go onto the first *Love Island*, which I turned down. I'd even been offered to shoot for the front cover of *Playboy*, which I also turned down.

The most exciting news was that I had done my first proper

photo shoot for a woman's magazine. Clothed. Fully fucking clothed. Me, *clothed!* A real model. I actually couldn't believe it. No one seemed bothered about my scars now that I'd made a name for myself. I was so happy to get paid to keep my top on.

In light of this, I realized that I didn't need to go into therapy. I just needed more jobs where I dressed like a nun. But I started therapy because I was still carrying around so much shame, and as I wrote in my 2006 diary, I was suffering from anxiety, and I wanted to analyze myself and know what sent me off the rails when I was younger. I wanted to understand why, and I quote, "I've always felt the need to have a guy in my life."

And it was the guy I'd just let back into my life that I found myself talking about in my sessions. "I love him so much, more than I've loved anyone, but...he can't stop lying—silly things, like where he is. There are always so many inconsistencies in his stories. But I can't tell because he's so good at twisting and changing the story. I'm thinking about buying a lie detector," I said.

My therapist, Kate, looked at me like, *Girl, when you're thinking about buying a lie detector because you think your boyfriend can't stop lying, I think you need to leave his ass and spend that money on YOU.*

After I acknowledged her disapproving look, I felt the sudden need to defend Theo. I told her how he kept asking me to marry him and that if we put his lies and shady behavior to the side for just one minute, he was actually a great boyfriend, and I loved him so fucking much.

What can I say? I was an addict.

I was an addict.

But I didn't say I was an addict because I *didn't know* I was an addict. I didn't know my brain's reward system was reacting to him the same way a heroin addict's brain responded to heroin. I was being hijacked by dopamine and my underdeveloped frontal lobe, and this meant I lost all control.

In many toxic relationships, there's a back-and-forth between positive reinforcement (affection, attention) and negative experiences (arguments, rejection). The uncertainty deepens the attachment—it doesn't lessen it. It's the same reason heroin is addictive. The emotional highs and lows weaken the prefrontal cortex, just like with substance addiction, making it harder to think clearly and break free. Even when you know the relationship is unhealthy, the compulsion to reach out, stay connected, or get their approval can feel impossible to resist.

But it's also so much more layered and complex than that. As much as I was addicted to Theo, he represented something that I knew so well, something familiar—he represented home.

In the emotional sense—the chaos, and in the symbolic sense. He was my people. My tribe.

We had been back together for a month when Christmas approached. A few days before, Theo gave me a set of keys to his house in Kent and a ring that looked very much like an engagement ring, so much so that it was one.

"What's this?" I asked.

"What do you want it to be?" he said.

I put it on my wedding ring finger, petrified. I had no intention of getting married at twenty, but I didn't want him to feel rejected.

He spun me around. "I'm the luckiest man alive," he said.

Christmas Day rolled around, and we spent it together at his house in Kent. He got himself a pit bull puppy as a pre-Christmas present, and we named him Bailey.

We were a little family.

I played with Bailey in the kitchen while I cooked. Halfway through, I realized we didn't have any Yorkshire puddings—and one can't have a Christmas dinner without Yorkshire pudding, so I sent Theo to see if any shops were open. While he was out, I continued playing with Bailey, when Theo's landline rang. I picked it up.

"Hello?" said a girl's voice.

"Hi?" I said.

"Is Theo there?" she asked.

"He's gone out. Can I take a message?" I said.

"Who are you?" she said inquisitively.

"... I'm his girlfriend," I replied, feeling guilty for saying it, since technically, I was his fiancée, but I had no intention of telling anyone that, and anyway, who was this girl calling Theo's phone and asking who I was? Who the fuck was she? "Who are you?" I asked curiously.

"Well, that's funny because ... I'm his girlfriend," she replied.

Huh?

"Since when?" I asked.

As it unraveled on the phone while Theo was out getting Yorkshires, he had been dating this girl our whole relationship.

Our entire relationship.

The girl—it had all unfolded so quickly I didn't get her name, but it turned out to be Amy. The girl, Amy, told me all the details of how Theo had taken her to "his" apartment in Canary Wharf, which was actually *my apartment* in Canary Wharf. I had been out of town working, and he'd had sex with her in *my* bed. *In my bed.* On my fucking Egyptian cotton sheets. I wanted Amy to be lying, but she told me details of my apartment that you could only know if you had been there. We figured out the dates, and I remembered how I'd returned home from that work trip to find my whole apartment covered in candles and rose petals. Theo had even purchased me a pair of Alexander McQueen shoes as a gift. An "I missed you" gift that wasn't an "I missed you" gift but an "I fucked another girl in your bed" gift.

Of course he denied it. Said the girl was "crazy." And if I had a penny for every guy who has said that, well, I'd be Bill Gates.

I iced him out. I refused to talk. He called. He texted. On New Year's Eve, he showed up at my front door, begging for me to listen. He camped outside for hours. Patsy was inside with me, and we chose to ignore him. So he kept calling. He called and called and he wouldn't stop, so I changed my number.

A few nights later, as we entered the start of 2007, an unknown number flashed on my phone. I answered because it was usually my bank, and I had no reason to think it was Theo. However, some idiot had given him my new number, putting a huge damper on my new year, new me, new vibe. He was drunk—possibly high—slurring his words and rambling so fast that most of it was nonsense. But one thing came through loud and clear before I hung up: Since the night he sat outside my apartment, he'd been on a four-day bender and hadn't been home.

Which put me in a compromising position. Because if Theo hadn't been home in four days... *who was looking after the puppy?*

"I can't believe we're doing this," Patsy said as we sat in her car outside his house.

"All I'm gonna do is feed Bailey if he isn't home. Just keep the engine running in case he is. I don't want to talk to him."

I still had the set of keys he'd given me. I'd left in such a hurry when we broke up that I'd forgotten to return them.

I knocked on the door, terrified, shouting Theo's name through the letterbox before finally putting the key in and stepping inside. The house was dark.

"Hello? Theo?" My voice echoed as I braced myself, heart pounding, afraid I'd walk in on him with another girl. I switched on the living room light—nothing: no Theo, no Bailey. I started to regret coming here.

What was I doing? Did I think I was some sort of superhero here to save the day? I considered turning back when I heard it— soft puppy whimpers from the kitchen.

I pushed the door open, and the stench hit me first. Covering my nose with my shirt, I looked down to see Bailey, filthy and ecstatic, jumping up and down in what was clearly days' worth of his own mess. He had no idea. I bent down, stroking him, murmuring, "It's okay. You're okay. It's all okay."

In a panic, I tried to clean the piss and shit off his feet with a tea towel. I was so overwhelmed and frazzled that I started raiding the kitchen cabinets for some dog food. I found a box, and without thinking, I put the food under my arm, picked Bailey up, and ran out of that house soooooo fast and straight back to Patsy's car, and yelled, "DRIVE!"

"WHAT THE FUCCCCCCCKKKKKKKKKK! I thought you were feeding him. I didn't know we were kidnapping his dog!!!!!" Patsy screamed, her voice high-pitched and fast, as she hit the gas.

I explained the state of the kitchen and all the piss and dog shit at hyper-speed because I thought I'd stopped breathing. My adrenaline was running wild, and the car journey felt chaotic as the reality of what I had just done hit me.

"Shit. Fuck. What was I supposed to do? Leave him there? Not knowing if or when Theo is going to come back? What if he dies????? I can't let him die, Pats!"

Neither of us knew the best way to handle this situation. The question of what to do when your ex-boyfriend goes on a bender and leaves his puppy alone at home for nearly four days wasn't one that came up that often, funnily enough.

I wish I could tell you that Theo came off his bender—was distraught by his behavior, begged for forgiveness, gave Bailey a good home, chalked up our relationship to immaturity, and we both went on happily with our lives. But it only seemed to get worse. And given Jamie had thrown a glass bottle in my face when he found out I was dating Theo, I guess I should have been prepared for it, but I wasn't.

After I rescued, stole, or kidnapped Bailey—whatever you want to call it—I didn't hear from Theo at all. I texted him from the car, something along the lines of *I went by your house, Bailey was alone, so I took him with me. He's safe. I can look after him until you come off your bender.* But he didn't text me back. I began calling him nonstop, but he didn't answer, so I panicked that maybe he was dead in a ditch. I called his mother, Michelle, who—sidenote—was the spitting image of the actress Laura Dern.

She assured me Theo wasn't dead, as she had just seen him. Oh, how the tables had turned. He was the one ignoring me now. So I gave up calling him.

I took Bailey to my mum's house because, well, she still fed me and did my laundry. I figured my little sister, G, could play with him.

I often stayed there—despite owning two properties before I was twenty—because living alone scared me. I wasn't used to the silence or a bed that didn't shake from passing trains.

Two mornings later, I still hadn't heard from Theo, and I needed to get my laptop, so I left Bailey with my mother and little sister and returned to my apartment.

When I arrived back, I wondered if I was suffering from dementia and had forgotten to close my front door—because it was wide open. Then I noticed that the wood around the lock had been clawed away aggressively and ripped open by a crowbar. Scratched into the door was the word "slut."

Jesus fucking Christ, Theo, I thought.

I put my door keys between my left fingers as I tiptoed into my hallway, quietly and carefully treading slowly on the wooden floor. I could already see that the living room had been destroyed and that my main TV had been stolen. But I checked the rest of the apartment to ensure no one was there. Then I made my way into the living room to see the mess. I took a mental note of the things I knew had been stolen. My laptop, my televisions, and a couple of other electrical goods. The drawers on my black gloss TV stand were open, and my belongings were thrown on the floor—a copy of my 2007 calendar that had just topped the Amazon bestseller list, along with some paperwork from the sofa I'd purchased. I turned to the small adjoining kitchen, and that's when I noticed a big, sharp knife near the entrance to the kitchen. I knew straightaway that it most definitely didn't belong to me. I bent down to inspect it but was careful not to touch it.

I went downstairs to talk to Mo, who worked at the front desk, to see who had come into the building while I was out. I told him what happened, and he said he would check the CCTV and find out. As I walked back to my apartment, my phone buzzed— Patsy was calling. I picked up to hear her grieved voice.

"The back window of my car has been smashed by a brick!"

Both of us suspected it was Theo.

As I reentered my apartment, the intercom by the door rang, and I told Patsy not to worry, that I would sort it out and would call her back. I picked up the intercom, and it was the building manager, Steve. He had gone through the CCTV, and they had something to show me. I went back downstairs and entered the back room, where they kept the monitors.

"We went through who entered the building last night and spoke with Tobias, who was at the front desk, and it appears you know the guy who came in," said Steve.

I looked at the screen, and there he was… *Theo*, walking out of my building with my television in his hands. He walked past Tobias, who nodded, and then around the corner, out of sight.

Steve fast-forwarded the video. I watched Theo reenter the building and exit again five minutes later with a big blue Ikea bag filled to the brim. I could see my laptop and another television poking out the side.

"He entered around ten p.m....said to Tobias that he owned half of your apartment...bloody cheek of it...and then he tried to get the spare set of keys. Tobias said that he couldn't release them without your permission, but since he had seen him with you before...well, he said he could go and see if you were in but that he had called up to you, and you hadn't picked up the intercom." Steve paused, then added, "Sorry, he wasn't to know—"

"It's fine," I said, choking and leaving the room.

Dad came to fix the front door and install a new lock. Deborah came up with him and wrote down a list of everything that had been stolen. I was so panicked. So unbelievably panicked that the contents on my laptop, my photos, my videos, journal entries would all end up online, that I couldn't stop pacing the living room. It was password protected, but Theo knew the password. I didn't have anything shocking on there. No sex tape or anything. I did have a very compromising VHS-C tape with footage of me giving Theo a blowjob and whatnot, but I checked and it was still in my second bedroom, hidden where I'd left it. The thing I was worried about, naively, were unseen photos from projects that hadn't been released—that would cost me tens of thousands in contracts—and the series of photos of me drunk on the toilet. Photos of me pissing, where I'm pretty sure you could see my vagina. If these photos were released online, well, my life would be over. My career donezo.

"He's obviously broken into your apartment as retaliation for taking his dog!" Deborah said, crouching to inspect the mess on my floor.

"What was I supposed to do? Let Bailey starve to death?" I said, running my hands through my hair. "I texted him that I had Bailey, and I've called him, and he hasn't picked up!"

"You're just gonna have to keep calling him," Deborah said.

I was so furious at Theo and myself that I wanted to throw my body against the wall. I agreed to call him, but warned that he would lie.

"He can't lie. There's evidence," Dad yelled from the hallway while fitting a new lock.

I assured Dad that Theo *could* lie—that if there were awards for world-class bullshitters, he'd win. "He'll probably say he has an identical twin and *that's* who broke in." As soon as I said it, I had an idea. I'd record the conversation as evidence of his lies. I ran into my bedroom and found the little recording device I'd been using for these elocution lessons my manager convinced me to sign up for so I could stop sounding like I was born in a gutter. I called him. He didn't answer, so I called again. No answer. On the third try, he picked up, and I hit record...

As soon as I asked him where my stuff was, he accused me of stealing his. Naturally, I thought he was talking about Bailey, so I said, "If you'd answered your phone...you would have known that Bailey was with me at my mum's house—"

"*Where's my TVs? Where's my laptop?*" he said.

"Your TVs?" I couldn't tell if he was mocking me or what. It took me a good three minutes of going back and forth with him to understand that he was *accusing me* of the exact crime *he* had just committed.

I knew he was a liar and a cheat, but these were some ninja manipulative tactics that I'd never seen before. He was projecting and using DARVO (Deny, Attack, Reverse Victim, and Offender), but I didn't know that. I was so disoriented. Like, wait, what? That's not what happened. My brain was struggling to process the absurdity of being accused of the crime *he* had just committed. I kept thinking if I just explained myself, if I could prove my innocence and clarify the truth, he'd realize his mistake.

At one point I got so angry, I yelled down the phone, "WHY ON EARTH WOULD I NICK YOUR TVS? WHERE WOULD THEY BE? WHY??? WHY WOULD I NICK YOUR TVS? Now...I...I just reckon you're making it up because you've fucking stolen all my stuff."

"I'm making it up? Are you having a laugh? Number one, I haven't stolen your stuff, yeah—" he said.

"Well, number one, *you have* stolen my stuff—"

"Shut up a minute, yeah..." Theo yelled.

"I've got CCTV of you—" I chime in before he can finish.

"Do ya think I care? I don't give a fuck! Listen, that's what ya hav' to learn 'bout me is I don't care. I knew...I know there was cameras. I do not give a fuck! I walked straight in and straight out. Listen, the bes' fin' you can do is call the police and get me put in prison 'cause I'm goin' to *kill you* when I see ya. Listen, I didn't come up to take your stuff. I came up for YOU last night...to beat your fuckin' head in. See, if you was there, you wouldn't have been talking. I would have ripped your head off, and I would have gone to prison for a couple of years. 'CUZ I DON'T CARE. I walked into your flat knowing that the reception people saw me and knowing that I would get done forever for what I was gonna do to you. I want to make this really clear in your little head that I came for *you*. And I'm gonna get ya, I promise ya. Sorry to threaten ya, but I'll get to you in prison as well. This isn't it. It's not stopping. I've still got to get on top."

I took a long breath in and didn't say anything. Suddenly I was that little girl in the back of the car with her dad, learning to muffle my tears. Learning to stay quiet to calm his anger.

The conversation went around in a circle, and the following days, Sunday, Monday, and Tuesday, were caked with stress. Theo and I spoke on the phone as I recorded more conversations. By Wednesday, I realized I wasn't getting anywhere, and I sat outside the police station for an hour, sweating, trying to gather the courage to go in. When I finally did, I found myself sitting across from two male officers, reporting the crime.

"It's considered 'domestic,'" one of them said. "Not much we can do. Domestic cases aren't taken as seriously."

I'd spent an hour outside, forcing myself to walk through these doors, only to be told *this*.

"He broke into my home. With a knife," I said, shoving the recording device toward them. "Listen to this. He says he came to kill me."

One officer glanced at it, then shrugged. The other took the voice recorder, then spoke casually.

"The building could press charges for the front door since you don't own it. That's probably your best shot at getting him charged." I stared at them. Wondering what planet I was living on.

"Oh, cool, so everything inside the apartment I can't do anything about because I dated the guy. But the door—thank you for enlightening me with the fact I don't own it—I can get the building to charge him for breaking it?"

"Yes," the officer said.

By Thursday I'd racked up hours and hours of phone conversations with Theo. At some point—I don't remember when exactly—he softened. He seemed to have mentally flipped a switch, and the accusations stopped.

"Why haven't you wanted to talk like this until something happened to you?" he asked. I held the phone in front of me and looked at it. I knew I had to choose my words wisely—that saying the wrong thing could set him off, and somehow, though it had taken me many years to truly accept it, I knew that when it came to men like this, I would have to be the one to surrender, and by that, I mean apologize—to relinquish control.

"I don't know...I'm sorry for not talking to you when we broke up. I should have," I said. And that was it. That's all it took, me saying sorry for not talking to him after I ended things. *Not him saying sorry, but me.* He agreed to give me my laptop and TVs back, on the condition I handed over Bailey. "Just give him his dog back and be done with it! It's not going to end otherwise," Mum said, convincing me. I was reluctant. I knew she was right, but I didn't want to do it. "Sometimes you just do things for an easy life," she used to say when succumbing to my dad. I hated that I was doing the same. Theo went to my mum's house and she handed Bailey over like it was a drug deal. A day or so later, Dad drove me to Theo's in his van. I walked to the front door and rang the buzzer. I stared at him, but he wouldn't look at me.

"Here's your front door key," I said, putting my hand out.

"Thanks," he said, taking it and leaning on the doorframe.

"How's Bailey?" I asked.

"Great," he said. "I don't know why you think I can't look after my own dog."

I looked away. It was obvious *why*, but I knew better than to say anything. When I turned my eyes back he finally met my gaze. I searched the eyes of the man who'd dragged me through hell for some sort of remorse, or even love, but I couldn't find it. I'd passed up on a slew of decent, desirable men for this. What the fuck was wrong with me? Was my self-esteem really that low?

"I'll get your stuff," he said, breaking eye contact and heading inside.

A few minutes later, he returned and handed me my laptop, an old phone, and some other electronic devices. "Hold on, I'll grab your TV," he said, returning inside. He gave me one back, and I chose to forget about the other one. I only cared about the laptop and those drunken photos of me on the loo.

We said goodbye to each other. I loaded the items into Dad's van. Tears welled up as we drove away. I was so relieved that it was all over and that I hadn't ended up trapped with this man. So relieved.

I honestly felt like I'd dodged a bullet.

The Crime with No Name

January 2007. I wake to the vibrating of my BlackBerry. I check the caller ID. "Nic T" flashes on my screen. I look at the time in the corner with one eye still glued shut. It's nearly 1:00 p.m. I contemplate whether or not I have the energy to answer. I might still be drunk from the tequila shots I was slamming down my throat at 4:00 a.m. like it's a goddamn sport. I want to be a person that gets up early and goes to the gym. I want to be like Nic T, who has her life together, gets up at the crack of dawn, and has twenty-five things done before lunch, but I'm not. And I feel internal shame about it, so I pick up and put on my best "I've been awake for hours" voice. "Yo, yo, what's up?" I say, suddenly realizing my voice sounds like a man who smokes two packs a day.

"Did I just wake you?" Nic T asks. From the noise in the background, I can tell she's out and about, which makes me feel even worse, but I don't want to lie. I need to accept who I am.

"Yes," I say, followed by "Jesus, I sound like a dead donkey. Must be all the cigarettes." I try to clear my throat.

"Did you go out last night?" she says, sounding like she's in a busy store and is not paying attention because she's reading the ingredients on the back of a milk carton.

"Yeah...I went to some dumb club, made out with some actor, ate a Big Mac on the way home, and vomited in the toilet. It's not a good night unless you vomit down the toilet," I joke and think about how I want to eat a sausage and egg McMuffin and watch reruns of soap operas on the TV I got back from Theo three days ago.

"Anyway, what are you doing?" I ask. "You sound distracted."

"Listen," she says, like a detective in a movie that's about to tell me my mum has been murdered. I panic. I've been terrified of a phone call like this my whole life, you know, the ones that come in the middle of the night and change everything. Even the word "listen" makes my heart leap out of my chest.

"I just got off the phone with Dave Reed..." She pauses, distracted again. I'm desperate to know where this is going. Dave Reed is a manager who looks after Katie Price, aka Jordan, aka the most famous woman in England who used to be a Page 3 model.

"And...?" I say, slowly waiting for her to explain.

"...and apparently, you're on the front cover of the *Sport* because of a sex tape...I'm in M&S right now trying to buy it," she says. I feel like someone has put their hand down my throat, pulled my heart out of my chest, and tied it around my neck, but I think this must be a joke. She's winding me up. We always wind each other up. This is so clearly a joke. I wait for her to laugh and say, *Got you!* But she doesn't.

"Don't wind me up, Nic. I'm too fragile to be fucked with," I say, sitting upright and pushing the duvet off of me. My palms are clammy. I don't feel okay.

"I swear to God I'm not fucking with you! I'm trying to find out what it is…" She pulls the phone away from her. "Excuse me, where are your papers?" There's a faint voice in the background, but I can't hear what they're saying. She sounds like she's walking.

"Nic!" I say, my voice sharp. "*What did Dave say?!*" I jump out of bed and begin pacing.

"He called me and said Keeley is on the front cover of the *Sunday Sport*…something to do with a sex tape? Did you make a sex tape?" Her voice went up at the end with a mix of shock, judgment, and disbelief.

"*No!*" I tell her. "I didn't fucking make a sex tape…I mean, I know I get my tits out for a living, but jeez, I don't want anyone to see me fucking! I turned down shooting the cover of *Playboy* not to show my vagina! I'm trying to move away from Page 3, not into porn!"

I immediately start thinking about the tape I have hidden in the second bedroom that has footage of Theo and me on it, but I'd checked after the break-in and it was there. I'm sure of it. And my laptop didn't have a sex tape on. Only those photos of me drunk on the toilet. I couldn't think what else it would be.

"I can't see it…Hold on…" Nic T pulls the phone away from her again and starts talking to someone. "Do you sell the *Sport*?"

I can hear a man saying, "If we sell it—it will be here."

"They don't sell it," she says, irritated.

"Fuck, fuckkkkkk, fuck, fuckkk." I slam my fist into the wall. My head starts spinning. I'm so utterly confused and feeling out of control that Nic T is talking, and I have absolutely no idea

what she is saying. "I'm gonna go to the store and see what it is…
I'll call you back," I say as I hang up. I run up and down the hallway once, twice, three, four, five times. I grab my keys, wallet,
coat, and a pair of Ugg boots and run out of my apartment like
I'm escaping a blazing fire. I can't shake this nagging feeling of
dread.

A sex tape?

A sex tape?

A FUCKING SEX TAPE??

The nearest store is on the corner, and I run into it at full speed
and scan the newspaper section on the bottom shelf, searching
for the *Sunday Sport*. There's the *Daily Mail*, the *Sunday Times*,
and the *Daily Star*, and then finally, I spot it. *The Sunday Sport*.
And suddenly, in a matter of moments, my life is flipped upside
down. I'm on the cover. *On the front page of the* Sport *newspaper*.
My stupid face is looking back at me. I'm wearing this low-cut
black dress from the red carpet of *FHM*'s 100 Sexiest Party, and
the headline reads: KEELEY HAZELL IN HOME PORN VIDEO. I can't
breathe. My lungs are tight. My hands are shaking. I feel like I've
been shot repeatedly—just *bang. Bang. Bang. Bang.*

There are four screenshots of me from the video and the words.

Read her naughty sex confessions.
See her stripped naked.
See her outrageous sex act, and finally, see her having sex.

I throw cash down on the counter and stumble outside the
shop. I open the paper and scurry through the pages, landing
on a picture of my *vagina*. There it is—*my vagina*. A screenshot

of my legs spread wide open and my fucking vagina printed in black-and-white.

I know where this was taken; I know the hotel room. These are screenshots from the two vacations Theo and I went on. It's footage from the tape I have hidden in my second bedroom. We'd taken an old-school '80s VHS video camcorder away with us, thinking it would be funny and cute because it was the same video camera our parents had when we were little. It was so retro that it took tapes. Little ones that I had no idea how you converted. We filmed ourselves—welcome to our hotel, this is the beach, that type of thing. I had been filming our hotel room when Theo got out of the shower naked, and I ordered him to get on the bed, and I gave him a blowjob. I was trying to be sexy. I handed him the camera, and he pointed it at me, and in the back of my mind, I was thinking, I'm going to watch this back so I can see if I'm any good at this. The same way I watch a video of me doing a headstand!

But anyhow, none of that mattered because it was *my tape*, and it had always been in *my possession*. Even Theo said, "I don't want anything to do with this tape because if it goes missing, I don't want to get blamed." But *now here I fucking was in a newspaper with my legs spread open and my vagina on display like it was sports stats from yesterday's football match!* It didn't make any sense.

Nausea takes over my whole body, and I straight-up vomit. I hold the cheap newspaper in my hands, its blackness rubbing on my fingers as a watery substance pours out of my mouth. After, I try to inhale, but instead, my knees come out from beneath me, and I collapse to the ground in tears. I put my hand against the wall of the newsagent's to steady myself. The paper is in front of me. The pages blow open in the wind. I grab ahold of it to stop it from blowing away. I try to read the article, but I can't. I'm hysterical. I scream as loud and as hard as I can. "THEO, YOU FUCKING PRICK!!" Every curse word comes out of my mouth along with beggings and pleadings for this to all be undone. I cry like I've never cried before. I can't stop crying. It's like everything I've ever bottled up is pouring out of me.

I'm a total mess. I don't care that I'm outside on a busy street. I don't care who sees me.

Porn Star

was thirteen the first time I saw porn. Tracey, one of the Grove Park girls, took me inside an older guy's house—her drug dealer, midtwenties, joint hanging from his mouth. He asked if we wanted to watch a Snoop Dogg music video, and we said yes. He pulled out a videotape, popped it into the player, and pressed play.

A pirated video started playing. Snoop Dogg appeared on-screen. Then a naked woman. Then another naked woman. Then a woman with a dick in her mouth. Then an orgy.

I'd spent hours watching MTV music videos before Dad left and we could no longer afford cable. I had seen a lot of slow-motion grinding, but never actual shagging.

I sank into the black leather chair, feeling a wave of embarrassment followed immediately by laughter. The man sat on his sofa, smoking a joint, watching the porno with deep concentration like he was watching a David Attenborough documentary. I didn't know where to look. It didn't turn me on, and after a while I started to get scared that he might be getting funny ideas about doing this with Tracey and me, so I urged her to leave.

The next time I saw porn was when I was eighteen—a Jenna Jameson DVD called *Where The Boys Aren't 16*. It was girl-on-girl, and I watched it with a football player who we'll call Hank.

Hank, like most boys around me, was obsessed with wanting to sleep with multiple women at once, as if one girl couldn't possibly be enough. He wanted more, more, more. This made me feel inadequate, like no man would ever be satisfied with just me. And, to be honest, that did seem to be the case, since the majority of my boyfriends had cheated.

The thing I noticed most when discussing porn with Hank—and boys like him—was how they spoke of the women in it. They desired them, sure, but only in the moment. They were disposable, interchangeable. I remember lying next to him, intimidated by Jenna Jameson's perfect physique and saying, "God, she's so beautiful."

He grunted, "I like it when the other girl shoves her fingers right up her pussy. I'd like to see another girl do that to you."

I looked at him as if to say that would never happen. "Would you date her?" I asked.

(I know what you're thinking; there was a lot of chat happening for two people watching porn, but I was intrigued by the whole thing. It didn't turn me on as much as it made me question what men actually wanted—and, by extension, my own self-worth.)

"Nah," he said, trying to kiss me. "I'd shag her, but I wouldn't date her."

"Why?" I said, almost offended on Jenna's behalf.

"Why would I date a porn star?" He said it like that was the dumbest thing he'd ever heard. Adding, "I don't want to date a girl who gets dicked all day by other dudes, or other people have seen getting railed. Why would I do that?"

His response made me feel insecure about my profession as a Page 3 model. Did men feel the same way about me? Would anyone want to date me when other men have seen me nude? Would no one love me because of it?

At nineteen, my friend Suzie called me up distraught that she'd found a stash of adult-film DVDs in her boyfriend's bedside table.

"Why does he have these?" she asked.

"I don't know. Anything odd in there?"

"There's a lot of anal. Some girl-on-girl... There's just so many DVDs," she said, confused. We spoke on the phone for hours, trying to understand when, how, and why he secretly watched them. Was sex with her not enough? Was it cheating? We didn't know.

Later, she confronted him, and they got into a fight. She told him she'd break up with him if he didn't get rid of the DVDs or if she found him watching them again. After that, Suzie, our other girlfriend, and I were sent into a frenzy whenever we had a boyfriend. We searched in the shoe boxes to find our boyfriend's secret stash as evidence of their infidelity and would call each other up in a tizzy. "I've found a porno. What do I do about it? Do I dump him?"

Porn was a threat or something to be managed. Rules were put in place within each relationship to protect ourselves from it.

For most of my girlfriends, porn made them feel like their

boobs were ugly, their vaginas flappy, and that they needed to run straight to the salon and get a Brazilian. And even I, who one might think would be magically shielded from these comparisons, gracing the front covers of men's magazines and being praised for my body, felt the same.

My boobs didn't feel big enough, my butt wasn't round enough, and my face wasn't beautiful enough. Ironically, out of all the girls I knew and were friends with, the models were the most insecure about their bodies, because every part of our physique was dissected, scrutinized, and held up for judgment.

At twenty, my thoughts on porn were this: If I caught my boyfriend watching it, I'd be angry and upset. Porn stars aren't a threat because men want to shag them in secret but never take them home to meet their mothers. Female porn stars are to be envied for being so able to put themselves out there sexually and not feel ashamed. I don't enjoy sex as much as a porn star, and I felt like my performance in the bedroom is terrible by comparison. Some men and women love watching porn—which is fine, but I have no interest in it outside of educational purposes. And even then, every position I've seen has already been tested and deemed disappointing.

But for all my hang-ups about porn—about what it meant for relationships, how it shaped the way men saw women, how it shaped the way women saw themselves—I never imagined I'd end up on the other side of it, that I would become the unwilling participant of a "home porno" spread against my will. And from there on out be called a porn star. And get treated like one.

*   *   *

From the moment I dragged myself off the sidewalk in tears, I knew the question would be "How did it get out if it wasn't you?" Followed by "Why did you film yourself in the first place?"

Short of telling whoever asked me these questions to fuck off and die, I would need answers. To the latter I could say, *Don't we all record ourselves to improve? To see what we're doing? I film myself boxing to refine my technique—why is filming myself having sex any different?* To the former, I didn't have an answer. Truth was I didn't know. I ran back to my apartment, into my second bedroom, and went to my hiding place—an old camera box filled with random manuals and odd items. To my surprise, it was there—the VHS-C tape Theo and I had used to film ourselves was right where I'd left it. I'd never made copies or transferred it to my laptop. There was just this one tape I'd hidden when we returned from vacation.

My mind was spinning. *Had he stolen it and put it back when he broke in?* I was so confused. So filled with hurt and anger, that I called the guy who'd so clearly maneuvered this whole thing. I don't know what I was gonna say; I just felt like I had to do something. I dialed Theo's number, but instead of a ringtone, I got an automated message. *"Your call cannot be connected at this time. Please check the number and redial."* The automated message played on a loop. *"Your call cannot be connected at this time. Please check the number and redial."*

That was the message you got when your line had been disconnected.

He'd changed his number.

I called his landline—the same thing. My anger turned to rage. I didn't know how else to reach him, so I called his mother. She picked up.

"Did he tell you what he did?" I cried. She clearly knew and felt awkward.

"I don't know what to say, Keeley. You kids," she said, dismissing it like it was youthful mischief. *YOU KIDS?* I wanted to scream that it wasn't "us kids." It was her son—the one *she* had raised to be a monster, but instead I hung up and collapsed, sobbing until my eyes ran dry—like windshield wipers scraping across glass without fluid.

That evening I packed a bag and went to my mum's. I will never forget the look on her face when she opened the door—pure defeat, followed by shame. "Well…" she said, shaking her head. I waited for her to say, *Something like this would only happen to you*, but instead she asked if there was anything I could do about it. I didn't know.

I'd called my manager, Jon, when I was outside the store in the middle of my sobbing. "My ex-boyfriend…sex tape…the cover…*Sunday Sport*…" I said, trying to string words together and breathe. He was finding me a lawyer, and in the meantime, I spoke to Dave Reed, the man who'd called Nic T and told her about it.

"Awww, babe, I'm so sorry. It's just awful. I can't even imagine what you're going through. I've got clients that release these things themselves, but as I said to Nic T this morning, I was so surprised when I saw it 'cause you're not about all that," he said.

In retrospect, I wished I'd savored his sympathy. Because an "I'm so sorry, it's just awful" from a man who worked with women who profited off their own sex tapes was about all I was going to get. Every other man treated it as a business transaction or assumed I'd released it myself. That was the consensus at the time. *All women* with sex tapes were the ones who leaked them. Even I thought it. *Oh, how brainwashed I was!*

The following day, sleep-deprived and delirious, I received the tragic news I was back on the front page of the *Sport*. I met my manager, Jon, and my lawyer, Adam—two middle-aged white men with posh accents—at a members' club in central London. I was too busy trying not to cry. My face was blotchy and swollen, my eyes hollow, and my skin suddenly erupted in pimples, as if my body was protesting. I was still trying to process the whiplash of it all—twenty-three days ago I was engaged; nine days ago Theo had broken into my apartment. On Saturday night, I was kissing a guy in some misguided attempt to move on. By Sunday morning, my entire life had changed. And now, on Monday, I was here—betrayed, vulnerable, exposed—sitting across from two men who had no idea what any of this felt like. And still the unanswered question of how my ex got the tape.

"They showed the judge your topless photos and said you wanted this," Adam said, his voice neutral, but the words "YOU WANTED THIS" were so intensified he might as well have been hovering over me and yelling them. He had been in court that morning. Despite the injunction, the paper still ran the story on the front page that morning. I barely had time to process it before realizing I was now suing the newspaper and the third-party distributor who sold the tape.

All of them men. Middle-aged, slightly overweight, balding men.

"I turned down shooting for the cover of *Playboy*," I said in a state of delirium, hoping it would prove that I didn't want this. "Why would I turn down the cover of *Playboy* to release a sex tape? What would I get out of this? It makes no sense."

My lawyer looked at my manager but said nothing. I was feeling more infuriated than I had ever been in my life. "And how did my ex get the tape? Why aren't we going after him? He was the one who did this," I said.

As my lawyer explained, this was a privacy and copyright case. *A privacy and copyright case.*

Because in 2007, it was yet to be considered a crime. It was soooooooo far from becoming a crime that it didn't even have a name. Revenge porn is what it would eventually be coined a few years later, and years after that, in 2015, in England and Wales, it would become a criminal offense with a sentence of up to two years in jail.

But as I sat with my lawyer and manager on a cold day in January, it was merely a privacy and copyright case. One I was told I had little chance of winning. Since it was looking like I might not be the copyright holder, and as for my privacy, well, did I deserve sexual privacy? That seemed to be the question no one could answer and why the other side had taken my topless photos in front of the judge. I visualized these men standing with my photos, saying: *I mean look at her. Everyone's already seen her tits. Of course she wants this. We all know what girls like this are like.*

"All we know is that your ex gave the *Sport* a preview of the tape sometime last year in November, but he didn't sell it to them until recently, and then they paid him ten thousand pounds. He said that he owns the copyright to it, that it was his tape and his video camera. We can't prove that you own the original tape. And we're not going after him because he hasn't got any money," Adam said.

I had a lot to say about this, but I said, "*November?*" The guy had asked me to marry him in December!

"Yes, then he went quiet on them."

I vividly remember when it hit me that Theo had copied the tape while we were in a relationship. I sat back in my chair in utter disbelief, knowing this was collateral. The whole thing was preemptive. Preplanned. I'd hidden the tape as soon as we got back from vacation, but clearly when I was out of town working, he searched every inch of my apartment, found the tape, copied it, and put it back exactly where I'd hidden it. I couldn't get over it. I'd had sex with a *villain*. The guy had slept next to me and said he loved me knowing he'd copied the tape.

"Look, I'm just working with the law, but I'm telling you— you don't want to go to court. If the other side proves your ex holds the copyright, you won't be entitled to a penny, and they'll continue to sell this thing," Adam said. He pulled out a piece of paper and slid it across the table. "The other side wants to settle."

The other side was the third-party distribution company and the *Sport* newspaper, which claimed they had no money. I was unaware of this at the time, but the paper was owned by billionaire David Sullivan, a man who had built his fortune on low-budget porn films. The same year his paper marketed and profited from my stolen tape, he sold the *Sport* for £40 million. And if you believe in small-world coincidences, here's one for you: The same man whose empire profited off my worst nightmare is now the chairman of West Ham United, the football team owned by my fictional husband, Rupert, in *Ted Lasso*—a show I would go on to act in.

Adam exhaled. "I'm gonna nip to the loo. Look it over—we'll discuss when I get back." He got up and left.

My manager, Jon, and I sat there in silence for a second. I felt like I was going to burst into tears at any moment.

"Talking about it brings attention to it. If anyone asks you a question, you ignore it. The best thing to do is remain silent," he said, adding, "We want this to go away as quickly as possible."

"What about my side of the story? It's so fucked up that my ex was even allowed to do this," I said, my voice sharp.

"Doesn't matter," Jon replied. "If you say anything, more people will look up the tape. You don't want that."

I sat back in my seat, infuriated. "Let me get this right. So my ex breaks into my apartment, says he's going to kill me, sells a sex tape that he's stolen to a national newspaper, and all of these men get to make money off it, while the whole world thinks I leaked it and I just have to stay...*silent*?"

I felt like I was getting fucked left, right, and center. This wasn't just Theo fucking me over. This was a gangbang.

"People are going to think you released it regardless of what you say. So it's best if you say nothing," he said. If there was ever a moment in life when I thought the whole system was rigged, it was then, or maybe it was when Adam returned from the loo and I looked over what was being offered to me.

There were two options, Offer A: Settle this claim and stop selling the video. Offer B: Accept an advance of the royalty. Then it said, "The disadvantage of taking offer A is that it stops us but does nothing to address what is going on in the wider market," meaning it would stop them from selling the video, but it could do nothing to control the internet. Offer A was roughly the amount I'd already paid in legal fees, and offer B was three times the amount but less than I'd make for one campaign—both well below six figures. So, overall, they weren't exactly great retirement plans and given my career had just been cremated, it wasn't enough to live on.

I stared at the paper. I knew selling the tape could have been a way to make the best of a bad situation. It was out there, and no one could unsee it. Maybe the money would soften the pain? But the idea of profiting from my own violation, of going into business with Theo and the men who exploited me, felt unbearable. I couldn't monetize my own abuse. Something in me refused. I couldn't shake it.

As for going to court, my lawyer was heavily advising me against it. I'd already spent tens of thousands in legal fees. What if I sat in a courtroom and gave this *more* media coverage, listened to a parade of men rip me a new one, and I lost because I didn't own the copyright? I'd be hundreds of thousands of dollars in debt, I'd have to pay the other side's legal fees, and they would continue to sell the video.

"What are you thinking, Keels?" Jon said.

"I want to take option A. I want them to stop selling the video," I said.

"You know it will be out there on the internet for everyone to see…and if you take option B, they'll seek to control the internet," Adam said.

"I know," I said. "But that's the option I'm choosing."

I wasn't in the right headspace to make any decisions, especially twenty-four hours after this happened. I was also not equipped to handle the emotional ramifications or fully grasp how this would affect the rest of my life. I was twenty. Everyone else was making mistakes that wouldn't count. But this was as permanent as the scar on my face.

Adam tied up all the legal stuff. *The Sport* was ordered to stop selling it, but they'd already profited off it, and then it spread all over the internet like wildfire. All the money I made and then some went on legal fees trying to remove it from the internet, but as soon as I'd paid to have it removed, it just popped back up on another site. None of the men watching or sharing it gave a shit. And why would they?

In the media, there was a type of woman this crime was happening to: the Pams and the Parises of this world—women who either capitalized off their sexuality or openly admitted they wanted to be famous. And the world saw these women as a certain kind of woman for which they granted no sympathy because it was assumed that they leaked it themselves and... *wanted it.*

In the weeks and months following the legal battle, there was only one thing I wanted.

I wanted Theo dead. I thought about killing him. I even thought about hiring a hit man. *Truly, I did.* That was all I thought about once the legal battle was over. Then I realized I was incapable of killing anyone else, so I thought about killing myself. Which I also realized I was incapable of doing. That somehow made me feel even *more* pathetic, so I tried self-harm—holding ice cubes in my hands until they went numb. Turns out that's an anxiety-reducing technique that somehow didn't reduce my anxiety. Instead, I had panic attacks, full-on, *I think I'm dying in the middle of the store, please call me an ambulance* panic attacks. I could no longer sleep in my bed and slept on the floor with a knife next to me. I stopped eating real food and lived on junk. I chewed on the ends of my hair—which was either tasty or deeply satisfying. I smashed plates just like my mother without realizing the irony of such fate. I went to nightclubs with people I barely knew, let alone liked, and drank so much I'm surprised I still have a liver. I did photo shoots and cried in the toilet between takes. I cried walking down the street. I cried in the grocery store. I cried in every mode of transport—planes, trains, and cars. I cried until I couldn't recognize myself. Until my eyes looked permanently swollen and I had to wear sunglasses even when there were no signs of sun.

I stopped seeing my therapist because I was too ashamed to tell her about the tape, only to break down in the doctor's office and beg him to help me. I learned firsthand about depression, and even when my brain was foggy and unable to see through it, I did everything in my power to drag myself out of it.

I want to pause for a moment and say I'm beyond grateful to my NHS doctor, who referred me to a counselor in training during this time. I'm so thankful to have grown up in a country that provides healthcare for people like my family, who couldn't have afforded it. The legal and justice systems are perhaps a little rusty, but growing up without the added stress of knowing I could get hit by a car and end up in debt is one I'm grateful for. I also know that I was in a very privileged position to get the help I needed. Not everyone can afford that luxury, least of all my family. I didn't take the help I got lightly, nor my recovery. When despair hit, and I felt like I couldn't go on, I turned to hope. I started making lists.

Lists of public figures who had started their careers in porn. Lists of celebrities with leaked sex tapes that hadn't destroyed them.

Before the tape, I had grand ambitions for my career. I saw it as a game of chess, where every move had to be carefully calculated.

For someone like me, the career path was clearly paved. You made as much money as possible modeling for the lad's mags, and then you went into one of the two major reality shows. (You couldn't go on *Dancing with the Stars* because they were snobby about Page 3 models.) Hopefully, you did well, and the public loved you. Then you sold books you didn't write, flogged perfumes, acted in Christmas pantos, and released an album of songs where your voice had been autotuned. The other option—there were two paths—was marrying rich. Preferably a football player, or someone equally, if not more, rich, and immediately changing your surname to your husband's to disassociate yourself with your past.

These two paths were tried and tested and worked well.

I decided very early on that I was going to do neither. I wasn't going to play by the rules. I'd been taking acting classes once a week, determined to become a serious actress, strategically positioning myself to make it happen. When I made enough money to not be just surviving, I turned down jobs that didn't align with my vision. *Love Island*, etc. I knew I had to fight the stigma of being a Page 3 and glamour model, but I was prepared to take on the battle.

Once the tape came out, everything I worked so hard to build went up in a cloud of smoke. A fashion campaign I'd turned down multiple jobs to secure? Poof. Gone.

So I made lists to give me hope.

I needed proof that this wasn't the end, that I could survive this. That the career I'd been trying to build, with fashion campaigns and acting opportunities, was still on offer, even though it wasn't looking like it. That's when I found the story of a struggling young actor who, homeless and sleeping in a bus station, was offered $200 to star in a porn film. He took the money. Later, he went on to write and star in a movie. It received nine Oscar nominations. He got three wins, including Best Picture, and grossed over $200 million. The movie was *Rocky* and the actor Sylvester Stallone.

I bet no one was calling him a porn star.

I continued the list, and plenty of people were on it—football players, actors, politicians. When I added Colin Farrell, an actor I thought was devastatingly handsome, I realized they were all men.

Women, of course, had sex tapes or started in porn and went on to build incredible careers—as businesswomen, as reality stars. But they weren't winning Oscars. They weren't selling movies they'd written.

I studied my list, trying to pinpoint the pattern, but something about it stayed just out of reach. Was it because men were celebrated for being sexually promiscuous? Or because, even though I found Colin Farrell devastatingly handsome, I had no interest in watching his sex tape? And if I had, would it have changed how I saw him? Would I have thought any less of him? Probably not.

* * *

I flew to Los Angeles for a men's magazine job a few months later. I was still getting jobs, but not the work I wanted. It was all about pushing the boundaries with how far they could take it sexually, with me bent over or eating strawberries and cream while the cream dripped all over my bare breasts. The days of shooting with the hottest fashion photographers were long gone and when the photographer I was shooting with asked me to be "more sexy," I burst into tears and walked off. I called my manager, Jon, and said I'd pay them the money back. I was very sensitive. I hadn't kissed anyone since the actor I'd made out with in a club the night before the sex tape came out, and I had zero desire to be sexy. I was celibate, by choice or default, I didn't know. And every time I had to pretend to be sexual in any way, it made me feel overwhelmed. So I did what people with money do when they feel overwhelmed—I went on a juice cleanse.

I can't say I felt much better when I left—four days of drinking bitter green juice hadn't changed much. I was still overwhelmed. I drove back to Los Angeles and decided to stay in a hotel for a few nights, thinking that might help, but I had nothing to do and no real friends in LA, so I ordered room service and turned on the television. A twenty-six-year-old Kim Kardashian was all over the news. This was the first time I'd seen or heard of her. As I learned, her sex tape with the R & B singer Ray J had been leaked two months after mine. I popped an antidepressant in my mouth, took a bite of my burger, and watched her talk about her new reality television show with ease. Rumor had it she sued the company that released the sex tape and settled for $5 million for invasion of privacy.

Who is this woman? I thought, *and how did she manage that?* I felt a sudden wave of rageful injustice.

As I watched Kim talk, I felt a multitude of things—happy she was leveraging her tragedy into a "triumph" but also sad that if her sex tape was released without her knowledge, her leveraging of it somehow made the crime less serious.

There were also rumors that she released it herself. However, it was hard to decipher the truth in these rumors since that was the consensus of *all women* with sex tapes, and no one would think differently until 2014, when sexually explicit images and videos of women, mainly well-regarded actresses, were released in a mass hack. Then the consciousness would change, and people would begin to wonder if someone other than the woman could be responsible for its leak.

A part of me wanted the rumors about Kim to be true because if she had released it herself, Kim would have been in control. (One could argue that she was never in control and that playing into the oppressive systems only keeps the systems alive, but to release a sex tape yourself is a way of giving consent, and consent is the key difference between two people engaging in sex and *rape*.)

Thankfully rape is now recognized as a crime, but it wasn't always.

The more I watched Kim talking, the more I felt like maybe I'd made the wrong decision. If I lived in a world where women in sex tapes—willingly or unwillingly—would never be taken seriously, wasn't selling mine the only real option? Wasn't following the path of appearing on reality shows the smart choice? I could have spun my trauma into something profitable and sailed off on my small yet sturdy boat. Screw passion and artistic integrity. The world was never going to let me have it anyway. As I looked at Kim, I couldn't help but wonder...did I just fuck it all up?

Frustration bubbled up, and I grabbed the remote and switched the TV off. I knew if I kept watching I would get even angrier, so I decided to go downstairs to the bar to get a drink. I grabbed my wallet, phone, and room key, and then I realized that I had forgotten my fake ID and that I wasn't even old enough to drink. Men on the internet were watching me having sex, but I wasn't legally allowed to buy a drink.

That was a mindfuck.

When I returned to London, the football player, Hank, who I'd watched porn with at eighteen, asked me if we should watch my sex tape together. When I told him to "fuck off," he said, "Aren't you into me anymore?"

The nightmare that I'd been through didn't even register.

I'm jumping ahead, but I didn't have a romantic relationship until over a year and a half later, when I met Harry in a night-club. I was out with Nic T, who was no longer a Page 3 model herself but still told everyone we were. Harry, who looked like he was in a band with his skinny jeans, but also a surfer with his shaggy long hair, said, "I've actually never read *The Sun*." I was intrigued. A British boy two years younger than me who hadn't seen my tits in the newspaper, how could this be? He explained that his rah-rah, posh school had banned it. "They're not fans of tabloids," he added. And while I found this to be somewhat snobby, I liked that he hadn't seen me naked. Yet anyway.

Harry became my first boyfriend after everything. Our upbringings couldn't have been more different. He grew up in

Eaton Square, in a home worth £33 million. It had an elevator, a housekeeper, and bottled booze behind glass fridges. Dating him felt like I'd slipped through a crack at Charing Cross into a posher London where suddenly everyone spoke a different language. It was fascinating.

After the legal case, I'd taken my manager Jon's words to heart and decided to remain silent about the sex tape. I didn't bring it up, and neither did Harry. Everything was going splendidly until about four months in, when we went out for drinks with a group of his friends.

At the table was Will—a drunk TV host from a privileged family who clung to the conviction that it was his own talent and hard work that accounted for his success, dismissing the idea that privileged people so often do, that Daddy and Mummy, who both worked in the industry, had anything to do with it. He and Harry had been in a heated debate all night, and Will decided to make it personal. "Your girlfriend is a porn star," he said, seemingly disregarding the fact I was sitting there. Harry told him to shut up and stop acting like a prick, and Will turned to me and said, "I've seen your sex tape. Great work."

I thought about throwing my drink in his face. Instead, I downed it in one gulp, then got up and told Harry I'd be outside.

He followed a few minutes later. "I've never seen your tape. But I need you to know how hard it is for me. The shit I have to deal with. The shit people say."

I desperately wanted to crawl into a bathtub and cry. "How hard it is for YOU?" I said. "DO YOU HAVE ANY IDEA THE SHIT I HAVE TO DEAL WITH?"

"No," he snapped. "Because you won't tell me! You've never

spoken about it. But it's fucking hard. The shit people say. I get mocked and teased constantly." He put his hands through his hair, seething. "Not to mention the friends of mine that have watched you GETTING FUCKED."

That last line echoed with the horrid confirmation that I was forever going to be in a throuple. It would be—me, whoever I was with, and the tape. Theo hadn't just ruined my career. He'd ruined my love life.

After fighting for what felt like hours, Harry and I went to bed. I couldn't sleep, so I surfed the internet and emotionally cut myself by reading comments about myself on public forums. *It's funny how many page 3 girls have pretended to be upset when videos of them having sex have "accidentally" made it into the public arena, but they all seem to get over it quickly enough when their careers get the inevitable boost. It's as stage managed as forgetting to put on any knickers when you are wearing a short skirt near the paps. :rolleyes,* said *Sparkle*.

Yea... silly airhead, now where can I find that tape to laugh at her some more??? said another user, followed by, *Stupid girl....brains and beauty never mix with women.*

My source of deep psychological pain and trauma was entertainment. The comments were endless—debating whether I was good at sucking dick and whether I was attractive to begin with. Reading them only confirmed what I had long suspected about society and its views on women. Finding myself both subject and object of these revelations was excruciating yet unsurprising. That's how women like me were treated.

Some version of this moment would play out in every romantic relationship I would find myself in after Harry. In my midtwenties, an actor I dated—not publicly—had his agent, manager, and publicist worrying about how it looked, career-wise, if it were to come out that their star was dating a girl with a sex tape. I mean, what would the fans say? How would he be perceived if people knew he was dating *that kind of girl?*

Over and over again, I'd start dating someone, and I'd wait for the dreaded conversation to happen, for them to bring the tape up, and then, after having to explain that I didn't release it myself, that I wasn't a porn star and neither did I have plans to be one (not that there was anything wrong with being a porn star, I wanted to make that clear). I would get the same response. "Babe, that's so awful. I'm so sorry you had to deal with that." They would be sympathetic and display understanding until it slowly ate away at them like a ticking time bomb, tick, tick, tick, tick. BOOM.

Self-Serving Justice in a World Where Men Walk Free

found myself waiting outside a nightclub in Bromley. This was a month or so after the sex tape came out. I had rampant plans to meet an acquaintance and get shit-faced. I stood by the rope, waiting to go in, when I heard a guy say, "All right, Key." I looked over to see who it was, and standing on the other side of the rope, having just come up the stairs from inside the nightclub, was Theo.

Theo. My ex. Theo, the guy who'd fucked a girl in my bed. Who'd broken into my home with a knife. Who'd rummaged through my apartment to find the tape of us having sex. That guy.

The blood drained from my body. "What's happening? You going in?" he said like we were old friends who hadn't seen each other in a while. I couldn't believe it. I stared at that motherfucker like I was hallucinating. God, I had fantasized about running into him, but in those fantasies I was running into him with a double-decker bus.

I started shaking. I felt dizzy. I couldn't breathe. I wanted to punch him so fucking hard in the face, but I couldn't see straight.

It took every single bit of courage I had in me to walk over to him. I mean, *everything*. I looked him dead in the eyes. And then I opened my mouth and spat.

As my saliva sprayed Theo's cheeks his right arm rose and, in one quick motion, he slapped me as hard as he could across the face.

"DON'T YOU EVER SPIT AT ME, YOU FUCKING DIV!" he yelled, enraged.

I held my cheek with my hand, more from shock than the pain, but it had hurt.

"You're a fucking scumbag," I said.

That really set him off. "YOU STUPID FUCKING BITCH!" he shouted. "I don't know who the FUCK you think you're talking to." Then he went to slap me again. I ducked out of the way as the bouncer, who'd presumably witnessed the whole thing, intervened. He stood in front of Theo, facing me like I was the problem. Theo was cursing me out and the bouncer raised his voice. "Move away from the lad. You're not welcome here. You need to leave! *Fucking leave!*"

I looked at the bouncer in shock, like, *I need to leave? Not the man who just slapped me across the face? But me?* I could hear the music pumping from downstairs in the club. Theo was trying to talk to the bouncer. "Did you see that she spat at me?" he said. The bouncer was looking at me as if I'd spat at him, but kept repeating, "You aren't coming in. You aren't welcome here."

I stared at the two of them, Theo and this super-jacked-up bouncer, and screamed, "AND WHY WOULD I WANT TO COME INTO THIS SHITHOLE WHEN IT'S FILLED

WITH CUNTS LIKE YOU?" Then I ran off around the corner with enough rage to start a war.

Once I was out of sight, I called Patsy, and I rambled on and on as I walked the streets. I'd taken a taxi to Bromley because I'd planned on drinking, and now I didn't know where to go. The guy had fucked a girl in my bed, broken into my home with a knife, sold a sex tape to a newspaper, and slapped me across the face, and yet *I* was the one asked to leave the nightclub. *Nothing* would happen to him. Nothing. There would be no repercussions. Justice would never be served.

"I saw him driving around in a Range Rover earlier, proper thinking he's all that," Patsy said.

"*I get slapped, and he gets a Range Rover?*" I said in disbelief.

"He's a nasty little prick," she said.

A thought crossed my mind, and I started running.

"Where are you going?" Patsy asked.

"To the Sainsbury's parking lot," I said, catching my breath. If Theo had gotten a new car, I knew where he would have parked it.

"What color is it?"

"Black. Why?"

I stopped running and started looking over my shoulder. I was in the middle of the parking lot. I scanned the cars, looking for a black Range Rover. I spotted one and stopped. My whole body was rushing with adrenaline.

"Did you happen to see the registration number?"

"It's like LM something...I think there was a 0..." Patsy said.

"Defo his? Like he's not driving someone else's car?"

"Yeah. My brother knows the guy he bought it from."

"How much does a Range Rover cost, you reckon?"

"They're proper expensive."

"More than ten grand?" I said, knowing that's how much Theo had been paid.

"Oh, yeah, for sure."

"Even secondhand ones?"

Patsy clocked on. "What are you gonna do?" she asked nervously.

"You know, just take my money back," I said, rummaging through my bag. I was shaking uncontrollably, in full fight-or-flight mode. I pulled out my house keys and put my front door key in between my knuckles the way I would when walking home late at night. Ready to defend. "I'll call ya back," I said.

As I hung up, I could hear her say, "Don't do anything stupid!"

I didn't know if it was ironic that the car was parked in the *exact* same spot where Jamie had thrown a glass bottle in my face. In the same parking lot where I had smashed Theo's front windshield. I didn't know if I should ascribe any meaning to any of it in any of the ways we ascribe meaning to things: "fate," "it was meant to be," that sort of thing. The whole thing just felt so vividly unlucky and sad.

I tapped the key on the car for a second. Hesitant. I didn't want to lower myself to Theo's level. I wanted to be the bigger person and walk away. I didn't want to be the sort of person who used violence to solve things or who felt the need to retaliate in such an unlawful manner. Yet I wanted some form of justice. I had been embarrassed and humiliated in front of thousands—if not millions of people. I'd watched the career I wanted to build evaporate into thin air. I would be defined by this moment forever, and yet nothing would happen to him. He wasn't going to jail. He wasn't going to get fined. His career wasn't over. He got to ruin my life, buy a Range Rover, and let society blame me for his actions. And that just didn't seem fair, so I dug my key into the metal and dragged it along. I walked around that car three times, knowing he'd have to change every single panel. I dug the key in so hard, the metal on it wore down. I stopped at the hood and looked at it. My heart was pounding; it was the most alive I'd felt. If the world couldn't yet recognize this as abusive, then fuck the world. I knew.

I took my key and engraved C - U - N - T in all capitals. Then I walked off, wishing I'd had a lighter on me so I could have set that fucking car on fire.

I spoke to Theo once more after that. Three weeks later he called my landline at one in the morning sounding sickly proud of me for keying his car. "I knew it was you, because no girl is smart enough to key every panel," he said. I shouldn't have entertained it, but the phone call had jolted me awake, and when I heard his voice on the other end, I pushed my lips on the mouthpiece and immediately started singing "When the Sun Goes Down" by Arctic Monkeys. ("What a scummy man, just give him half a chance, I bet he'll rob you if he can...") I hung up and he phoned back. Adrenaline was pumping through me and I thought, *I need this asshole to tell me why.*

"I was just getting back at you—" he said.

"For what???" I snapped. "What exactly are you getting back at me for?"

"YOU SPLIT UP WITH ME FOR NO REASON!"

"I split up with you because you were shagging someone else

for our entire relationship, okay? *That's* the reason! THAT'S WHY I BROKE UP WITH YOU! And you...what...you want to put something fucking awful and terrible out into the world and destroy mine and my *family's* life because you're fucking"—I searched for the word—"jealous?" It didn't feel right, but I went with it. "Do you not realize how fucked up that is?"

"You were *laughing*!" he said in a high-pitched voice.

"I was laughing, yeah...because it was *expected*. Because I was such a fool for even trusting you. I was so fucking naive and stupid for being with you in the first place."

If I hadn't been so distraught, I might have started laughing again out of sheer disbelief. My laughing at myself for being an idiot for dating him had been interpreted as my laughing at *him*. He'd twisted his actions into a reaction rather than recognizing this for what it was: a choice he made. A deliberate decision to humiliate me publicly, to make the whole world laugh at me the way he imagined I'd laughed at him.

And it worked. His wish was granted.

The call went on with him trying to justify his actions. He explained that his friends had shown him my overly sexualized topless photos and articles where it said I was single. "Everyone was saying it," he told me. "Keeley's taking liberties." It was no different than one man telling another to "knock his wife about a bit" if she steps out of line. This was just the modern version—the 2007 act of oppression and abuse. As laws changed, men didn't evolve and realize the errors in their ways; they just found ways around them. And the world allowed it.

What did *you* do to make him hit you? Were *you* wearing

something slutty when he raped you? Why did *you* send him the topless photo? Why did you film *yourself* having sex?

These questions people asked in light of a man violating a woman guaranteed that Theo and his friends would never hold themselves accountable, because they collectively believed this was their right.

At one point, I'd heard enough excuses. And to be perfectly fucking honest, I was sick of men who couldn't process their emotions instead of taking them out on me. I slammed down the phone and unplugged it.

Tenergrief

always thought it was funny that it was called "glamour modeling" because there was nothing glamorous about the filthy, cockroach-infested hotel room in Tenerife that I was staying in along with Nic T and another Page 3 girl, Karla. This hotel was categorically the worst. Giving it a one-star Tripadvisor rating would have been generous.

Our employer, *The Sun*, realized that its readers preferred seeing us girls on a beach with our tits out instead of inside a studio, so once a month the paper would send us somewhere sunny to shoot photos for Page 3. This month they had flown us off to Tenerife, or "Tenergrief" as the three of us would rename it.

The paper employed around fifteen to twenty girls at any given time, and Sally, the Page 3 photographer, would split us into two groups and take half of us away for one part of the week, and then we would be switched out for the other group.

For a paper that had oodles of money, they paid us very little and gave Sally even less to take us away. We would be crammed into a budget hotel that barely had two stars and each be forced to share a room with at least one other model, sometimes more, depending on the location and the setup.

Sally decided who went in which group and who would share a room, and knowing that Nic T, Karla, and I were joined at the hip, she put the three of us together, which was the most exciting thing ever. The three of us loved each other. We were Page 3 breast friends. Thick as thieves. We were so excited to share. When we arrived at our room, we pulled the mattresses off the beds and put them into the middle of the floor like we were having a slumber party. There was a high chance that we would leave with fleas, or get crawled on by cockroaches, but we were getting paid to hang out with each other in Tenerife. It was amazing. This was by far the greatest perk of the job.

Once we moved the mattresses, Karla and I flopped ourselves down, and Nic T went to sort out the keys. I pulled a copy of *ID* magazine out of my bag and started flipping through it while Karla—on her mattress beside me—was on her phone text-flirting with a West Ham football player that Nic T had set her up with. There was a cockroach we had named Richard living under a glass in the corner of the room, waiting to be set free outside by someone other than the three of us. The surroundings sucked, but whatever, we were ready to have a fun time. We'd take a few photos and then just hang out.

Giddy with excitement, Karla started reading me the text messages the football player was sending her when Nic T came bursting through the door with Toni, a petite brunette who was on her first Page 3 trip as a test shoot to see if her photos were good enough to make it in the paper.

"Shaz is bang out of order because she is refusing to share a room with Toni because Toni is a stripper, and Shaz said she can't trust her with her stuff because she reckons strippers are thieves!" she yelled.

Toni awkwardly stood behind her. "I'm not actually a stripper. I tried it once," she said quietly.

Nic T had steam coming out of her ears. She and Shaz already had a tumultuous friendship. To be fair, everyone had a tumultuous friendship with Shaz because she was your friend one minute, and then she seemed to hate you the next. This was the final straw for Nic T, who was ready to go to battle for Toni. "I'm going to have this out with Shaz!" she declared, storming back out of the room. Karla and I looked at each other, like, *Oh shit, it's about to go down!* I threw my magazine down, she threw down her phone, and we ran out of the room ready to watch the drama.

We caught up to Nic T, who was on her way to the pool area to find Shaz, who was tanning in a tiny bikini on a sun lounger that looked like it was from the 1980s. Nic T approached her. "Toni just told me that you're refusing to share a room with her because you think she was a stripper and strippers are thieves," she said.

Shaz peered over her black sunglasses, looked at Nic T, and said, "I said I don't want to share a room with her."

"...because she's a stripper..." Nic T added.

Toni butted in to say once again that she wasn't a stripper, and the whole thing popped off. Nic T was shouting at Shaz; how dare she be such a judgmental hypocrite. Did she not realize that *she* took her clothes off for a living. Shaz yelled back to Nic T that it was her choice who she wanted to share a room with and to mind her own business. Toni started shouting, well, attempting to. "I'm not a stripper!" she managed before running off crying. A few of the other Page 3 girls appeared poolside and asked what was going on. Karla and I filled them in, and before you knew it, everyone had an opinion. And they were expressing them loudly. The general consensus was this: Shaz shouldn't discriminate against someone for stripping, and none of us should be made to share rooms with girls we didn't know. Therefore, Toni would have to find somewhere else to stay—and now Shaz looked like a mean bitch. Shaz fled to the other side of the pool and started crying. Karla and I exchanged a look, then sat down beside Nic T, who was visibly shaking and crying herself.

The whole drama made its way around the grotty hotel and to Sally, the photographer, who was married to the picture editor at *The Sun* and, therefore, had more power than God.

That night, all ten of us Page 3 girls sat around the dinner table, sharing some bread and aioli and talking about sex. We discussed blowjobs, anal, licking men's assholes, and who we were shagging.

Every girl sounded like they were Samantha Jones from *Sex and the City*. Complete nymphomaniacs who loved the D. Lived for it in fact. It was hard to tell if everyone was being honest or if they were just performing the idea of the modern, sexually liberated woman because it was cool.

"I haven't had sex in a very long time," I found myself saying, wanting to be vulnerable and honest. This was deep in my celibacy era, post–sex tape, pre-Harry.

"Me neither!" One of the girls opposite me squealed, "I haven't had sex in, like, six days!" On seeing her face and how completely baffled and shocked she was to have not had sex in all of six days, I felt no need to tell her that I hadn't had sex since Christmas morning fourteen months prior. I wanted her to have her moment. Six days to a sexually active nineteen-year-old was a long time. I couldn't outdo her.

Nic T and Shaz were sitting on opposite ends of the table, ignoring each other, when Sally, who'd just joined us, raised her voice to address the drama of the day.

"Nic T, this is the last trip you're ever coming on for Page 3," she said. The whole table fell silent. Nic T was in disbelief. We all were. It was a grand moment, sort of like we were on a reality show and had just found out who was eliminated from this round. I lowered my head, not knowing what to do or say.

"I'm being fired because...?" She went to argue but Sally jumped in.

"No! Stop, Nic," she said. She had a Northern twang that came out after a couple of glasses of wine. "I nearly flew home because of this drama, and this type of behavior is not acceptable and ruins the trip for everyone." Sally broke off some bread and took a sip of her white wine. No one said anything. "All of you girls need to be careful. If you want to keep your jobs, then you need to learn to behave. The only person who can do what she likes is

Keeley because *The Sun* will not fire her. When she is on the front cover, she sells papers. But the rest of you need to be careful."

The whole table turned to look at me. I didn't know what to do with my newfound privilege and power, but I thought it would be worth a shot to see if I could get Nic T's job back.

"She's not coming back, Keeley. Don't even ask," Sally said before I could speak.

Nic T got up from the table and ran off. Karla and I excused ourselves politely and followed.

"I can't believe she fired me!! I was just trying to help out Toni!" Nic T said through tears. "What am I going to do with my life now?" The tears kept coming, and I didn't know what to say. A girl had once been fired from Page 3 because she hadn't had her roots done. It was brutal. Even more brutal was that I suspected the real reason Nic T had been fired was because of her age, not the argument with Shaz. She was twenty-four, about to turn twenty-five, and that was ancient, practically dead in our industry. All the other models were eighteen to twenty-one. And before our time, the girls had been as young as sixteen, an age so young it makes me want to vomit. Still, it didn't change the fact that Sally had all of the power to make the decisions on everyone's career but mine. You misbehaved and you were out. It made me want to know how far I could push it.

A little while later, after Nic T had spoken to her new footballer boyfriend and stopped crying, she decided, in an act of rebellion, that we should all go to a strip club and befriend the strippers. We rejoined the group and waited for Sally to leave. Then Nic T said, "Hey, listen up. Simon gave me his credit card in case of emergencies, and I'm paying for everyone to go to a strip club. Lap dances on Simon!" Simon was the new boyfriend and had kindly offered to pay for our excursion. Everyone cheered. Shaz went to her room. Toni, who didn't make the cut, was already on a flight back to London Gatwick, and the rest of us headed out in search of a strip club to send Nic T off in one last hurrah.

Bizarrely, I don't know why, but Tenerife is filled with strip clubs. They're everywhere, so it didn't take us long to stumble upon one not far from our hotel. This place was huge, with a big neon sign and a fourteen-foot billboard advertising the strip club outside. I looked up and to my utter shock, there was a photo of me in pink lingerie. On the billboard. I was the face of the strip club. Me. Yes, *me*. My image, my body, was being used as "promotion," without my consent. Alan—the photographer from Tobago—had shot the photo for my website. The copyright was jointly owned by our company. The next day, I phoned him to ask how they had gotten it. "They must've ripped it from the site," he said. "It's very common. They want the sexiest girls, but they don't want to pay for them."

Here was Shaz, judging strippers as thieves, when it turned out the real thieves were the people profiting off our images. After that, I'd stumble upon my photo everywhere—on sex workers' business cards in photo booths in Vegas, on escort sites, even in a strip club in Thailand, but nothing as big or surreal as this billboard in Tenerife. And there was nothing I could do about it. Well, unless I wanted to spend a small fortune just to *maybe* get it taken down. I spoke with a few lawyers, who all said the same thing: "You'll spend more in legal fees, and even if you do see the inside of a courtroom, getting any compensation will be slim to none."

So: The strip club stole my photo, and Alan would eventually run off with the money I was making from the site. All in all, everyone made something off that photo. Everyone except me.

Lucky, my parents taught me sarcasm.

"Shit. Well, the cat's out the bag. I've been leading a double life as a striper in Tenerife," I said, pointing at my face on the billboard.

"Oi, oi, give us a dance," Nic T yelled, always one for banter.

We found another strip club around the corner, because I didn't want the punters to be confused. It was narrow, dark, and grimy. About five girls were working, all non–English speaking except one girl from England who wore round black glasses that reminded Nic T, Karla, and me of Harry Potter.

The girls greeted us warily like we were a bunch of escorts there to steal their business. The English girl with Harry Potter glasses asked cautiously if we were in the right place. We literally had to reassure them that we were the ones looking for a private dance. We weren't trying to steal their clients; *we were* their clients. Nic T flashed Simon's credit card around. "Put it all on this," she said.

The English girl with the Harry Potter glasses said she would have to ask her boss if it was okay to give us girls a lap dance because no group of women, or women without men, had ever come into a strip club and asked for a lap dance before. This was a first. We were a first. She didn't even know the rules on whether or not she could dance for us.

We hung around by the bar and watched as she walked over to

an older mobster-looking man in the corner and said something to him; he looked over to us, and we waved. He whispered something to her, and she walked back over to us and said, "Come with me." Most of us scurried off into a room and sat in chairs lined up in front of a mirror—a long line of Page 3 models waiting to be danced for. Karla decided to stay at the bar area; she was busy sexting the football player and didn't care to have a stranger grind all over her.

The English girl with the Harry Potter glasses danced for each of us for a few minutes, and we asked her questions. How long have you been living in Tenerife? Do you do this full-time? How'd you get into it? We were more interested in getting to know her than anything sexual.

After the dance, we stood by the bar area, ordered drinks, and watched the girl on the main stage dance. Nic T slid up next to me and put her mouth close to my ear. "Okay...so I've just found out that this place isn't just a strip club..." *No shit*, I thought. All you had to do was take one look around this place to know something dodgy was going on.

"It's a drug front, isn't it?" I said.

"No," she said.

"Money laundering ring?"

"What? No," she said, looking around to make sure no one was listening. "Well, it's sort of...I don't know how to say this... a brothel? Like, you can pay the girls to hook up!" She added, "I've always wondered what hooking up with a girl is like."

"Same," I said.

"You should try it."

"Pay one of the girls to hook up?" I said in a high-strung voice. I don't know why it felt so outrageous, but it did.

"I'm sure they'd much rather hook up with you than some dirty old fat man with a crooked little smelly dick."

I screwed my face up. "I don't know. They might be into that. Maybe they're not into pussy," I said. I was having some sort of moral conundrum that Nic T was going to pick holes at.

"Why don't you do it?" I asked.

"I'm not going to cheat on Simon," she said, getting out her phone and texting him. "But I just said you might, and he offered to pay for you. Personally, if I were selling myself for money, I'd rather have sex with one of us than a man. This is how they make money." Nic T flung her brown hair back. I admired her gesture. Football players made obscene amounts of money, and these women seemed to make very little, so there was something I liked about liberating these women through monetary gain— but something about paying someone to hook up felt icky. The transactional nature didn't sit right with me. Yet I had always wondered what hooking up with a woman might be like, so I contemplated it.

While I was dating Jamie, I wrote a handwritten letter to *Cosmopolitan* magazine. It was two pages long, and I went into detail, exclaiming how much I hated sex. WHAT AM I MISSING???? I wrote in all caps. WHY DON'T I ENJOY IT AND EVERYONE ELSE DOES???? WHAT IS WRONG WITH ME???? I ended my two-page letter asking if they could please write back to me to let me know why I didn't enjoy what Hollywood movies and songs painted as the greatest thing ever. All of my friends seemed to love sex. I loved kissing. Kissing was one of my favorite things on the planet. I was sexually attracted to men, at least, I thought I was, but I just hadn't found my groove in the act of it. (It would take me until I was twenty-six to have my first orgasm through sex and my big "aha" moment.) I was relying on *Cosmopolitan*—the ultimate voice of all things sex—to give me the answers. If *Cosmo* didn't know what was wrong with me, who would? But they didn't reply, and I was none the wiser. Stumbling around having boys fuck me like they were a power drill digging for gold while I received no gratification.

Then the sex tape happened, and the thought of having sex with anyone made me physically sick. The faucet of my sexuality had been flipped right off. I might have been topless in magazines looking like I was ready to take a dick or two, but I wasn't exactly in the headspace to "bone." I also wasn't trying to live like a nun forever. I wanted to crack the code.

So, there I was, in this strip club that doubled as a sex work establishment with Nic T's boyfriend, Simon, willing to pay for me to...you know, get back in the game. It felt like the perfect chance to explore my sexuality and desire. Maybe I'd even discover something about myself. I mean, what if I was queer? I'd never hooked up with a woman, so how did I know that I wasn't a lesbian? The only porn I'd really enjoyed was female-on-female. (Wasn't that a telltale sign?) I had steamy fantasies, and let's face it, some people don't figure out they're gay until they're in their fifties. I hadn't enjoyed sex with a man. Maybe I liked vagina?

So that's how I agreed to break my celibacy: that and the three shots of tequila.

One of the Page 3 girls, Julia, had hooked up with girls before so naturally, I consulted her. "Why don't I come with you?" she said casually, like we were going shoe shopping. "I'll show you the ropes." It seemed smart to have someone experienced with me, so I agreed. I wasn't sure I was attracted to Julia, as beautiful and as sexy as she was, I didn't feel anything romantic. Then again, I no longer trusted my own attraction. Look where it got me with Theo.

We picked a lady and headed to the back room. We had fifteen minutes—plenty of time for me to have sex with two women and discover if I was actually gay.

The three of us entered a small room at the back of the strip club that contained a bed with white sheets. There was a mirror on the wall opposite. It wasn't the nicest place on the planet, but it was better than our hotel room, I can tell you that. Julia removed her clothes freely, keeping nothing on but her knee-high boots. The stripper/sex worker got on the bed naked. I stood nervously and giggled as I watched the two girls hooking up. I slowly took off my jeans and T-shirt and awkwardly tried to insert myself. Julia, who, unlike me, was so free sexually, was having a whale of a time, and so was the stripper/sex worker. (But really, who knew if she was having a good time or not or if she was just performing for the money?)

I jumped in the middle, and the two women started sucking on my tits, and I returned the favor by sucking on theirs. Then the stripper/sex worker started caressing my clit, and Julia went down on me. I thought I'd get into it. In my imagination this was going to be the sexiest night of my life. In reality, I felt zero sexual arousal whatsoever. It felt foreign and mechanical. I felt nothing. I decided that I should try and spice it up by giving one of the girls oral sex, so I positioned myself in between the stripper/sex worker's legs and took a deep breath.

I looked at her vagina, willing myself to touch it or do the things one is supposed to do when their head is by a vagina and consent has been given. I just couldn't. I started to feel dizzy and overwhelmed and saddened by the whole experience. Seeing a vagina this close reminded me of seeing my own in the newspaper and what a devastating moment that had been. I couldn't get that image out of my head. *My vagina in black-and-white in a newspaper.* That's when I spiraled. My chest started tightening, my heart was pounding, sweat dripped freely from my armpit down my side. It was a familiar feeling, I knew what was happening. I was having a panic attack. A full-blown panic a few inches from another woman's vagina. I know there is no ideal place to have a panic attack, but being in a strip club in Tenerife in the middle of a threesome was definitely up there with one of the worst places to have one. Julia and the stripper/sex worker seemed unaware of my distress. The two of them were going for it. They looked like they were in a porno, and I just lay there like a lemon waiting for my heart to slow down and for the whole thing to be over. Luckily, Simon had only paid for fifteen minutes because soon a man knocked on the door and said, "Time's up."

I got dressed immediately and found Nic T by the bar. "I don't think I'm gay," I said.

"Tell me everything!" she yelped in excitement.

"Well, it was interesting," I said.

"Give me the details! Did you...?" she said, putting her fingers in a V shape over her mouth and sticking her tongue out in between them.

"No!" I said, suddenly self-conscious.

"What? Why not?" she asked, disappointed. I told her that I

couldn't bring myself to do it and that sadly the fantasy in my head didn't match the reality.

Much later, when we returned to our hotel room, I thought, well, isn't life having a right old laugh. I'm unknowingly the face of a strip club down the street, my image selling sex, and yet I can't find a shred of enjoyment in it. It seemed so comical that on paper, two Page 3 models and a stripper having a threesome was a titillating, erotic experience. A scene tailor-made for the male gaze, one that would make a male friend of mine move his head from side to side like his brain was malfunctioning when I told him about it many years later. But in reality, it was far from erotic.

I was so confused by my own sexual desires. My wants and needs. I had no fucking idea who I was. Up until this point, consciously or otherwise, I'd been performing and living out someone else's fantasy of sex. Even the tape, to a greater or lesser degree, had been my attempt to live up to the idea of me. I wanted to be Samantha Jones from *Sex and the City* and sit at the table and speak about sex like the other models.

But I had to admit the truth. The sex I enjoyed the most was alone with a vibrator. It was quick, there was no mess, and I didn't have to move my legs into positions that made my inner thighs ache. And maybe I needed to have sex with two women to figure that out. But there is freedom in knowing that. When it comes to sex, the only empowerment there is, is knowing your truth. When it comes to yourself, the only freedom is knowing who you are.

I guess that's the part I hadn't figured out.

Part Three

Woman

LA: A Love Story of Sorts

came to the decision to quit glamour modeling and move to Los Angeles slowly—then all at once, like sliding a piece from a Jenga tower, only to watch the whole thing collapse with a single pull. *Well, if there's any way to overcome trauma*, I found myself thinking, *it's to quit your job, book a flight to a faraway place, and never return.* Then came the inevitable wave of doubt. What if I quit, end up forty, broke, and have to move back in with my mother? Then I'll be kicking myself that I didn't cash in while I still had the chance.

The responses to my desire to quit highlighted an interesting class disparity. People I had come to know from privileged backgrounds, such as my boyfriend Harry, would say, "Just quit. Follow your passion; everything will work out. Jump, and the net will appear." Meanwhile, individuals from where I grew up would respond, "What do you mean you're thinking of quitting your job? What are you going to do? How will you make money?"

In the end, I took a leap of faith, trusting some invisible net would find me. I quit modeling and moved to Los Angeles to study acting at a year-long conservatory. I'd fallen in love with it week after week in my Friday-night drama class. Although pursuing such an unstable career without my naked past seemed crazy, it felt like I must be clinically insane to pursue it given all the scandal I'd have to fight against. But alas, I wasn't one to follow the rules, and when I saw a mountain in front of me as daunting as Everest, I felt compelled to climb it, even if I was unprepared and unequipped—even when it left me bleeding out on the side of it.

Upon my relocation, I found an apartment by the Grove, an outdoor shopping mall with cheery music and a water fountain that puts on a show—it is, in other words, the most sickening place on the planet.

By LA standards, the school I signed up for wasn't far from my new abode. But one of the pitfalls of Los Angeles is that you need a car to get anywhere, and parking is, quite honestly, the quickest way to increase your cortisol levels.

On my first day, I arrived early, signed in at reception, and watched returning students stand around, discussing Chekhov like he was some sort of vodka. "Chekhov is just so...smooth," one student said.

"Yeah, but if you consume too much at once, you'll start questioning the meaning of life."

I made my way to my first class, nervous. It was called sense memory, an acting technique in which you memorize an object to re-create it when it's not there. I had set clear goals for myself before studying acting, and when I say "goals," I really only had one: I wanted to learn to cry on cue. That's all I desperately wanted.

I sat in a fold-up chair with my eyes closed, surrounded by twenty-five other people, and re-created a lemon. That was the first item we were assigned. After that, we would graduate to a coffee cup, and, if we were really lucky, we'd move on to a place.

Six weeks in, I was bitter, still stuck trying to re-create a lemon, and I started questioning everything. If I could taste a lemon when it wasn't in front of me, didn't that make me psychotic? If I *couldn't* fully believe a lemon was in front of me, did that mean I was a terrible actor? Was I ever going to learn how to cry—let alone on cue?

For all my unanswered questions, I must have been doing something right because a week later my teacher, Lou, graduated me from lemon to coffee cup, and a week after that to place. This, I was told, was a big deal.

The place I was asked to re-create was my childhood bedroom. In reality, I was still sitting in that same fold-up chair, but in my imagination, I was on the floor of the room I had shared with Deborah in the prefab. Mum entered, wearing a yellow Adidas sweater. In every version of this exercise, she was always wearing that sweater. I knew exactly which one it was, though she hadn't owned it until we moved to Grove Park. But that didn't matter— I focused on the sweater because being in that room brought up so much emotion, and I didn't want to feel any of it.

I was torn. I wanted to learn to cry on cue, but I didn't actually want to be back in that bedroom feeling all the sadness I felt. And it didn't help that the girl behind me was wailing uncontrollably in my ear.

I was jealous of her wailing. She was so fucking good at it. I wanted to cry like that. And somehow it made me feel like a failure knowing that she was the same age as me—twenty-two—her parents had paid for her to be here (as was the case with 99 percent of the students), and the most trauma she'd experienced to date was the death of her goldfish when she was twelve. She hadn't even lost a grandparent. She was so shiny, so unscathed by life, yet she cried like it was nobody's business, and it annoyed me. I tried to have compassion for her. Most people who had the luxury of spending thousands and thousands of dollars to sit in a cheap fold-up chair and cry had led very middle-class, privileged lives, but instead, I felt worse. Here I was with all this trauma, and while I'd moved across an ocean to overcome it, the least I could do was use it for my art. The girl behind me lost her goldfish and could cry like her whole family had been murdered, and I'd seen the remains of my friend's head in the road and I couldn't produce a single tear.

I let out a little whimper of frustration. Crying on cue is a skill I so desperately wanted, but I'd already cried so much the last couple of years that going through the emotion was something I didn't want to do to get the skill of crying on cue. The girl behind me vamped up her wailing as I faintly heard our teacher, Lou, say, "What can you feel, taste, and touch?"

I can feel, taste, and touch failure, I thought, while I opened my eyes and slumped back in my chair, defeated.

After the exercise, we met with our teacher individually for a one-on-one. When I sat down in front of Lou, he asked how it was going. I said that it was going terribly and that I needed to know how to cry on cue.

"What are your acting ambitions?" he asked.

I told him I wanted to be a serious actress. "If Meryl Streep and Glenn Close had a baby, that's who I want to be," I said with a straight face.

He laughed so hard, his stomach was shaking.

"You're naturally funny. Have you read any Neil Simon?"

I said I had no plans to be a comedic actress and had been blessed—or cursed—with the gift of trauma, which I wanted to give the world and only star as a heartbroken widow in war movies. I actually didn't say that last part, but I thought it, which we all know is basically the same thing.

Once I finished my talk with Lou, I made my way downstairs to join the other students my age for lunch.

As I sat eating my Subway sandwich, I was just another unknown, twenty-two-year-old, hungry for knowledge, given the chance to become whoever I wanted to be. In England, I rarely met boys my age who didn't know who I was. In America, no one knew me. And I loved it. But as much as I loved having any fame or prior knowledge of my life stripped away from me, well, for a few months at least, I struggled with how different I was from everyone else. Everyone kept talking about where they went to college and what they'd majored in. I learned more about Wisconsin and Michigan State and a guy called Rob Weinstein from the class of '07 than I ever needed to. Conversation focused on what they would do now that their parents were making them get jobs. "My dad said he'd take me off the family plan if I don't start working," a girl said, and I wondered what it must have felt like to have someone else pay for my phone bill other than myself.

There were other Brits in the school, of course. We're everywhere. We pop up in every country because our natural instinct is to colonize. It's in our blood. But again, there were Brits who could afford to move to Los Angeles and go to acting school because of their family and had grown up in a completely different socioeconomic environment, and there was *me*, who had dated these kinds of posh Brits but wasn't one of them and couldn't identify. Nor relate to their skiing trips or hardships.

People bond over similarities and shared experiences, and no one I met could relate to my life. They weren't setting cars on fire, robbing cabdrivers, and popping ecstasy like Smarties. (I'm not sure I've mentioned the last part to date, but at this point, you know more than they did.) I wasn't explicitly telling the other students everything about it. I remained elusive about my past as part of my strategy to leave it where it ought to be, *in the past*. And this seemed like a great way to avoid confronting it. But the year was 2009, the internet was thriving, and society—or maybe it was just people in LA who were trying to get ahead—were googling every single person they met. I had no doubts that I'd been googled. I just didn't know for sure because no one said anything.

It wasn't until I was back in Lou's class trying to re-create my childhood bedroom that I suspected he knew about my past.

After avoiding my feelings in the fold-up chair for the entire hour, I sat with Lou, and he asked me if I'd seen the movie *The Brown Bunny*, starring Chloë Sevigny.

"I haven't. What's it about?" I asked.

"Watch it when you get home," he said. "I think it will be good for you."

When I got home that evening, like the good student I was, I rented the movie, which had premiered at Cannes, sat back, and watched. My face dropped when I saw the very explicit scene in which Chloë Sevigny performs oral sex on the writer/director/lead actor and then boyfriend, Vincent Gallo, on camera. I couldn't tell if Lou was trying to say that I should star in movies like this or if he was trying to be encouraging, saying, "Hey, if

Chloë can star in a movie where she gives head and can still have a career, then maybe you can, too."

Still, I knew then that he *knew*, and then I had to deal with the embarrassment of wondering if he'd watched the sex tape. How would I ever look at him the same way? It wasn't long after *The Brown Bunny* that it became apparent that everyone *knew*. I could tell by the sudden changes on everyone's faces. *The looks.* Oh God, the looks that changed from one day to the next. And while I knew that they *knew*, no one would say anything, and it felt like I was carrying an elephant on my shoulder that everyone could see but was too embarrassed to acknowledge.

I needed somewhere to exist without being "the Keeley with a sex tape and topless photos on the internet." Somewhere to process everything or, better yet, not process anything at all. The way I usually dealt with this was by getting shit-faced, but I had a rude awakening when I found out everywhere closes at 2:00 a.m. in LA. Everywhere. All bars and clubs kick you out and shut their doors at two. I thought this was Hollywood; the place was known for debaucherous parties and fun, and now I was learning that everyone went to bed at 2:00 a.m.!? That's when parties get started in Ibiza. At 2:00 a.m. in London, I was backing shots and trying to make out with an entire football team, not leaving and going to bed.

I decided that maybe this city-imposed curfew was a good thing, as it would allow me to lay off the booze for a bit. (It worked until I discovered house parties.) That was how I found myself in the West Hollywood Library after school hours. Avoiding alcohol and people.

You should know that the West Hollywood Library wasn't just any library. This place is a temple, straight out of the pages of *Architectural*

Digest: big glass windows, a fancy staircase. I would go and sit in silence with my laptop and read books on acting and screenwriting and journal for hours. Having friends is great, but have you ever sat in a room full of people where no one talks to you? It's heaven.

So, among books and people seeking shelter, this is how I started my love affair with writing. I sat for hours and poured my soul onto the page through ill-formed and grammatically incorrect sentences and spellings. I almost forgot I was dyslexic. I had the most intimate relationship I've ever had with anyone, sharing all the tiny details about myself that I was hiding from others. I wrote everything that happened to me in present tense to live through it again. Then I got creative and hid my feelings in the structure of a screenplay, which I learned how to do from a book. I'd found a lover. A best friend. A companion. Someone to drive me crazy and keep me up all night. Someone to help me make sense of the world and my place in it.

The more I wrote about my experience and confronted it, the easier my sense memory class became. Writing seemed to be my intellectual processing of emotions, and acting was my body's.

For eighteen weeks, I worked on my childhood bedroom, re-creating every little detail of it in my mind: the bunk beds, the wallpaper, the window in the back. And every time I re-created it, the same thing happened. I sat on the floor, playing with my toys, when Mum entered the room wearing her yellow Adidas sweater. I see her and don't stop crying for an hour. Every day for eighteen weeks, I went back to that room in my mind, and I cried.

As for crying on cue, I forgot about it. I focused on feeling my emotions when they arose and becoming more aware of them. But now I'm curious whether I can do it. I just tested it out, and I managed to produce a tear as I write this. Oh, now there's another one.

The Agent Meeting

We enter a spacious office. KEELEY (early twenties) is sitting opposite a big-time talent AGENT (forties). He is looking at her headshot and résumé.

AGENT. Thank you for coming in. Have a seat on the couch.

KEELEY. [Sits down] No problemo.

AGENT. Keeley Hazell is your real name. It's not a stage name?

KEELEY. It's my real name.

AGENT. That's a really great name. Fantastic. When people want to become movie stars, they wish they were born with names like that.

KEELEY. It's what my parents were thinking when they named me.

AGENT. You should change it.

KEELEY. Oh, okay.

AGENT. Have you thought about changing it?

KEELEY. Well, I once thought about changing it to Oprah Winfrey, but turns out someone already took it.

AGENT. [Laughing] That's a good one! I'll come up with some names. Just with everything that's online, you don't want people looking you up and not hiring you.

KEELEY. Ah, right.

AGENT. It's just, there's all these photos and videos, you know? Just get a new name and it solves it.

KEELEY. Got it. Though, I like my name and I don't want to feel like I'm running away from my past. I'd like to bury it... but...

AGENT. You can with a new name. How about Audrey Monroe?

KEELEY. You know, I'll give it some thought.

AGENT. Keeley Moore? You come up with something. Anyway, like I've said before, I think you have something really interesting. You have all of these contradictory qualities that make you unique. You're intelligent... articulate... and I hope you don't mind me saying, but you're not what I expected for someone so... *sexy.*

KEELEY. [Uncomfortable] Thank you?!? People often tell me they're surprised when they meet me, typically because I dress like an eighty-year-old granddad.

AGENT. We look after a British actress who was on a TV soap for years, and now we've made her into a movie star.

KEELEY. I should get her agent's number.

AGENT. That's me.

KEELEY. Oh, I know it was...

AGENT. Anyway, you both have a similar essence. You have that…more than meets the eye thing.

KEELEY. Oh, I think I know who you're talking about…Kat? She's done amazingly well! You seem to work really well with women.

AGENT. Yes, Kat, she's doing *great*. She just booked a film franchise and she's set for life. *(Beat.)* Look, I want to be honest with you. I think you have something I could work with…but I'm hesitant to take you on because when I reached out to you, it was because I wanted to date you.

KEELEY. Oh, okay. [Inner thoughts: He wanted to date me? Wow, I totally thought he was gay.]

AGENT. I've got to jump into a meeting now, but there's a cocktail party later for Young Hollywood. Do you wanna come?

KEELEY. I can't. My BOYFRIEND and I have plans. But I'd love to work together.

AGENT. That's a shame. Well, have a nice life.

The Real Keeley

t began with me in a red swimsuit on a movie set. The year was 2014, and I was twenty-seven. I'd landed a small role in the sequel to a big blockbuster hit, *Horrible Bosses*. Playing "Rex's assistant." She had no name of her own. No backstory; she was just "Rex's assistant," or, as I learned when I was handed a skintight black dress that made my tits pop, his "sexy assistant." The role was as glamorous as it sounds. I had two lines in one scene, where I squeezed into that skintight dress and let my cleavage do more acting than I did. Then there was the poolside dream sequence scene, where I wore the aforementioned red swimsuit and said absolutely nothing. It wasn't exactly my big break, but a great credit for my résumé and a huge step up from "frozen girl," a role I played nine years earlier that required me to pretend I was frozen in a grocery store while a guy lifted my shirt up to sketch a drawing of my tits.

We filmed the red swimsuit scene at a luxury hotel pool a few hours outside of Los Angeles. The director placed me on the edge of a sun lounger next to J, a well-known American actor and writer nearing forty. "Pretend you're having the time of your life," the director said, before walking off. J smiled and nodded at my swimsuit. "I nearly wore the same thing," he said.

"It would've complemented your hair," I replied, noticing that J and the other male leads were all fully dressed.

We talked about our lives as you do when you're practically glued next to someone for hours. He told me he had a pregnant fiancée; I told him I had a boyfriend who was a pain in my ass. The conversation drifted from our romantic lives to our careers, and that's when J confessed that he recognized me from *FHM* magazine. He could vaguely remember the photos: pink bikini, brown hair. I'd been eighteen when I'd taken them. I teased him about it—asking why an American man had seen *such a scandalous magazine* in the first place. He playfully said he'd been to London and read it for the articles. I laughed, and that's when the conversation took a more serious turn. I told him that I had been trying, *unsuccessfully, it would seem*, to steer away from playing any part that was remotely sexy—adding that I only wanted to play roles that required me to be in a burka or at least a turtleneck. He sincerely and curiously asked *why*. I was never going to bring up the sex tape and tell him I didn't feel comfortable being viewed as "sexy" because of what had happened to me; even sitting here in this red swimsuit made me feel vulnerable and exposed. So I put it into a different context—less about me, but the larger social context. I gave him my whole spiel that society tells women they can't be complex human beings with contradicting qualities. "We flatten the feminine to individual qualities. You can be hot, but you can't be smart. You can be smart, but you can't be sexy. And once people view women a certain way, it's hard to change their perceptions; it's like trying to unsee a bad haircut—you just can't," I said.

J became amped up and engaged, ready to explore the topic of female inequality between takes and makeup checks. We discussed the many challenges women face. We spoke about pretty privilege and how I'd benefited from it. We spoke about the pitfalls of it. We spoke about an extremely attractive girl he used to do improv with who was gorgeous and funny, and because of this, all the guys wanted to date her and all the women hated her.

And somehow, five hours passed, and when the director yelled "cut" for the last time, we were still talking—this time about the script I'd written. It was about a British girl who moves to Los Angeles after a very public scandal and tries to reinvent herself. (I wonder where I got the idea?!) I was going to play the lead. A big production company had optioned it, and it had nearly been sold to a studio, but—here's a story that sums up Hollywood for ya: *They googled me and backed out.* One of the executives' exact words were "We just couldn't with all the stuff on the internet." I relayed the story to J, leaving out the part where the guy said, "I couldn't tell if you were a nude model or a porn star," but leaving in the part where they're owned by a kids' network.

"They loved the *idea* of reinvention on paper. They wanted to *sell* reinvention, but they weren't willing to take the risk on *my* reinvention," I said.

"Mmmm," he muttered, stroking his eyebrow.

After filming wrapped, J reached out and asked to read my script. I emailed it over, and he came back with notes, adding, "You've got the goods. You're talented." I considered forwarding it to the studio exec, along with a photo of me sticking my middle finger up.

*   *   *

The world of showbiz was rough, but I kept writing. I kept auditioning. And finally, a year later, I graduated from the red swimsuit and booked a recurring role as a maid who falls in love with the king on *The Royals*. I was thrilled.

The show shot in London, but they couldn't afford my airfare or hotel, so I paid my own way and stayed at my mum's house—the one I had grown up in, now fully decorated. (Acting in England does not pay as well as getting one's tits out, let me tell you.) Still, my work life was looking up, but my love life? Not so much. After I broke up with my pain in the ass boyfriend, I started to feel very cynical about love. This feeling was intensified one evening after filming, when I had dinner with my friend David. On the verge of tears, he said, "What if we never fall in love again? What if that's it for the rest of our lives?"

I should have prefaced it by saying he was going through a divorce. Even so, what he said struck a chord, and I looked at him with a face full of doom. *Oh, God, what if this is it?*

After dinner, I called Patsy and told her what he'd said. She replied, "Of course you're going to fall in love again." I hung up, thinking, *That's* exactly *what I said to David. I lied to him, she just lied to me, and now I know for certain I am going to be alone for the rest of my life.*

The next morning, I reached for my phone, checked my messages, and found one that would change my life.

It was from my friend David—a different David. (Sorry, half my contacts are named David. It's so much easier to have friends with the same name.) The message said, *Hey, you have an admirer. His name is Alex ****. He wants to take you out. Look him up.* I googled him and braced myself. He was surely either a seventy-five-year-old with face tattoos fresh out of jail or a polyamorous balding tech bro with thirteen children. When his photo loaded, I nearly fell out of bed. This guy was a thirty-year-old dreamboat. *Jesus*, I kept repeating as I looked at his photos. *Jesus*. I don't want to be shallow or objectify a man, but *Jesus*.

I read a little about him. Actor. Humble beginnings. He seemed perfect. Why was he interested in me? There had to be a catch. I texted David back, *I just looked him up. What's the catch?????????? Does he have six toes? A camp at Burning Man? A gambling addiction?*

David said there was no catch and he was lovely. So Alex and I exchanged numbers and started messaging. He was away on location in Baton Rouge shooting a movie. I was filming in London all summer, so we had our first date on FaceTime. It was love at first sight or *love at first FaceTime*. The chemistry between us was palpable. It seemed to travel through the phone and into my stomach. He was so warm and genuine. And a complete romantic. *Romeo and Juliet* was his favorite movie. When he was twenty, he had a tattoo of an *X* and a dotted line placed on his arm for his wife to sign. He'd already planned his wedding and his children's names.

Once all the fundamentals had been established, Alex said in his Midwestern accent, "Y'know, I saw you in *Horrible Bosses 2*, and I googled you, but I went to Instagram right away, and I didn't see all the other stuff. Only after I messaged you did I go back to Google and click on the video tab. And I thought, whoa, did I just message a porn star? And can I date a porn star?" He started laughing and then offered me an explanation. "My dad is a pastor." I laughed along with him but lowered my eyes because I knew what he'd seen was the sex tape, and no matter how much money I'd thrown at trying to erase it, that godforsaken thing lurked in shadows like a ghost that just wouldn't fuck off and die.

He picked up on my sudden dip in emotion. "Oh, shit, sorry, did I just upset you?"

"No. *Yes*. Well, Jesus fucking Christ, your parents are going to think you've lost your mind if you take me home!" I joked, wondering if I should just hang up now and save myself the trouble of having his family think he's dating Satan.

"Don't worry. They think I lost it years ago," he said, smiling.

We looked at each other through our devices, and I genuinely had a moment when I thought I'm going to do it. I'm going to tell him the truth about the sex tape. I'm not going to wait for him to bring it up in three months' time. I'm going to explain how it happened now and get this over with.

"For the record, I hate blowjobs, I'm really shit at sex, and I'm not now, nor have I ever been, a porn star," I said.

Okay, so I didn't *exactly* tell him, but he did say something reassuring, that I was a thousand percent sure he was going to regret. "And you know what? It wouldn't matter if you were."

We spoke every day for nearly three months—thousands of messages and video calls. And two weeks after I returned to LA, he flew back from filming and, without a moment's hesitation, came straight from the airport to see me. I'll never forget when I walked into La Poubelle, my local bar, and saw him in person for the first time. He was sitting at the counter, even more handsome and charming in person. I pinched his arm to see if he was real. And he was real, all right. And I couldn't believe my luck. We fell madly, head-over-heels—we can't live without each other— in love. I'd never experienced anything like it. It was like time had stopped, and fireworks went off, and the only people on the planet were us.

We moved in together a month later. A few months after that, Alex purchased a tiny home for us to live in in a trendy and up-and-coming neighborhood called Highland Park, and we made a home. (If you want to know whether you truly love someone, try living with them for a number of years in a house no more than five hundred square feet.) Life was great. Things were looking up. I had a boyfriend. A home. A career. Then, in a blink of an eye, I woke up thirty-two, and had a full-blown meltdown.

Thirty-two marked ten years since I moved to Los Angeles, the city where dreams are made...or, in my case, slowly disintegrated. I kept getting close to booking roles—down to the last two—only to lose out to someone with industry parents whose nudes weren't floating around in cyberspace. Then the auditions started drying up. From near misses to one audition every six months. Then...nothing.

The only thing keeping me afloat was *The Royals*. I'd made my dramatic return at the end of season four, perfectly teed up for a full comeback as a series regular in season five, but then the show was canceled after its creator was fired over allegations of sexual harassment and misconduct. And just like that, I was a thirty-two-year-old actress in Hollywood who hadn't made it.

Meanwhile, Alex's career skyrocketed. A sought-after writer/

director had him in mind for a lead role in his new TV show. All he had to do was put himself on tape—and unless he completely fucked it up, the part was his. "I booked it," he said, one afternoon. I threw my arms around him in excitement. I was so thrilled for him, but he couldn't understand my frustrations. He was thirty-five and male. His career had been a series of green lights. When he stepped off the plane, he got signed by Ryan Gosling's agent. He never had to ask himself, "Is this person trying to help me or fuck me?"

In my moments of sheer panic, my new manager would try to lift my spirits. "Keeley, we just need a role that is *you*," he'd say. "Like, if there were a series regular part for a funny, offbeat British gal, you'd nail it."

It became a running joke that I just needed to be cast as myself. Not exactly hilarious—I'd played myself in two films already. But it seemed insane that another role with my name on it would just come along. I'd played those Keeleys in my twenties when I was sort of famous, now I was a nobody.

Most evenings I wallowed on the sofa eating family-size bags of salt-and-vinegar kettle chips and bars of Hu chocolate and watching *Sex and the City*. Alex would come home and find me in this state; one evening he grabbed the remote and switched the show off. "You can't keep moping around watching this shit," he said. I would've been offended but I knew I needed to snap out of it. So I went full self-help on my depressed ass: I practiced manifesting. I listened to so much Tony Robbins, I could hear his voice in my sleep. *The Secret* became my bible as I tried to "retrain my brain" to "think positively." I did everything—yoga, a silent retreat. I even prayed, and I'm an atheist. I got back into acting classes and worked on my craft, and every night I would light a candle before bed, get on my knees, and say: *I want to be a lead on a TV show.*

But no matter what I tried, I always ended up on the sofa, binge-watching *Sex and the City* and crying that my career was over. At least I had my relationship with Alex, I told myself. We'd been together about three and a half years and were building a life together until one evening, as we were cooking dinner, he said the words no city girl ever wants to hear:

"I want to live on a ranch in Colorado."

Momentarily, he shocked me out of my depression. He was my life. We'd discussed the future, but nowhere in our plans was Colorado. I was certain I wanted to spend my life with him, but *what the heck was I going to do on a ranch? Raise chickens? Milk cows?*

We decided it was time for a chat.

"Are we *doing this.* Are we getting married or are we…breaking up?" Alex said. I never thought I'd hear "marriage" and "breaking up" in the same sentence, but okay.

We talked about marriage and kids and where we would raise them.

The more we spoke, the more apparent it became that we wanted completely different lives. I missed London. I missed feeling like a sardine on a Saturday, walking down Oxford Street shoulder to shoulder with thousands of people. He wanted to be in the open fields with no houses in sight. He wanted a wife who was going to stand on the side of the stage while he played. I wanted to be on the stage, playing. He wanted a woman to facilitate his dream, and I wanted to facilitate my own. I was so addicted to standing alone and holding on to my individuality that I'd never even posted a photo of us together on social media. Never walked the red carpet with him. I knew that being in a public relationship with a handsome, successful actor would give me credibility and change how people viewed me, boost my career even, and yet I refused it.

I felt so flawed and fucked up. Here was a man who loved me, who could provide an extraordinary life for me and a family, and what was I holding on to? My nonexistent career? My independence? My longing for Nando's?

We went back and forth for nearly six months, deluding ourselves that we could make it work. We planned our wedding one minute, and the next we were lying in each other's arms, crying. "I want you to be happy. Go live your dream."

I loved this man more than I'd loved anyone, and the heartbreak that consumed me was unlike anything I'd ever experienced. I felt like I was losing my best friend, my family, and I didn't want to let go. I held on to his legs like I used to hold on to my mother's and begged him not to leave me, but in the end we both knew it was over, and we had to cut the cord. He was the one to do it. And I was a mess. Ripped to pieces. I'd just lost the love of my life to livestock.

As a temporary solution, I moved out of the home I shared with Alex and into a garage that had been illegally converted into an "apartment"—and I use that term generously. It had a single bed, a mini fridge, a microwave, a toilet, and a shower. That was it. No kitchen—just the bare essentials. It felt less like a place to live and more like a survival bunker for someone who had severely miscalculated the apocalypse. It was a weird time in my life. The fear of turning forty and moving back into my mother's house began to feel less like a fear and more like my reality.

What's addictive about Hollywood and why it's so hard to give up is you're only ever one phone call away from having your life changed. All the stories you hear are from actors who've made it. They sit on talk shows and tell the host how they auditioned for ten years and nothing, and then, boom, they're the face of the new Marvel franchise. You don't hear the countless other stories of the people who *nearly* made it. And because it's not based entirely on talent, even if you can't act, you think, *Well, it could be me if I just keep on trying.*

Truth was, I didn't know if I had it in me to keep on going. I didn't want to live in a garage my whole life and give this career another ten years and get nowhere, but I didn't know what else to do. Weeks were passing by and nothing was changing. I was lying on my bed one evening, doomscrolling Instagram, comparing myself to others and thinking I'd fucked up my whole life, when a message popped up. It was J, whom I'd met all those years ago. He told me he'd written a part for me in his new TV show.

I was flabbergasted.

Gobsmacked.

Overjoyed.

A month or so later, J and I met up in a Mexican restaurant to discuss the part he had written for me. We ordered chips and margaritas, and he told me about the TV show. It was a football show set in England. It would film in London. J was going to play the lead, Ted, a cheery and optimistic American football coach who'd come to coach a British football (soccer) team, which, if you haven't figured out, is an entirely different sport. The whole thing sounded charming, but honestly, I was desperate to know what the part that he'd written for me was. Was it big? Small? Did I get to keep my clothes on? I'd just stuffed a big handful of chips in my mouth when he said, "The role is Keeley. She's one of the leads." I was so stunned, I nearly choked.

"I want it to be meta," he said, picking up his margarita and taking a sip. "I love the idea of you playing *you*. The character is more than she seems, you know. She did Page 3 and lads' mags, and she's been pigeonholed because of that. People write her off because of her past, but she's going to prove that she's so much more than that. Our first conversation inspired it... She's foxy, smart, funny, and at a crossroads in her career. I've been fortunate to see that side of you, but the public hasn't. When we meet her, she's dating this football player who's just not right for her, and she knows it."

I was absolutely mute. I couldn't get words out of my mouth, so I picked up my margarita and tipped the last of it down my throat. Then a huge, gigantic smile spread across my face. "Yes." I said, "I'm in. Where do I sign?"

J told me not to get too excited. The show hadn't been picked up at this point, meaning, it was just a script waiting to be sold, but the idea of me being a lead in a TV show was enough to make me wet my pants with excitement.

As soon as I left the restaurant, I phoned Patsy up to tell her.

"And the role is Keeley?" she said.

"Yeah," I said.

"So you'd be playing yourself?"

"I think it's meant to be a bit like *Extras* and I'm Barry off *EastEnders*."

"That's so f-ing cool!" she said.

J sent me the pilot script to read—which was amazing. I gave notes and suggested rewrites for some of Keeley's lines so they'd sound more like me. I prayed that the show would get picked up, and eventually it did.

It was incredible news.

I was ready—no, born ready—to play this part. All I had to do was convince a group of executives that I *was* Keeley.

"Casting decisions aren't solely mine. They're done by a committee, especially the pilot," J explained on the phone. I knew this to be true from filmmaker friends who'd been forced to cast A-list actresses in roles meant for "unknowns" like myself. Still, it felt like the role was mine. I mean, it was named and based on me; who else could play me better than, well, me?

I auditioned. I auditioned again. According to J, I was at the top of the list, but casting wanted to see another scene. In the third and final round, J read with me. In the scene, he fed me a burger while I pretended to be on a photo shoot, dressed as a sexy animal. It made me laugh—back in the day, a bunch of Page 3 models had done a shoot where they were all dressed as animals, and one had to be a pigeon. A topless pigeon. It killed me. We couldn't stop laughing.

As I waited to find out if I got the part, I did a visualization exercise where I imagined playing this version of myself. I thought about what this meant for me personally and what it meant on a larger scale for society. The tabloids could no longer call me a "glamour model." I was about to be an *actual* actress. And *God*, that meant people would have to question their biases about someone like me.

It really felt like everything I'd endured—the sex tape, the breakup with Alex—had led me to this moment. The moment I played Keeley on TV. The moment my entire life changed. I just needed confirmation that the part was mine, so when a text with J's name flashed on my screen, I opened my phone immediately.

What would happen if someone else got cast as Keeley and you got offered another part? it read. I felt like I'd been punched in the chest. I didn't know what to say, so I responded with *I don't know* and a struggling emoji. Followed by *I don't want you to be stressed. It will go whatever way it's meant to.* I was being Zen on the outside to keep my confidence up but inside, I wanted to rip my intestines out. What would happen if someone else got cast as Keeley?! What would happen was that I was going to die! I CAN'T HAVE SOMEONE ELSE PLAY *ME* ON TV. I WILL DIE. *DIE!!!*

The next week was brutal as I waited to find out if I got the part. I was so anxious to know anything, so desperate for confirmation, that I glued my phone to my side and answered immediately when my manager called.

"I have news..." he said.

I took a deep breath, squinting my eyes in anticipation. I told myself this was it—my one shot. If I didn't get cast to play myself, I was quitting. I had to. If I couldn't get this role, I had no chance.

"Go on…" I said, squeezing my eyes shut.

"They've gone out on a direct offer to an actress who hasn't auditioned."

My heart dropped into my stomach as the words echoed in my head. *Who?* I demanded. He told me her name. I knew who she was, a relatively known actress whom I'd met once with Alex. I went straight to Google to look at her. I stared at her photos. She had the same hair color, eye color—even a similar nose and face shape. But that's where the similarities stopped. She carried none of the baggage I dragged around like an overstuffed handbag. Her Wikipedia page told me everything: Her dad was a famous film director, her mother was a film producer, and she'd been educated at a prestigious private school with a celebrity alumni list as long as my leg. I stared at the page, my right hand hovering over the keyboard in total disillusionment.

Before I could fully accept the reality, my phone started buzzing again. My manager yelled in excitement, "She turned the offer down! You're still in the mix!" I let out a long exhale, and put my face in my hands and cried with relief. But the hope was short-lived because five minutes later, he called back.

"Er, *well*, I've found out that she turned down the offer as a play to get more money. But I don't know if they have it. Hold tight. It's so close to being yours!" I hung up, my mind spinning. *Of course they have the money—they're one of the richest companies on the planet! She knows it. Her agents know it. This actress is about to get rich playing me, and what do I get? A reminder that I didn't grow up with rich industry parents?*

I was on edge for days as I waited for my manager to call me back. The stakes were the highest they'd ever been. Finally, his name popped up on my screen. I took a deep breath and crossed my fingers.

"Tell me," I said.

"They've raised the cash," he said. "She got the part of Keeley."

I hung up the phone. "Noooooooooooooo!" I screamed as I immediately hurled myself into a ball on the floor. I thought about what my mum said after the car crash. "Something like this would only happen to you." And I squeezed myself harder into a ball. I was so close to having my entire life changed. Centimeters away. And now it was gone. What was I going to do? I'd told all my friends about this part. What was I supposed to tell them? That I was such a shit actress I couldn't even get cast to play myself?

I lay on the floor of my shitty apartment in ruins. I felt so stupid for even believing it could be mine. I was so dumb to think that the world was ever going to allow me to be more. I was the chick people laughed at for having her tits out in the paper. The fool whose career was ruined because her ex-boyfriend released a sex tape. *A fucking joke. I'm good enough to be a character, but I'm not good enough to play her.*

A few days later I was still processing the fatal blow when J called while I was in the car. I answered reluctantly. "I'm sorry," he said. He told me he didn't want to cast anyone who hadn't auditioned, he would have cast me months ago if it had been solely his choice, but the actress set to play "me" had a bigger résumé. Hearing this didn't help. *Of course she had a bigger résumé. While I was digging through phone booths for coins so I could eat, her dad was casting her in his films!*

I wanted to scream.

J reminded me of the small role he wanted to offer me a few months from now and asked if I could write a new sample script to be considered for the writers' room. "A Keeley origin story." He still very much wanted me to be part of the show, even if it wasn't playing the role he'd written for me. I told him that I was done with acting, and the only thing I had in me to write was my obituary.

When I hung up, I smashed my fists on the steering wheel and blasted a song so loud, I couldn't hear myself think. And as I pulled up to my apartment with Aretha Franklin blaring, I got a huge reminder of how close I'd been to success. In fact, I'd been sleeping next to it for almost four years. My jaw swung open. Directly opposite my apartment window was a gigantic billboard of Alex. It had freshly been put up like some cruel, sick joke. It was his face—his ridiculously handsome face—next to his costar's, looking like they were about to kiss.

I couldn't believe it. In fact, I *didn't* believe it. I kept opening my window every five minutes to check if it was real.

Every time I left or came home, that billboard was waiting for me, an enormous, inescapable reminder of how much I missed him. How much my heart ached. How alone I was without the one person who could soothe me. And how all my dreams had fallen to the wayside while Alex was living out his right in front of my window.

Once I didn't get cast as Keeley, I decided that acting could go fuck itself. I threw my copy of *The Secret* in the bin, vowing it was bullshit, and on a whim, I applied for a job in television. It was a behind-the-scenes position at a production company that funded, developed, and produced TV, mainly in the reality space. It was never my dream to work behind the scenes in reality television, especially when I've been offered so much to star in it, but I couldn't let all this ambition go to waste, so I decided to put my all into this job. I was going to work my way up the ranks to be a producer on one of the shows the company I worked for produced, *Love Island*. Who needs to make shit tons of money playing a fictionalized version of myself on TV when I can potentially produce the greatest reality show of all time? I can relocate to Mallorca and tell the contestants, in a voice resembling an eighty-five-year-old woman, "Back in my day I was offered six figures to go on the first one."

A few months into my new job, I received a call from my manager. "I've just gotten an offer for a small role on the show you auditioned for."

"Didn't you see on TMZ? Acting and I are donezo," I replied, ducking outside, just so I could turn the offer down. But a week later, when I was drowning in unanswered work emails and completely overwhelmed with the duties of having a real job, I couldn't help but wonder if I'd made a terrible mistake, so I called Nic T.

"Babes," she said, "how much are you getting paid at your job now?" I gave her a rough figure. "And how much are you going to get paid to do this acting gig?" Again, I gave her the figure.

"So, two weeks from this acting gig is the same as five months'

salary at your job. That means you've got four months and a fortnight to find something else." It was a very logical answer. Very
Nic T. But I told her it wasn't about the money—since it wasn't
exactly a financial game changer. I wouldn't be buying a home
anytime soon; it would barely buy me a shed.

"What's it about, then?" she asked.

"My career," I said.

"Yeah, and I thought you wanted to be an actress?"

"Well, I did," I said. "But it hasn't happened, has it?"

"We're literally talking about you getting offered an acting
role," she said, matter-of-fact.

I felt like an idiot. Yes, this was an acting gig, but an acting
gig that came at a high price. I'd have to be on set with an actress
playing "me" who was getting paid hundreds of thousands of dollars to do so, and I just didn't know if I could be around her without getting all Tonya Harding and wanting to take her out by the
knee. I know, *I know* she didn't do anything wrong. None of this
was her fault. It was just the idea of anyone morphing into some
version of me made me want to explode. I mean, I was the one
who had to do all the heavy lifting of being Keeley, for God's sake!

I asked everyone I knew for their opinions. I even talked to my
dying plant. The next morning, as I was sitting in my office sending an email, my phone lit up. Jack, my hot, successful rebound,
had sent me a text about my whole conundrum. Well, it wasn't
exactly a text; it was an essay. I had to scroll four times to read
this thing. It was the sweetest message about how his mum had
wanted to be an actress and that the bug to act never leaves you.
He ended it with *While this is a small role and not the part that you
should be playing (I'm not sure how anyone else could play you; you're*

*quite a unique character, :)), it is still an opportunity to do the thing
you love. You've put years and years of your life into this; don't give up.*
I almost cried when I read it. I went into my boss's office and told
him I was quitting "because I couldn't give up on my dream of
being an actress to produce reality television." This moment has
always felt like a scene from a Nancy Meyers movie. Especially
when I lost the credit card belonging to one of the producers
and accidentally went home with my boss's, only to realize that
I hadn't actually accepted the part and that they might have cast
it. I texted my manager frantically, *Have they cast the part yet?????*

The very next morning, I flew to London to start filming. Only
when I was thirty-five-thousand feet in the sky did I realize I
didn't even know what the part was; I had zero idea who I was
meant to be playing, and I actually didn't care. This was no longer
about the acting but about limiting my suffering. I thought, *I'm
going to have to suffer watching this, so I can either suffer and be a part
of it, or I can suffer from afar.* It was happening with or without me,
and it felt better to be rewarded with a tiny bite of cake than no
cake at all. At least, that was my thinking. Less than forty-eight
hours later I was on set doing my best acting work by pretending
I was totally fine not being cast to play Keeley. Honestly, my performance was Oscar worthy. You should have seen it. It was better
than my acting in the show, which was bad. Just *awful*. Instead of
using this as an opportunity to prove how good I was, I sabotaged
myself on-screen with defiant disengagement. It's only now that I
wish I'd disengaged with a Scouse accent and some fake eyelashes.

The first scene I filmed was this huge gala scene. The actress playing "me" was in it and J introduced us. We briefly said hello, and then I watched as she sat next to her on-screen boyfriend, Jamie. I pinched myself to see if I was real and not in an episode of *The Twilight Zone*. One of the SAs sitting opposite me observed curiously, "There's a character called Keeley, and *you're* called Keeley. That's so weird!"

Everybody, it seemed, was baffled by this since the name Keeley isn't all that common, so to stop confusion, the director named me "real Keeley," and I found this amusing since people usually used the word "real" when discussing my tits, but now they were using it to differentiate me from the TV character version of myself that I'd auditioned for and didn't get.

During the time I was filming, my ex Alex got engaged. We'd remained friends after the breakup, so when his name popped up on my phone, I didn't think much of it. I'd just sent him a voice note a few days prior. I opened the message and the photo loaded. *A diamond ring.* From Tiffany. I was walking to get on the tube when my knees buckled. In a panic, I texted him back orange heart emojis and congratulated him. Then I sat on the tube and cried. I was still crying when he replied, *Live a life, Keeley. Figure out what you truly want. You don't want to be texting your ex about his engagement, I know that. I really do care about you, and you have a chance in this life to be truly happy. Do it.* This was followed by another text that said, *Sex and the City is fucking garbage and it poisoned your brain.*

That made my tears turn into laughter.

Less than a year later, the show came out. I watched the first episode alone on my laptop. The actress playing Keeley appeared on-screen. I wanted to be sick. She opened her mouth to speak, and for a second I thought her accent was a joke. Then I thought, *Wait, is that supposed to be my accent?* It wasn't the actress's real voice. I knew that much.

I thought watching someone else play Keeley on TV was going to kill me, and that was an understatement. Death would have been easier. What I went through was torture. Slow and painful, like I was being "fucked in the arse by a splintered cricket bat."

Call me a masochist, but I couldn't stop watching. The pandemic had struck. The world was crumbling. People were willing to fight to the death over the last roll of toilet paper. All the while I was watching a cheerier version of "me" thrive on television. On-screen Keeley shifted careers easily. One minute she was a Page 3 and glamour model, and the next she was being offered a job branding for the players. What was she going to do next, produce *Love Island*?

In television, there is a narrative technique called a "cold open." You start in the middle of a scene—no setup, just action—before cutting to the opening credits. If my real life had been a TV show—or, more accurately, a reality show during this time—my cold open would start with me, Real Keeley, on my knees in my London bathroom, rummaging through a bag of my old hair-dressing supplies to find a bottle of brown dye. I would savagely be slapping it all over my blonde hair like a woman covering a crime. You wouldn't find out *why* yet. After the opening credits, the episode would jump to me sitting on the toilet, scrolling my phone, reading that the actress playing Fake Keeley had just been nominated for an Emmy. "I'm the England football team!"

I'd mutter to no one. This will make more sense when you learn the Emmy nominations came out two days after England lost the Euro final on penalty shoot-outs. Then you'd see me on the tube crying while watching my audition tape. You might think, *Jesus, this girl cries on the tube a lot,* but if I've done my job, you'd understand why. Later you'd see me alone in my flat, wearing a black turtleneck and my gold Keeley name necklace, while trying to write. From a distance, I might look like a down-market Carrie Bradshaw. But I'd explain to the audience—over the phone to Patsy—that my gold name necklace has nothing to do with the one Carrie Bradshaw famously wore. "This isn't some cute *Sex and the City* idolization symbol!" I'd say. "Name necklaces came out of the ghetto, they're about identity, pride, and survival! I don't wear mine to be cute, I wear it 'cuz I'm from the fucking ghetto."

You'd see billboards of the show Fake Keeley is on everywhere. People dressed up as her for Halloween. Bumper stickers. Tattoos. Then me—watching Fake Keeley on-screen, also in a black turtleneck, also wearing a gold Keeley necklace. A voiceover would kick in: "*They say imitation is the sincerest form of flattery. But what happens when the imitation is leading a better life than you?*"

And at the end of the episode, we return to the beginning: me sitting on the sofa, watching Fake Keeley watching *Sex and the City.* I'd focus on Fake Keeley's dyed blonde hair, then on Carrie's, then back to mine. We'll flashback to me watching *Sex and the City* on the sofa. In my mind—which of course we'll see on-screen—I'll be trapped in a room of mirrors, all reflecting on each other or some kind of Russian doll nightmare. I'd switch the TV off, storm into the bathroom...and we're back at the beginning. On my knees. Dyeing my hair brown.

* * *

So, what began with me in a red swimsuit ended with *Ted Lasso*. The show became a hit. Not just a hit, but a big, jaw-dropping, award-winning hit—one of those hits that comes along every ten years or so. All the lead actors became rich and famous, and it changes their lives. I mean, it *changes their lives*. They buy houses and send their kids to the same private schools they attended, and have their own TV shows made. And go to the White House to meet the president.

As for me? The only change I noticed was when I went to order some food and gave my name for the order and the server said, "Oh, Keeley, like the character from *Ted Lasso*!" He mistook my look of horror for confusion and then asked if I'd seen the show. *Had I seen the show? Had I seen the show? Had he ever seen his face with a shiner?*

That's the other thing. While I was just someone who was "sort of famous for being *almost* famous," as *Ted Lasso*'s Keeley Jones liked to point out, *she* was reaping all the rewards. Keeley Jones defied the stereotype—proving that women can be multifaceted. She was charming and well liked—always solving other people's problems with wisdom not expected from a character who was a former glamour model.

I can only imagine how wonderful it would've been to play the Keeley who breezes through life never stigmatized by her past. Who people see for who she is and not the "airheaded starfucker" they believe her to be.

But you know what? I get to play the Keeley who has stumbled and struggled and survived. I get to play the greatest role of my lifetime—the Real Keeley, and here she fucking is.

Unlikely Feminist

When I was fifteen, I saved up two weeks' wages and bought a punching bag and gloves from the Argos catalog, on sale. I took the bus into town to collect them. I'd underestimated the weight of the bag, because when I arrived, the guy behind the counter looked me up and down and asked if I had a car to put it in. He laughed when I told him I was taking it back on the bus.

He thought I was joking.

When I started dragging the bag toward the door, he stepped out from behind the counter in shock and offered to help.

"I've got it," I said, refusing.

I most definitely didn't have it. That bag was heavy as shit. I'd barely worked out a day in my life, and this was the heaviest thing I'd ever carried, but I dragged it out of the store and onto the bus with more determination than I'd ever shown for anything.

Dad came and hung the bag up in my bedroom. I got my CD player out, put on my Eminem album, and slipped on my gloves. Then I smashed the shit out of that bag for a solid sixty seconds before nearly vomiting. My whole body trembled. I hadn't known you were supposed to wear wraps, so my knuckles were cut up, but I was shaking too much to get the gloves off. I lay on the floor, overwhelmed, staring at the ceiling.

I was so furious.

I grew up in a world of violence. A world of dominance. It was in the home and on the streets. I hated that. I hated that anyone could overpower me—that violence became a physical way to control, silence, and violate me. My desire to hit that punching bag wasn't about exerting dominance. It was about resisting powerlessness. I wasn't training to hurt anyone—I was training to not be physically hurt.

The instinct to go and get a punching bag was the same one that drove me to key Theo's car after he broke into my home with a knife and then sold a sex tape of me. It was an instinct that said this isn't fair. This is unjust. I don't know what I have to do, but as long as I'm alive, and it's safe, I will do something. I will fight back.

This sentiment, this pilot light, has left me beaten black-and-blue more times than not. When I walked into the police station to be told that the crime Theo had committed wasn't that serious because I'd dated him or when the legal system failed me by not recognizing my violation as a crime. Or when the world forced me into a narrative of self-blame and tarnished me with unfavorable labels that I couldn't do anything about. I didn't let that conviction leave me. *This isn't fair. This is unjust. I don't know what to do, but I will do something. I will fight back.*

That instinct first visited me when I was four and wanted a *Ghostbusters* backpack for Christmas. When Aunt Anne told me

I should play with a doll. Little me was literally saying, *Fuck this shit; I'm not playing by your stupid rules*, and so, without having the language to define it or the knowledge to understand it, I did something about it: I cut my hair off, dressed in boys' clothes, and became Kevin.

Of course, life isn't that simple. It doesn't matter how much you are willing to break the rules or how much you are willing to fight or mock the system; you still have to operate in a world under the constraints of the oppressive systems it upholds. The real world doesn't go away; domestic abuse, misogyny, inequality, and sexism exist. Women are affected by these things on a daily basis. And just because it's not happening to you doesn't mean it's not happening.

For most of my life, I've been labeled and pigeonholed. Growing up on a council estate made me a "certain type" of person. Being a topless model made me a "certain type" of person. I've been mocked and shamed for both. And while I can resist societal conditioning in some ways, I haven't always been able to shake its grip on me. Even when I could recognize and label it as such, I still couldn't stop it from affecting me. For most of my twenties, I was so deeply ashamed of what Theo did to me that I was ashamed to admit how ashamed I was. When people advised me to change my name, I often considered it. But I felt a deep resistance. I knew that changing my name would mean denying part of my history—denying how I became the woman I am today. Changing my name meant running away. And while I felt ashamed, I didn't want to run, hide, or pretend. I didn't want to change my name just to comply with societal rules and, in doing so, submit to the idea that I should feel ashamed or embarrassed for what had happened to me. That would have meant burying my shame instead of confronting it and conforming to the expectation that I should feel ashamed at all.

And while I've refused to conform many times, I've still had to survive under a patriarchal, capitalistic system that benefits some and not others. In a system that has been publicly shaming and oppressing women throughout history. In a system that is rigged.

I'm acutely aware that I am no different from the other girls I sat with on the wall in Grove Park, and yet, because I was born in a particular body at a specific time that society deemed my body and looks of value, I've led a very different life. Still, with its privilege came its limitations. Glamour modeling was just class oppression transmuted into sexual objectification. I just went from being a "chav" to a "bimbo" with money. And while money gave me freedom, access, and autonomy, it didn't free me from judgment over the choices I made to get that freedom.

Being a woman is messy. It's confusing. It's full of contradictions. Half the time I feel like I'm battling the perceptions, thoughts, and opinions that have been placed on me by society in order to strip them away and see who I really am underneath. I'm constantly asking myself questions like: Do I even want a romantic partnership, or have I just been conditioned to believe that I should have one? Do I want a boyfriend so society values me more and other women don't view me as a threat, or do I want one because we're hardwired for connection, so it's an innate need? I even ask myself questions that seem shallow like: Do I want to pump Botox into my forehead? If so, is it because I'm really horrified to see my face with lines? Or because sometimes I have to be public facing, and if every single woman has pumped their face with it, I'm going to look old and haggard in comparison and, therefore, work less because the world values beauty and youth? And if I do this, will it make me less of a feminist? If I age naturally, does that do anything for society, or am I the only person it affects?

I think we need to ask ourselves these questions in order to understand who we truly are without all the bullshit placed on us. Sometimes you won't have an answer. Sometimes you'll have an answer and it won't be the one you like. Sometimes you'll be sick of asking yourself questions.

Knowing yourself is not clean-cut or easy. Neither is feminism. It's flawed just like human beings. But it isn't about being perfect. It's about refusing to let the world decide who you are. It's about buying the punching bag and learning to fight back even if you don't win. It's about cutting your hair and renaming yourself Kevin, so that others can't define you. It's about reclaiming your voice when others have taken it away from you. And it's about listening to that voice inside that says, this isn't fair, this is unjust, and I don't know what I have to do, but I will do something. I will fight back.

Acknowledgments

Writing is typically a solitary task, and I spent hours, days, weeks, and months staring at a computer screen in various locations because I moved *eight times* across three cities while writing this. Still, I didn't end up with the published book you're holding without the support and encouragement of others.

Thank you to everyone at Hachette, especially my editor, Suzanne O'Neill. It meant so much to work with not just a female editor but an entire team of brilliant women across all aspects of this book: design, copyediting, production, audio, and all the other areas that go into making this book happen. To my manager, Van Johnson—you were the first person who encouraged me to write. Thank you for believing in me. And to my agent, Joe Veltre—thank you for being unlike the agent I write about.

Sal Romeo, who is no longer with us—I wish I could share this with you. Thank you to David Walliams, Emma Holly Jones, and Franklin Leonard for being so generous with your time and support. Nicola Tappenden—for surviving my topless years with me. Patsy, my partner in crime—thank you for your support, enthusiasm, and eternally optimistic outlook. And finally, to the people who bought this book hoping to see tits—congratulations on making it this far through a book with no nudity.

About the Author

Keeley Hazell is a writer, actress, and former glamour model known for being one of the UK's most successful Page 3 models. She has graced numerous magazine covers worldwide and transitioned into acting after studying at the Lee Strasberg Theatre & Film Institute in Los Angeles, appearing in films *Horrible Bosses 2* and *Like Crazy*, among others, and the TV show *The Royals*. She was also a writer and actress on Apple TV+'s award-winning TV show *Ted Lasso*, where the lead character of Keeley is named for and based on her. *Everyone's Seen My Tits* is her first book. She currently resides in New York.